Rediscovering the American Midwest

Series Editors: Jon K. Lauck and Patricia Oman

The Midwestern Moment   Jon K. Lauck, ed.
The Forgotten World of Early Twentieth-Century
Midwestern Regionalism, 1880–1940

A Scattering Time   Sara Kosiba, ed.
How Modernism Met Midwestern Culture

Pieces of the Heartland   Andy Oler, ed.
Representing Midwestern Places

Making the Midwest   Jon K. Lauck, ed.
The Formation of Midwestern Identity, 1787–1900
   Forthcoming

A Scattering Time

A Scattering Time

How Modernism Met Midwestern Culture

Edited by
Sara Kosiba

Hastings College Press | Hastings, Nebraska

© 2018 by Hastings College Press

All rights reserved. No part of this book may be used or reproduced in any manner whatsoever without permission from the publisher, except in the case of brief quotations embodied in critical articles and reviews.

Copy Editors
Bruce Batterson
Kit Grode

Book Design
Patricia Oman

Paperback   ISBN-10: 1942885520   ISBN-13: 978-1-942885-52-8

Hardback   ISBN-10: 1942885512   ISBN-13: 978-1-942885-51-1

Manufactured in the United States of America.

Text is printed on acid-free, chlorine-free paper.

Contents

Sara Kosiba	Introduction Midwest Modernism Is Not an Oxymoron	ix
Jennifer J. Smith	Autobiography, Modernism, and the Midwest	1
Ross K. Tangedal	That Time in Chicago Midwestern Memory in Nella Larsen's *Passing*	17
Meg Gillette	The Davenport Renaissance What Was It, and Why Does It Matter?	33
Marcia Noe and Meghan O'Dea	From Davenport to Provincetown Floyd Dell, George Cram Cook, and Susan Glaspell Develop a Radical Theatre Aesthetic	49
Sara Kosiba	Breaking Binaries Deconstructing the "Revolt" and Reassessing Midwestern Literature and Art	71
Harmony Jankowski	Dance Pioneering Ted Shawn and His Men Dancers Tour the Midwest	87
Dustin Gann	The Unrepentant Outsider Emanuel Haldeman-Julius and the Creation of a Nationwide Audience	101
Gregory S. Rose	The Midwest as a National and International Economic Powerhouse by 1920	119

Contents

Paula Wisotzki	Revolt in the City Labor and Art in the Urban Midwest	141
Gregory Gilbert	Federal Art in the Midwest in the 1930s and the Meeting of Rural and Urban Cultures A Challenge to Grant Wood's "Revolt Against the City"	163
Dimitrios Latsis	MoMA's Wood Regionalism and the Midwest at the Heart of the Modernist "Beast"	187
Lara Kuykendall	John Steuart Curry Regionalism at War	207
	Contributors	227

Sara Kosiba

Introduction

Midwestern Modernism
Is Not an Oxymoron

John Updike once claimed that midwestern writer Dawn Powell's work was "doomed to a perpetual state of revival."[1] Unfortunately, Powell's home region suffers a similar fate as her literary legacy. The region seems in a perpetual state of rebuttal: rebuttal against continued accusations of revolt, rebuttal against continued characterizations of the region as simply "flyover country," and rebuttal against continually flattening platitudes of the region as "America's heartland."

The essays in this collection refute the lingering idea that the Midwest had little to do with the cultural and artistic trends of early twentieth-century modernism, a claim that limits our understanding of the Midwest as a region and its place within national and international culture. Too often, students and scholars see modernist innovations and trends as exclusively European-centered or occurring only in major metropolitan areas. For example, in the art world, "there is a ubiquitous fiction in American art histories that narrowly ascribes the rise of modernism in this country to activities in New York and a few other cities along the East Coast."[2] Too often, regionalism and modernism are also seen as antithetical perspectives. John N. Duvall begins his essay on "Regionalism and American Modernism" by noting, "Any attempt to link regionalism to American modernism may seem, at first blush, a perverse enterprise. After all, definitions of modernism tend to cast it as nearly the antithesis of regionalism. If regionalist fiction between the 1890s and 1910s typically focused on matters of domesticity in rural localities, modernism was an international movement, encompassing fine arts as well as literature."[3] While Duvall's essay goes on to examine an expanded period of regional writing beyond the 1910 cutoff mentioned here, his comment notes a prevalent attitude scholars and students often have regarding regionalism and modernism: Regionalism is often classified as restrictively rural and provincial, whereas modernism is worldly and cosmopolitan. Yet, by moving beyond those reductive classifications and expanding our minds to new perspectives and possibilities, we, as readers, gain a much broader view of regional interactions with modernist ideas.

Much of the experimentation and innovation we associate with modernism did take place in Europe, but many of the American writers, artists, and intellectuals who lived and worked there, expanding our definition of the modern and new, were midwestern. And among those who stayed and innovated on American soil, those in the Midwest were quite often very aware of international and national events and developments in art and culture. In both cases, while influenced by the changing cultural climate here and abroad, the local maintained a lingering presence. For someone like Ernest Hemingway, writing in Paris cafes about Michigan, stories that would eventually become part of his avant-garde collection *In Our Time*, "in one place you could write about it better than in another."[4] In the center of modernist innovations and conversations in Paris, Hemingway was still drawing upon his midwestern roots for material. In a talk given in Kansas City, Missouri, on "The Artist of the Middle West," Grant Wood advocated an American style of painting that moved away from imitating foreign influences; however, he noted that this new style of painting would still value contemporary innovation, as "Modernism has added too many powerful tools to the kit of the artist to be forgotten."[5] This interplay of the local and the national or international is too often overlooked in discussions of a modernist artistic presence in midwestern writers, artists, and intellectuals. Scholarship such as in the essays included here show the continued need to move beyond limiting expectations and stereotypes of the Midwest and acknowledge a Midwest that is creative, dynamic, and diverse.

Midwestern nostalgia, particularly in the early twentieth century, is significantly tied to a modernist sense of place evoked by rural and urban spaces. Modernist writers often focused on the past or what was lost as part of their attempt to better understand the present moment: "A type of remembrance or fixation on a place, person, lifestyle, time, or artistic practice: such is the nostalgia of literary modernism, which invokes the past not to restore it, as much as to measure and perhaps challenge the present."[6] Chicago was a significant location for many midwestern writers and artists in the early twentieth century, and the city would often live on in memory or represent a key symbolic moment to be interpreted or reassessed years later.

Essays by Jennifer J. Smith and Ross K. Tangedal address the power of the city and the nostalgia it could engender. Smith examines how Sherwood Anderson and Margaret Anderson both look back fondly on their time in Chicago in their memoirs. It was the location where both writers could fully develop their artistic careers and solidify a critical and artistic identity. For Margaret Anderson, the creative climate in Chicago served as an ideal spot for founding the *Little Review*, a little magazine that would achieve a respected place within the modernist publishing canon. Sherwood Anderson also embraced the literary circles the city had to offer, writing later in life about the sense of inspiration and possibility characterizing his time there. He described engaging conversations with fellow writers such as Floyd Dell and how interactions with other artists in the city shaped his writing. Smith assesses how both Andersons merge fact and fiction and play with time in their recollections, creating autobiographies that are both self-interpretive and indicative of modernist style. Tangedal's essay expands our understanding of Nella Larsen's *Passing* by applying close textual analysis to pivotal early scenes in Chicago that establish key contrasts in the novel and shape the narrative that follows. Larsen's birth and childhood in Chicago would shape her early perceptions of race, and the greatest argument for the impact of those experiences is her return to the city for formative moments in both of her novels. Irene Redfield and Clare Kendry share a Chicago childhood, and their reunion at the top of the Drayton Hotel in *Passing* brings all the complexity of those early experiences into the complications of their contemporary lives. Focusing on Redfield's memories and reactions, Tangedal analyzes the way Larsen carefully uses language in those early Chicago scenes to establish contrasts that resonate throughout the novel. He notes that the ambiguous identity of the city, a place both of possibility and yet of conventionality and restriction, makes Chicago an ideal location for establishing and assessing Irene and Clare's divergent perspectives.

Historically, Davenport, Iowa, has never had the same prominence and creative reputation as Chicago, but two essays in this collection argue for it as a center of innovation and inspiration. Meg Gillette examines the cultural milieu of Davenport in the early twentieth century: "At a time when Paris was becoming famous for its 'lost generation,' New York for its bohemian Greenwich village, and Harlem and Chicago for their respective 'renaissances,' Davenport writers were actively promoting their own literary group and city" (39). Far from a sleepy midwestern city, she notes, Davenport experienced significant population boom and variety of individuals, from immigrants to writers to socialists, who populated the city with cultural diversity. While the mix of politics, ethnicity, and artistic temperament still bred conflict at times, Davenport was clearly a city of people engaging with contemporary ideas and exploring new forms of expression. Focusing more intently on some of those literary lives in the city, Marcia Noe and Meghan O'Dea explore the Davenport foundations that inspired the plays of Floyd Dell, Susan Glaspell, and George Cram Cook. All three writers were founding members of the Provincetown Players, a prominent early twentieth-century theater group. Noe and O'Dea trace how Dell, Glaspell, and Cook built on early social and political experiences in Davenport to craft plays that invoked modernist conceptions of time and that reflected on contemporary ideas and concerns.

While modernist ideas are clearly present in the literature of early twentieth-century midwestern writers, modernism in the Midwest was present in many other artistic genres and disciplines, as well, and too often we fail to contrast or examine those diverse responses. My essay argues for reassessment of the "revolt against the village" trope so commonly applied to early twentieth-century midwestern literature by arguing for a more careful reading of Carl Van Doren's original essay coining the term and for a broader assessment of how the concept of "revolt" has limited our understanding of both midwestern literature and art. Authors and artists viewed as more critical of midwestern rural life or small towns, those viewed as "in revolt," were often seen as more modernist or cosmopolitan, but reducing our readings and interpretation in that vein ignores the nuances and complexities of work that embraced the region. Modernism was playing out in interesting ways in texts and paintings that that stayed "loyal" to the Midwest, and more consistently viewing art and literature from the region in that way will more accurately broaden our perspective on midwestern culture.

Expanding that sense of artistic diversity in the region, Harmony Jankowski's essay covers what initially seems like familiar ground: pioneering efforts on a midwestern frontier. However, the pioneers in her essay are not traditional midwestern farmers but instead male dancers. Jankowski's exploration of Ted Shawn and his Men Dancers highlights the efforts of Shawn and his troupe to break stereotypes regarding the place of men within modern dance. As they toured the Midwest in the 1930s, they succeeded in breaking stereotypes that implied dancing was solely a feminine activity and opened the minds of those in small and large cities to the possibilities in modern artistic dance. Jankowski highlights an important contribution to our understanding of early twentieth-century dance history and also reveals a more nuanced view of artistic life in the Midwest.

While the Midwest had once been a strong center for publishing, by the early twentieth century it had been clearly eclipsed by the East Coast dominance of New York City and Boston. Nevertheless, that did not stop Emanuel Haldeman-Julius from building a successful publishing operation in Girard, Kansas. As Dustin Gann explains in his essay, Haldeman-Julius originally came to Girard when the socialist newspaper he was working on, the *Appeal to Reason*, relocated there in the hopes of rooting itself in an industrial and immigrant-heavy region. As local economics changed and the paper foundered, Haldeman-Julius purchased a controlling interest in the paper, revamping its focus and expanding the publishing mechanism behind it. His publishing company never merged perfectly with local politics and perspectives in Girard, but Gann describes the significant success Haldeman-Julius had in creating a large mail-order business emanating from the center of the country. Particularly through his Little Blue Book series but also through other publications, Haldeman-Julius's publishing efforts significantly shaped early twentieth-century politics and culture on a national scale.

Economic prosperity in the Midwest helped to shape and energize the region's status on a national scale and helped foster many of the artistic and cultural innovations of the time. Gregory S. Rose notes that while the northeastern United States may have had financial and intellectual status in the early twentieth century, "the Northeast could not match the breadth and depth of the Midwest's production-based economy" (120). In his essay, Rose examines the region's transportation structure, agriculture, population distribution, urbanization, and industrial efforts to show how prosperous and powerful the Midwest was in the early twentieth century. Many midwestern states ranked in the top five for areas like wheat and steel production. That economic power argues for more centralized value for the Midwest as opposed to the marginalized status often applied to the region.

The importance of industry and agriculture in the Midwest was not lost on the visual artists in and from the region. Paula Wisotzki and Gregory Gilbert explore the way those industrial or urban images contrasted artistically with the rural or agricultural point of view in the 1930s. Wisotzki focuses on the depictions of urban and rural labor in 1930s visual art, noting how modernist artistic techniques often introduced abstraction and innovation into realistic depictions of life. Highlighting prints and paintings by a number of diverse social realist artists, such as Morris Topchevsky, Francis Robert White, Harry Sternberg, and Carl Hoeckner, Wisotzki notes how the urban labor portrayed in their art differs significantly from the agricultural labor found in works of regionalist art of the time. She sees the efforts of those social realists as far more modernist and progressive, incorporating visual political commentary that sympathized with the plight of the American worker in the 1930s. Gregory Gilbert also sees political motivation in the urban and rural contrasts in early twentieth-century midwestern painting. While Grant Wood hoped the artistic programs generated by the New Deal of the 1930s would provide an opportunity to explore regional diversity, Gilbert highlights how the programs actually reinforced a cultural homogeneity counter to regionalist preferences. He examines several murals sponsored by the Works Progress Administration to demonstrate how those urban and rural images served that larger political goal. However, Gilbert also notes how Wood critiqued modern ideas and methods within his rural landscapes, maintaining some rural distinctiveness in the midst of the push for nationally representative art.

New Deal programs gave way to other challenges as the United States navigated the tumultuous years before and during World War II. Dimitrios Latsis examines how American art in the 1930s, particularly art from the Midwest, played a significant role in shaping perceptions of modern art. Latsis notes the national and international reputations of painters such as Grant Wood, Thomas Hart Benton, and John Steuart

Curry and their representation in many exhibitions and museum collections. He reveals how the careers of Benton and Wood, in particular, carried over into documentaries produced in the 1940s and 1950s that began to nationally canonize American artists of the early twentieth century. Ultimately, while regionalism in American art would continue to be critiqued throughout the rest of the twentieth century and quite often fall lower in favor, Latsis chronicles the persistent appearance of works by Wood, Benton, and Curry into the twenty-first century. This confirms, according to Latsis, a persistent place for these artists amid discussions of modern art.

While regionalist art may be accused of fascist tendencies or applauding an idealized rural life devoid of progress and diversity, the influence of war shifted the aesthetic styles and ideological priorities for many regionalist writers and artists. Lara Kuykendall traces the influence of war on the work of John Steuart Curry. As a student during World War I, Curry was slow to participate in the conflict, and it ultimately ended before he played any significant role. Curry would maintain some of that ambivalence about war as World War II approached, crafting anti-war paintings that reflected on the cost of war and its effect on the population. Kuykendall notes that after Pearl Harbor Curry's perspective changed significantly. The artist began to use the rural landscape and the midwestern farmers he knew so well to create war propaganda and assist in mobilizing the population in support of the war. Later, Curry would explore the lives of wartime medical personnel. In both cases, Kuykendall highlights the nuance within Curry's work as he maintained his personal discomfort with the pain and tragedy of war while still supporting the national war effort. Curry's wartime art provides an opportunity to reflect on how regionalist works were shaped by the fragmentation and complexity of early twentieth-century conflict.

These essays confirm an observation made years ago by scholar John T. Flanagan that midwestern literature (and I would argue art, dance, and other art forms or cultural responses) contained "a strong indictment of the status quo, a criticism of the social and economic life of the age."[7] For modernist art and culture emerging from or addressing the region in the early twentieth century, this is very true, particularly if we read "criticism" as an interrogation of the status quo and not necessarily a negative one. Instead of a region passively clinging to nostalgic visions of the past, the Midwest has always been a dynamic intersection of the past and the present, the old-fashioned and the modern, the conservative and the progressive. If we take the time to reflect on the diversity of perspectives included in this collection, we move one step further away from those lingering perceptions of a bland, homogenized Midwest and closer to a clearer, more accurate discussion of the region's past, present, and future.

Notes

1. John Updike, "An Ohio Runaway," *New Yorker* (February 20 & 27, 1995): 262.
2. William H. Robinson and Christine Fowler Shearer, "Against the Grain: Modernism in the Midwest," in *Against the Grain: Modernism in the Midwest* (Massillon, OH: Massillon Museum, 2010), 10.
3. John N. Duvall, "Regionalism in American Modernism," in *The Cambridge Companion to American Modernism*, ed. Walter Kalaidjian (Cambridge: Cambridge University Press, 2005), 242.
4. Ernest Hemingway, *A Moveable Feast*, ed. Seán Hemingway (New York: Scribner, 2009), 17.
5. "Grant Wood Explains Why He Prefers to Remain in the Middle West in Talk in Kansas City," *Cedar Rapids Sunday Gazette and Republican* (March 22, 1931), in *Grant Wood Scrapbook 01*, Figge Art Museum Grant Wood Digital Collection, accessed October 28, 2017, http://digital.lib.uiowa.edu/cdm/ref/collection/grantwood/id/1030.
6. Tammy Clewell, "Introduction: Past 'Perfect' and Present 'Tense': The Uses of Modernist Nostalgia," in *Modernism and Nostalgia: Bodies, Locations, Aesthetics*, ed. Tammy Clewell (New York: Palgrave, 2013), 6.
7. John T. Flanagan, "The Reality of Midwestern Literature," in *The Midwest: Myth or Reality?* (South Bend: University of Notre Dame Press, 1961), 82.

Jennifer J. Smith | Autobiography, Modernism, and the Midwest

Margaret Anderson, founder of the avant-garde magazine *Little Review* (1914–1929), described her arrival in the Midwest's biggest city from Columbus, Indiana: "Chicago: enchanted ground to me from the moment Lake Michigan entered the train windows. I would make my beautiful life here. A city without a lake wouldn't have done."[1] She "came to love Chicago as one only loves chosen—or lost—cities. I knew it in every aspect—dirt, smoke, noise, heat, cold, wind, mist, rain, sleet, snow.... And I was in love. My first love—I should say, my first real love. And it was a great love—great in everything including disappointment. But, oh, how I was in love."[2] Her view from the train and the romance with which she depicted the city parallel those of many of the artists who came to Chicago from small midwestern towns between the 1880s and the 1920s. She loved great conversation, and in Chicago, she found it—in living rooms, in the little theaters, in the 1913 Armory Show, in bookstores, and among the little magazines cropping up all over the city. Chicago was instrumental in providing the template of collaboration and conversation that drove the *Little Review*'s experimentation. Her friend and fellow midwestern transplant from Clyde, Ohio, Sherwood Anderson, whose many novels and short stories include *Winesburg, Ohio* (1919), characterized the Chicago scene as a "Robin's Egg Renaissance" of the arts and literature. He speculated, "So many of us began there, got our early impressions of life there, made friends there. Had we stayed in the home nest, in Chicago, when it all began for so many of us, the Robin's Egg might have hatched."[3] Chicago was the space between Columbus and Clyde and all that lay beyond; and yet, it was more than a stopover. Both Margaret Anderson and Sherwood Anderson characterized the city as home to unparalleled inspiration.

As Chicago attracted artists from the Midwest and beyond, writers had the task of explaining what was new about their work and about this place, which seemed equal parts innovation and grime. They did so, most famously, in fiction and poetry, but they also did so in autobiography. As writers such as Sherwood Anderson and Margaret Anderson moved from emerging to established authors, they turned to autobiography to frame their achievements on the literary scene. In this chapter, I will examine how these two figures wrote about the Midwest, modernism, and their artistic personae in Margaret Anderson's *My Thirty Years' War* (1930) and Sherwood Anderson's *A Story Teller's Story* (1924) and posthumously published *Memoirs* (1969). From these autobiographies, there emerges a hyperbolic emphasis on Chicago as both exceptional and liberating. The autobiographers recount artistic collaborations and rivalries, and they praise and damn their peers in crafty, often hilarious, terms. The writers cast themselves as arbiters of the new and extol honesty and frankness as virtues of true art, even if the life-writings are themselves part fiction.

For a long time, modernism, defined by its cosmopolitan ambitions and responses to urbanization, was synonymous with cities. In recent decades, scholars have offered a reappraisal of modernism in relation to rural and newly suburban spaces as well as outposts around the globe. Chicago, associated with the middle and the west, occupies a unique space in accounts of modernism. At the turn of the twentieth century, it was a city of largely white migrants from small midwestern towns, like Margaret Anderson and Sherwood Anderson, as well as immigrants from Europe. In the 1940s and 1950s, first- and second-generation transplants of the Great Migration transformed Chicago modernism yet again. Chicago's modernisms have strong ties to the Midwest as a region, to urbanization and industrialization, and to novelty, especially as the city was being newly made in the wake of the Chicago fire and was home to innovative city planning and architecture. Chicago's modernism has been derided—even by some of its practitioners—as aesthetically middlebrow, and, indeed, Chicago writers are not quick to dismiss middle-class readers. And yet, if modernism is the aesthetic response to modernity, then Chicago is pivotal. From the 1880s through the 1920s, the city enjoyed writing and art that alternately embraced and rejected the very institutions from which it emerged: the proliferation of arts and social clubs, the retail megastores, the support of newspapers and magazines, the influence of the visual arts, experimental theaters like the Little Theater, and social justice outlets such as Hull House.

Optimism ran high in Chicago, imagined as a city of the present and the future. Chicago had little history, having been founded in 1840, but it experienced rapid growth in industrialization, population, and geographic sprawl. It was the nation's fastest growing city of the late nineteenth century, and its arts scene reflected that foment. The city's newness correlated to the interest in giving language to urban alienation and industrial (dis)order espoused by modernists. Chicago was up for grabs in its meaning, and, in their autobiographies, both Margaret Anderson and Sherwood Anderson attempted to give shape to its shores, skyscrapers, and scribblers.

Her founding and curating of the *Little Review*, from 1914 to 1923, and his composition of *Winesburg, Ohio* remain their most lasting contributions to modernism. And yet, it is their autobiographies that give us the best insight into how they conceived their artistic personae and productions. Craig Monk argues that modernists saw autobiography as an act of criticism, constituting a "formidable framing gesture"[4] whereby an increasingly heterogeneous readership might understand the writer and his/her works and contribution to modernism. Autobiography as a genre, then, exists at the intersection of the accessible and esoteric, the twin pulls of which Chicago modernists were especially attuned to: "If modernism developed with elitist principles in ascendance, it was also forced to entertain broader, populist impulses in a desire to reach and influence an audience."[5] Margaret Anderson's impulse to reach a broad audience is evident in her inclusion of advertising language and strategies in the *Little Review*, as Mark Morrison suggests, as well as the many letters she published in the magazine and in *My Thirty Years' War* from an engaged, although often annoyed, reading public.[6] Sherwood Anderson recounted in his *Memoirs* the vitriolic letters he received following *Winesburg* for its perversion and immorality. Although he reminded his readers that sexual desires are universal, that he received and responded to so many such letters reveals his ambition to reach middle-class readers. Both Margaret Anderson and Sherwood Anderson are situated within a tradition of Chicago modernism, ranging from Theodore Dreiser to Richard Wright to Stuart Dybek, which blends esoteric experimentation, social commentary, and accessibility to reach a broader audience than other cosmopolitan modernisms.

Further, autobiography addresses one of modernism's most persistent features: an evolving understanding of psychology and the role of language in making the self. In autobiography, the writer's "act of textual composition has been his experiencing his past self as at once the same as his present self, continuous with it, and yet strangely, uniquely, as other to it."[7] Both Margaret Anderson and Sherwood Anderson collapse time and space in writing of their lives. They talk about formative experiences, such as moving to Chicago and early publication, in light of the public figures they later became. Moreover, the "self-mythologizing portraits of the artist"[8] of modernists including Gertrude Stein, Ernest Hemingway, Marcel Proust, and James Joyce, among many others, "[expose] the idea of self-creation as delusion."[9] In their autobiographies, Sherwood Anderson and Margaret Anderson drew portraits that point to their own omissions. For instance, Sherwood Anderson prefaced his *Memoirs* by relating why he would not write about his four marriages, and Margaret Anderson alluded to her long relationship with Jane Heap, co-editor from 1916 and main editor from 1923, in oblique terms. The erasure or elision of sexual histories, for artists so intent on treating sexual desire with frankness, insinuates that these accounts are partial and unstable. Maria DiBattista and Emily Wittman argue that such constructions of self are particular to modernism; for modernists, life-writing does not need to follow chronology or be comprehensive.[10] Rather, it might focus on a brief period of the author's life as in Hemingway's *A Moveable Feast* (1964) or it might focus on a "life-altering problem"[11] such as F. Scott Fitzgerald's *The Crack-Up* (1940). As such, "Modernist autobiography troubles the 'bios'—the life-matter—and the 'auto'—the grammatical and existential first person—of the form."[12] Further, the genre troubles period distinctions that cite an end date or period as definitively modern, as these works often appear much later than the presumed height of modernism. Both Margaret Anderson and Sherwood Anderson composed multiple autobiographies, signaling how the analysis of self and story of a life undergo constant revision. Irving Howe, writing of Sherwood Anderson, diagnosed two symptoms of Chicago's literary scene that bear out in their autobiographical writings: "the search for personal and creative freedom, and the attempt to nurture a distinct Midwestern consciousness."[13] For this reason, autobiography as a genre provides insight, if not totally reliable, into how these writers conceived these twin aims.

Margaret Anderson casts the founding of the *Little Review* as a dramatic moment of divine inspiration brought on by insomnia:

> I had been curiously depressed all day. In the night I wakened. First precise thought: I know why I'm depressed—nothing inspired going on. Second: I demand that life be inspired every moment. Third: the only way to guarantee this is to have inspired conversation every moment. Fourth: most people never get so far as conversation; they haven't the stamina, and there is no time. Fifth: if I had a magazine I could spend my time filling it up with the best conversation that the world has to offer. Sixth: marvelous idea—salvation. Seventh: decision to do it. Deep sleep.[14]

Fully formed yet vague, welcoming yet caustic—Anderson's account of the magazine's inception mirrors her curation of modernist aesthetics in the *Little Review*. She despised groups but fell in with Floyd Dell's Chicago salon; she found Theodore Dreiser tedious but considered Sherwood Anderson a marvelous talker. As she set up her office in room 917 of the Fine Arts Building (designed by Frank Lloyd Wright), she solicited start-up money from Boston and New York. Anderson began the *Little Review* in 1914 in Chicago with the aim to make the magazine the "international organ" for the "new prose."[15] The *Little Review* emerged from the Chicago Literary Renaissance to be one of the chief arbiters of avant-garde modernism. With Ezra Pound's addition in 1917, more British and European artists found their way onto its pages, including James Joyce's *Ulysses*, which appeared in serialized form in twenty-three installments from 1918 to 1920 and for which Heap and Anderson faced charges of obscenity. When it stopped publishing in 1929, twenty-three schools of art from nineteen countries had appeared in its pages.[16] In addition to literature, the editors published experimental visual art, criticism, philosophy, and treatises about music and musicians. Anderson's recounting of the magazine's inception and her personal experience in the city reflect two central aspects of modernism: the individual as a source and topic of ineffable inspiration and the formative space of Chicago.

As the passage about the inspiration for the *Little Review* intimates, the primacy of the individual and the celebration of inspiration were inseparable for Anderson. She was enamored with those artists and friends she considered extraordinary. To understand the kind of modernism Anderson curated, it is useful to know what kind she disdained; she turned her ire to a fellow Midwesterner working in the realist tradition. Although she called Sinclair Lewis "amusing and ardent,"[17] she had little patience for Lewis's attachment to everyday people and settings. She read *Main Street* (1920) one night in a "mountain village in the Pyrenees."[18] She describes how she stayed up

> all night with it in an accumulative rage. Could this be the book that had caused an outcry in recognition of its art? There is no art in it. Its photography is faithful and insignificant. Its truth is unimportant. Faithful photography has never been proof of art—nor has faithful psychology. The psychology of 'Main Street's people is representative, not special ... which can be traced to Lewis' theory that everyone is like everyone else, that everyone is interesting. No great book has ever been built on such a premise.[19]

In her condemnation of Lewis, Anderson projected a vision for her own little magazine and artistic persona: to only publish and sponsor art about extraordinary people and beautiful aesthetics.

Anderson repeatedly characterized herself as the ultimate exceptional person whose aesthetic sensibilities exceeded her ability to communicate them:

> I have never tried to explain the *Little Review*'s point of view to anyone—except a few artists—without being accused of didacticism, dogmatism, fanaticism, aestheticism, exoticism, a debauch of art for art's sake. (I never know what was wrong with art for art's sake. Should it be art for money's sake? Is there something the matter with art that it dare not exist for itself alone?) It is certain that the *Little Review* has printed work that will not hold up as art. This is inevitable. But I have always accepted or rejected manuscripts on one

basis: art as the person. An artist is an exceptional person. Such a person has something exceptional to say. Exceptional matter makes an exceptional manner. This is "style."[20]

These passages—about Lewis's failures and Anderson's commitment to exceptionalism—illuminate how she placed the individual artist at the center of art itself. The work she selected celebrated—and even fetishized—the self above all else. She endorsed artists whose bombast equaled her own. Her philosophy was that an interesting person will necessarily create beautiful art. She deplored Lewis's attempts to make the quotidian beautiful because her aesthetics depended upon the difference between the quotidian and the exceptional. In this, Anderson encouraged a brand of modernism that centered on the creation of a personality that infuses artistic expression. As such, her autobiography is typical of other modernists working in the genre. Modernist autobiographies are full of bombast and embellishment in service of placing themselves as the locus of the new. *My Thirty Years' War*, written years after her direct involvement in the magazine had waned, is hardly authoritative or reliable. She conflated long passages of time, misrepresented her age, and dismissed many important points. However, her autobiography shows how the creation of a self and a place is necessarily a fiction—but a fiction that fueled modernism.

Given this framework, Chicago may seem an odd choice for Anderson. Anderson's story is like many other artists of the period; she grew up shuffling between homes in central Ohio and Indiana. Finding bourgeois, middle-class life boring and stifling, she made her way from Columbus, Indiana, to Chicago. She came to the city in 1908 on the advice of a columnist, Clara E. Laughlin, with *Good Housekeeping,* to whom she had written an angst-filled letter. Laughlin invited her to the city to discuss life and art and, ultimately, set her up with a job. Over the years that followed, Margaret Anderson wrote book reviews and worked as a book clerk in a shop connected to *The Dial*, where she also found a job. It took a couple of tries for Chicago to stick, but she found purpose and vigor in the city. Her formative years and the emergent Chicago arts scene prove that the city fostered the exceptionalist inspiration she sought.

Anderson's early days in the city were consumed by stage performances as she had a mania for theater and music. She prided herself on being the most excellent member of an audience, which fed her sense that she had an innate gift for editing—from hotels to homes to clothes to concerts. She explained that her "incessant, unavoidable observation, this need to distinguish and impose, ... has made me an editor. I can't make things. I can only revise what has been made."[21] And so, in Chicago, Anderson edited a circle of friends who energized the early years of the magazine: Floyd Dell, Maxwell Bodenheim, Ben Hecht, Carl Sandburg, Edgar Lee Masters, Sherwood Anderson, and Eunice Tietjens and Harriet Monroe of *Poetry*. Chicago, with its arts scene made up of midwestern migrants, provided the ideal conditions from which the new art could emerge.

Conventional interpretations of the *Little Review* maintain that Ezra Pound was largely responsible for the experimentation and loftiness of the magazine. More recently, feminist critics have recovered the foundational role Anderson and Heap played, and they do so, in part, by turning to Anderson's autobiography for evidence. "Anderson and Heap's interests in contemporary literature and art, in social critique, and in artistic and intellectual freedom" were, according to Jayne Marek, "aspects of a radical spirit the two women shared that deliberately created a forum for unconventional expression and 'conversation'"[22] within and outside the pages of the *Little Review*. Those early years established the experimental framework that made it an outlet for Pound and his cohort, the Imagists, anarchists, and the eccentricities of artists like Marcel Duchamp and the Baroness Elsa von Freytag Loringhoven, whose erotic Dadaist poetry was a source of ire to both Pound and the censors.

Margaret Anderson was so anxious to publish uncompromising art that the September 1916 volume included thirteen blank pages with the caption "The September issue is offered as a Want Ad." Such escapades were part of the youthful, idealistic persona Anderson corroborated in the autobiography. Another such incident happened in Chicago in those early years. The *Little Review* was always extremely cash poor, with low subscription rates, no pay for contributors, and—in this particular moment—dwindling ad sales and patron support due to the anarchist content. Lacking money for rent, Anderson settled on a plan to camp on the shores of Lake Michigan, north of the city, in tents. She, her sister, her nephews, Harriet Dean (a radical staffer and lover), her maid and the maid's son set up five tents with wood floors and stayed from May to November. Anderson described herself as "lyric"[23] during this period, and indeed she was in her prose. She painted herself as a romantic, tragic figure spending a lovely, stormy Chicago summer camped for her art, lamenting only that she could not get her piano to the beach. In the first issue during this period, the *Little Review* published original poems by Vachel Lindsay, correspondence from Amy Lowell, an essay on Futurism, and book reviews of Fyodor Dostoevsky, Henry James, Mary Antin, and W.B. Yeats. Such was the variety that arose from the banks of Lake Michigan. And she welcomed Sherwood Anderson as a guest to the tents, writing, "Sherwood Anderson came to express his approval and to tell stories around the camp fire."[24]

Both writers elegized the height of Chicago's modernist moment as being one distinguished by its delightful conversation, often with each other. In conceiving of the magazine, she talked with others, including Floyd Dell and Sherwood Anderson: "Floyd and I talked of Pater and of living like the hard gem-like flame. Sherwood Anderson used to listen to us in a certain amazement (resembling fear).... But I liked Sherwood—because he, too, was a talker and of a highly special type. He didn't talk ideas—he told stories. (It sounds bad but the stories were good. So was the telling.)"[25] In her autobiography, she quoted Sherwood Anderson's essay, "The New Note," at length; the short essay, which was published in the inaugural issue of the *Little Review*, called for honesty and truth in writing. He recurs throughout *My Thirty Years' War* as a champion of the magazine and friend to Margaret and Jane, but she tempered her friendship and admiration with this damning quip: His "continued subjectivity ... leaves him in the state of vague romanticism about himself that he undoubtedly enjoyed at the age of ten."[26]

That sense of vague romanticism recurs throughout Sherwood Anderson's autobiographical writings. In his *Memoirs*, he wrote less frequently of Margaret Anderson, stating, "And there was the fascinating figure Margaret Anderson. I knew her when she burst forth with her Little Review, wrote for her first number, wrote for the old Dial when it was published in Chicago, became a part of what was, for a time, called 'The Chicago School' of Writers."[27] His memoirs presumed an exclusively masculine point of view, and while men from the Chicago scene were blazoned in Whitman-esque lists, women, especially Margaret Anderson and Harriet Monroe, received individualized attention as remarkable and out of the ordinary. Such vaunting of the writer as a heroic, male figure is not specific to his autobiography and occurs throughout the texts of male modernists working in the genre, which illuminates why Margaret Anderson cast her work as the product of other worldly inspiration and unceasing energy, rather than the calculated, controlled, and embattled work it often was.

There is also a dimension of the geographic to their self-fashioning, as one can see in Sherwood's comments about her in *A Story Teller's Story*. When they met again in New York, he said, "When I went to see them we had much fun together and Miss Anderson and myself had in common a fondness for clothes and for strutting a bit on the stage of life that drew us closely together but being at bottom fellow Chicagoans we were bound not to take each other too seriously."[28] He recognized a conscious, flamboyant performance of personality in them both, but he diminished the import of that staging in light of their Chicago roots. They had both left Chicago to try New York, and their anxieties about Chicago's working-class identity and presumed provinciality manifested themselves in two distinctive modes: He rendered them folksy co-conspirators, and she defended Chicago as New York's superior in conversation and originality. He did not associate them with their respective small towns but with the city that gave them ink and conversation.

Unlike Margaret Anderson, who spent only a few passages on her life before Chicago, which she casts as confining and tyrannical, Sherwood Anderson devoted a bulk of *A Story Teller's Story* to the youthful incidents that animated life in Ohio before he came to Chicago. DiBattista and Wittman describe how "[t]o accommodate the fluidity and the variousness of life and how it feels to be living it, modernist autobiography often tampers with sequence and chronology, sometimes abandoning the very idea of eventfulness in favor of recounting memories or anecdotes that evoke the emotional and moral texture of ordinary experiences."[29] This could be a thesis for Anderson's *A Story Teller's Story*. The 1924 autobiography, written while he awaited a divorce in Reno, consists of scenes and moments from childhood that tell of everyday experiences and interactions, particularly with his father, that, Anderson argued, were formative to his understanding of the story teller's centrality to both the decline of agrarian life and the rise of industrialism, which were the twin pulls of his aesthetics. He described how in Ohio a new narrative of "Get on. Make money. Get to the top"[30] emerged, which was fueled by factories, automobiles, jazz, and movies. Anderson's obsession with fanatical industry (both his own and the culture's) was a recurring theme in his fiction, essays, and autobiographies. The only respite from the fever of industry and social mobility came from writing, and he venerated the "Makers of paper" and "exclude[d them] from all the curses I have heaped upon manufacturers when I have walked in the street breathing coal dust and smoke."[31] Such meditations repeat throughout *A Story Teller's Story* as he made sense of his own vexed position as a recurrent advertising writer and former factory owner. And, it is with some resignation but also pride that he reflected on his time in New York after Chicago: "I was not too young anymore and could not make myself over to fit a new city.... I was a man of mid-western towns who had gone from his town to mid-western cities.... To the end of my life I would talk with the half slovenly drawl of the mid-westerner."[32] Age and place recur as formative to the writer's persona. Not much happens in *A Story Teller's Story*; instead, he positioned these reflections on the creation of a mid-western self in the context of industrialization. The very uneventfulness of the book as well as the conversational tone aligns it with a modernist tendency to meander and examine without teleology or revelation.

The *Memoirs* maintain his signature breezy storytelling mode, which Margaret Anderson so enjoyed. For the *Memoirs,* Ray Lewis White prepared an edited, critical edition in 1969 from the nearly three thousand manuscript pages that Anderson worked on, in fits and starts, from 1933 to 1941, when he died of peritonitis during a trip to South America. Originally published in 1949 with edits and excisions from Paul Rosenfeld, the 1969 edition reveals an unfinished opus. That the text is revised, expanded, and unfinished fits Anderson's vision of the memoirs, even if he did not live to oversee their completion and publication. White's edition follows a loose chronology, keeping to the spirit of design Anderson intended: In 1939, he returned to his *Memoirs* stating, "The idea is really ... to do an autobiography in a new way, not in the life of the teller but in lives that touch his life ... much as I used the figure of George Willard in Winesburg but carrying the idea into more mature years."[33] White argues that, like *Winesburg,* "each essay [is] complete and separate from contiguous material."³⁴ In the preface, Anderson wrote that he had "striven for frankness" and avoided chronology and personal development in favor of portraying "the life ... of a certain period in American life."³⁵ In this, his *Memoirs* could not be more different than Margaret Anderson's, which focused on her unique experiences and encounters.

He dedicated almost one hundred pages to his time in Chicago, and he spoke of the city as fostering creativity and conversation. "It was a time of something flowering in Chicago and the middle west," Anderson remembers, citing Edgar Lee Masters's *Spoon River Anthology*, Lindsay's poetry, Dreiser's *Sister Carrie*, and the *Little Review* as evidence, that in Chicago "was a time of excitement, something seemingly new and fresh in the air we breathed."³⁶ He also remarked on how conversation was a mainstay of the Chicago scene, as he recounted the nights spent at the Dells' small apartment or his own. Of Dell, he said, "When he was on the subject of literature he talked I thought brilliantly. I had never before heard such talk. How it flowed from him."³⁷ His memories of Dell echoed Margaret Anderson's; Dell championed his early works and became a kind of patron to the emerging writers of the Chicago scene. Anderson's *Memoirs* characterize his time in Chicago as "the gayest and happiest I have ever known" distinguished by a "feeling of brotherhood and sisterhood with men and women whose interests were my own."³⁸ He claimed that the times in Chicago were ones in which he had not yet known artistic jealousies, writer's block, disappointment in his craft, or the ambition for earning money from writing. That sense of unfettered, not-yet-realized possibility echoes in the pages of *Winesburg*, especially in the ending when George Willard departs his small town for an unnamed city, presumably Chicago. Throughout the stories, anticipating something is better than experiencing it; whether it is leaving Winesburg, falling in love, having sex, or becoming a writer, the characters routinely experience disappointment when their dreams are accomplished. Such is the tone of Anderson's memories of Chicago, where his art was on the verge of blossoming but had not yet been tainted by lackluster books and broken friendships.

As he recounted the composition of *Winesburg*—some of the early stories were printed in the *Little Review*—he, too, focused on rapid, ineffable inspiration as crucial to making "the new prose":

> And so the stories came, in this rather strange way, into existence. I had, in relation to them, a somewhat new feeling. It was as though I had little or nothing to do with the writing. It was as though the people of that house, all of them wanting so much, none of them really equipped to wrestle with life as it was, had, in this odd way, used me as an instrument. They had got, I felt, through me, their stories told, and in their own persons but, in a much more real and satisfactory way, through the lives of these queer small town people of the book.[39]

He alluded to the artists with whom he boarded on Cass Street near the Loop. He called the people with whom he boarded "the unsuccessful Little Children of the Arts,"[40] and he credited them for inspiring the *Winesburg* stories, although he later described them as stemming from his small-town experiences. In these divergent accounts, he collapsed the distance between town and city; Chicago liberates writers to treat their hometowns honestly.

At the beginning of this chapter, I noted that Sherwood Anderson compared his time in Chicago to a "Robin's Egg Renaissance" that he lamented ever having flown away from. The homely, natural metaphor of the robin's nest suggests something not fully formed, fragile, beautiful, and full of possibility. That is exactly the sense one gets from reading about Chicago in these autobiographies. So, why did most of the writers—including Margaret Anderson and Sherwood Anderson—leave? What drew them East and then to Europe and the South? Sherwood Anderson implied that Midwesterners cannot be taken seriously. Margaret Anderson stated that the "greatest city of America" was New York and "the greatest artists of the modern age"[41] were in London and Paris. However, not everyone left. Harriet Monroe stayed, and *Poetry* remains a powerhouse publication. In the 1940s, new writers—including Gwendolyn Brooks, Margaret Walker, and Richard Wright—emerged from the South Side, casting the city's modernism through another lens and from another milieu. Sherwood Anderson's Robin's Egg Renaissance got it right: These artists were at their best in Chicago when life was full of possibility and fragile in its infancy. Chicago was the place where both Sherwood Anderson and Margaret Anderson became enamored of conversation that prized honesty. It is here that they attempted to understand that ineffable source of inspiration that characterizes many modernists' conception of writing. From their arrival on westbound trains to working in the Fine Arts Building, Chicago was like the artists they admired: exceptional, conversational, and idealistic.

Acknowledgment

I am indebted to the NEH Seminar *Making Modernism: Literature and Culture in Twentieth-Century Chicago, 1893–1955*, led by Liesl Olson, whose book *Chicago Renaissance: Literature and Art in the Midwest Metropolis* (New Haven: Yale, 2017) informs and inspired this essay.

Notes

1. Margaret Anderson, *My Thirty Years' War* (New York: Horizon Press, 1969), 13.
2. Ibid., 32.
3. Sherwood Anderson, *Sherwood Anderson's Memoirs, A Critical Edition*, ed. Ray Lewis White (Chapel Hill, NC: University of North Carolina Press, 1969), 317.
4. Craig Monk, *Writing the Lost Generation: Expatriate Autobiography and American Modernism* (Iowa City, IA: University of Iowa Press, 2008), 12.
5. Ibid., 14.
6. Mark Morrison, "Youth in Public: The *Little Review* and Commercial Culture in Chicago," in *The Public Face of Modernism: Little Magazines, Audiences, and Reception, 1905–1920* (Madison, WI: University of Wisconsin Press, 2001), 133–66.
7. Maria DiBattista and Emily O. Wittman, Introduction to *The Cambridge Companion to Autobiography*, ed. Maria DiBattista and Emily O. Wittman (New York: Cambridge University Press, 2014), 7.
8. Ibid., 11.
9. Deborah Epstein Nord, "Victorian Autobiography: Fathers and Sons," in *The Cambridge Companion to Autobiography*, 97.
10. Maria DiBattista and Emily O. Wittman, Introduction to *Modernism and Autobiography*, ed. Maria DiBattista and Emily O. Wittman (New York: Cambridge University Press, 2014), xi.
11. Ibid., xii.
12. Ibid., xii.
13. Irving Howe, *Sherwood Anderson* (Toronto: William Sloane, 1951), 71.
14. Margaret Anderson, *My Thirty Years' War*, 35.
15. Ibid., 136.
16. "The *Little Review*," *Modernist Journals Project*, http://www.modjourn.org/render.php?view=mjp_object&id=LittleReviewCollection

17. Margaret Anderson, *My Thirty Years' War*, 77.
18. Ibid., 79.
19. Ibid.
20. Ibid., 134.
21. Ibid., 58.
22. Jayne Marek, *Women Editing Modernism: "Little Magazines" and Literary History* (Lexington, KY: University Press of Kentucky, 1995), 99.
23. Margaret Anderson, *My Thirty Years' War*, 91.
24. Ibid., 91.
25. Ibid., 39.
26. Ibid., 141.
27. Sherwood Anderson, *Sherwood Anderson's Memoirs*, 316.
28. Sherwood Anderson, *A Story Teller's Story* (Ann Arbor, MI: The University of Michigan Press, 2005), 351.
29. Maria DiBattista and Emily O. Wittman, Introduction to *Modernism and Autobiography*, xiii.
30. Sherwood Anderson, *A Story Teller's Story*, 84.
31. Ibid., 293.
32. Ibid., 347.
33. Ray Lewis White, Introduction to *Sherwood Anderson's Memoirs*, xxiv (quoting Anderson).
34. Ibid., xxxv.
35. Sherwood Anderson, *Sherwood Anderson's Memoirs*, 3.
36. Ibid., 337.
37. Ibid., 339.
38. Ibid., 344.
39. Ibid., 348.
40. Ibid., 350.
41. Margaret Anderson, *My Thirty Years' War*, 136.

Ross K. Tangedal | That Time in Chicago
 | Midwestern Memory in Nella Larsen's *Passing*

"That time in Chicago." The words stood out from among the many paragraphs of other words, bringing with them a clear, sharp remembrance, in which even now, after two years, humiliation, resentment, and rage were mingled.

—*Passing*[1]

I don't have any way of approaching life ...
it does things to me instead.

—Nella Larsen[2]

Nella Larsen's *Passing*, published to controversy in 1929, exists as a testament to narrative, textual, and regional ambiguity. Scholarship surrounding the novel centers primarily on three major contexts: racial identity, feminine identity, and sexual identity. Yet, the most undervalued and least discussed issue regarding the text is Larsen's attention to region and how it manifests textually. The main flashpoint of the novel—Irene Redfield's reunion with Clare Kendry—occurs on top of the Drayton Hotel in Chicago, Illinois. Larsen, who brilliantly distills the Harlem Renaissance, the New Negro movement, interracial marriage, lesbian desire, and maternal ambivalence at various intervals, equally uses Chicago as a central determinant for Irene's actions and identity. Larsen's Chicago flashback ("Part One: Encounter") represents a literary experiment in place that merges with her discussions of race, sexuality, and identity. Chicago is a hot, sensuous place, "with what small breeze there was seemed like the breath of a flame fanned by slow bellows";[3] she uses the city as a place of spatial memory, in which Clare Kendry returns to Irene's present through the past and becomes the destructive catalyst to her eventual destruction. Like many writers, Larsen recognizes how a city can function as both a personal ambiguous space and a collective memorial space. The episode in Chicago provides a distinctive narrative effect not unlike F. Scott Fitzgerald's use of the region in *The Great Gatsby* (1925) or Booth Tarkington's use of the encroaching midwestern city in *The Magnificent Ambersons* (1918). Like Larsen, writers of the Chicago Renaissance (which peaked in the 1920s), featured powerful expressions of the city. The narrator of Theodore Dreiser's *Sister Carrie* reminds readers that "the city has its cunning wiles," and its forces "unrecognized for what they are, their beauty, like music, too often relaxes, then wakens, then perverts the simpler human perceptions."[4] Chicago awakens, then perverts Irene Redfield's memory, its cunning wiles too strong for her to reconcile. Chicago is a crucial narrative element in Larsen's portrayal of ambiguity, both real and imagined, and through the complex textual interplay between past and present, readers bear witness to a writer's attempts to manifest regional identity at a time of great upheaval. *Passing* as a novel "passes" in several ways, yet the most inconspicuous subversion is the role Chicago plays in Nella Larsen's experiment in memory.

In *Chicago Dreaming: Midwesterners and the City, 1871–1919*, Timothy Spears defines the booming city's "restlessness, displacement, excitement, and dread"[5] at the turn of the twentieth century. He argues that "Chicago's significance rested most of all on its opportunities for *self-making*,"[6] and few cultures were more attuned to the idea of self-making at this point in history than African Americans. Historian Davarian Baldwin highlights the differences between the popular New Negro movement centered in Harlem and the New Negro movement in Chicago that resulted from the Great Migration in the early twentieth century. He argues,

> while Harlem thinkers advocated self-determination and cultural autonomy, Black entrepreneurs, war veterans, artists, politicians, and intellectuals in Chicago attempted to build a separate economic and institutional worldview known as the "metropolis." The "metropolis" model was to be driven by a symbiotic relationship between Black producers and consumers to secure community control of ideas and labor.[7]

The blending of economics and intellectualism was precisely the kind of freedom Chicago offered, for "the most important point about Chicago's 'metropolis' model is that the economic framework is not distinct or separate from the production of the arts and ideas, and in fact it was *the* site for a more comprehensive New Negro consciousness."[8] Just as Baldwin presents Chicago historically as a space of crucial history in the determination of African American consciousness, Nella Larsen uses Chicago as a center around which her memories (and the memories of her characters) coalesce into a larger concept of racial ambiguity.

Born prior to the Great Migration,[9] Larsen spent the first sixteen years of her life in Chicago before moving to Nashville, Tennessee, in the fall of 1907, where she attended Fisk University, a historically black college.[10] In *Nella Larsen: Novelist of the Harlem Renaissance*, Thadious Davis argues that her "falling out of place and concomitant seeking of place began in Chicago, where, within an immigrant social context, constricting circles of race and gender ran against the grain of opportunity and assimilation."[11] George Hutchinson, in his biography, *In Search of Nella Larsen: A Biography of the Color Line*, describes Larsen's Chicago as "a sprawling chaos sprung from the ashes of the great fire of 1871."[12] Having begun life in a "disabling fluidity,"[13] the young Larsen's Chicago childhood included several moves and name changes. More predominantly, her unresolved "double patrimony—skin color, class position, family connection—would become egregious factors affecting her spatial movement, social mobility, and self-perception in the decades ahead."[14] Davis points out further that Larsen "distanced herself from her Chicago past. For most of her acquaintances during the 1920s and 1930s, it simply did not exist."[15] Similarly, Hutchinson notes that the city "left an enduring imprint on her personality," making Larsen "keenly sensitive to the stigma of blackness."[16] Though Chicago was becoming an artistic and economic foundation for African American identity, for Nella Larsen the city represented the ambiguity of her youth, the fractured self at the center of her genius, and the space of memories she'd sooner forget.

Given Larsen's precarious past in Chicago, we can see why she would feature the city so prominently early in the narrative. Larsen immediately develops the ambiguities deep within Irene Redfield, since she lives in Harlem, the predominantly black neighborhood in New York that sparked the Harlem Renaissance, while Clare Kendry lives in

Chicago, a city of multiple cultures, races, and peoples. *Passing* is a novel of conflict, a story of ambiguous feelings, emotions, races, sexualities, and memories, and there is no better place for Larsen to fixate on these ideas than in Chicago, her space of "disabling fluidity"[17] and "sprawling chaos."[18] By choosing to use Chicago as an interlude rather than the main setting of the novel, Larsen amplifies the unique hold the city has over Irene (and over Larsen herself). After a short introduction to Irene Redfield, readers are thrown headlong into a sweltering Chicago summer, "a brilliant day, hot, with a brutal staring sun pouring down rays that were like molten rain. A day in which the very outlines of the buildings shuddered as if in protest at the heat."[19] Historian Dale Kramer notes that "traveling notables chose one or more of the epithets from the standard hellbox" when describing Chicago: "raw, ugly, chaotic, turbulent, brutal, frenzied."[20] Each of these epithets plays a role in Larsen's vision of the city, just as her own Chicago past teemed with chaos and turbulence. Irene recently received a letter from Clare Kendry, a childhood friend, whom she recalls being "hard and apparently without feeling at all; sometimes she was affectionate and rashly impulsive. And there was about her an amazing soft malice, hidden well away until provoked."[21] Hutchinson contends that Clare, "[inciting] both entranced admiration and dread, when she suddenly reappears as a beautiful and sophisticated adult, she is the nearly perfect human embodiment of a fetish."[22] Irene fetishizes what she cannot have in Clare, and Clare relishes her ability to retreat from and return to her true racial identity any time she pleases.

 Moreover, Irene focuses on one line in Clare's letter, a line that seems to dominate the remainder of the novel: "For I wouldn't now, perhaps, have this terrible, this wild desire if I hadn't seen you that time in Chicago."[23] With the words "wild" and "Chicago," Irene remembers her youth on the south side of Chicago.[24] She unfurls her own history against the backdrop of Clare's "wild oat" father, a father who had been brother to two abusive aunts.[25] Clare is taken away by her aunts to the west side, which leads to abuse and mistreatment, and she eventually tells Irene,

> "the aunts were queer. For all their Bibles and praying and ranting about honesty, they didn't want anyone to know that their darling brother had seduced—ruined, they called

it—a Negro girl. They could excuse the ruin, but they couldn't forgive the tarbrush. They forbade me to mention Negroes to the neighbours, or even to mention the south side."[26]

In this moment, Larsen creates in Irene a subdued desire to relive Chicago through Clare's letter and later with Clare herself. Chicago provides the stage for Irene Redfield's identity crisis, where she acts out her desires and dysfunctions in equal and damaging patterns. However, Clare is responsible for thrusting Chicago back into Irene's domestic routine, or what Frank Hering calls "the fantasy of idealized domesticity's safety."[27] By breaking up that safe haven, the memory of Clare becomes the memory of Chicago, and the letter represents "a piece with all that she knew of Clare Kendry. Stepping always on the edge of danger. Always aware, but not drawing back or turning aside. Certainly not because of any alarms or feeling of outrage on the part of others."[28] There is no stopping Clare's existence, and therefore the existence of Chicago, in Irene's memory, and her experiences in the city fracture Irene's fragile identity.

A key element in Irene's reunion with Clare in Chicago is recognition. Having already established the hazy heat of a summer day—"Sharp particles of dust rose from the burning sidewalks, stinging the seared or dripping skins of wilting pedestrians"[29]—Larsen creates a blurred atmosphere filled with destructive and disorienting imagery. Irene walks the burning sidewalk when "before her smarting eyes a man toppled over and became an inert crumpled heap on the scorching cement."[30] The falling man, perhaps foreshadowing Clare's falling in the climax of the novel, also represents exhaustion on the part of Irene. Her roles as mother and wife and friend to Clare (once they reunite) lead her to the very ends of her strength and eventual destruction. However, a descent of that magnitude gains in gravity if witnessed (or recognized) by others. Larsen forecasts the descent with the man lying helpless on the burning pavement: "About the lifeless figure a little crowd gathered. Was the man dead, or only faint? someone asked her. But Irene didn't know and didn't try to discover. She edged her way out of the increasing crowd, feeling disagreeably damp and sticky and soiled from contact with so many sweating bodies."[31] Claudia Tate argues that *Passing* "must be deduced not merely from its surface content but also from its vivid imagery, subtle metaphors, and carefully balanced psychological inquiry."[32] At issue is Irene's perception of the city and the falling man, the heat of one leading to the cold death of the other. Larsen's narrative perspective obviates Irene as narrator—she is not the narrator; she is the actor—though Larsen filters every thought and action through her, as if she were the storyteller. Irene immerses herself (at least in memory) within the sweltering Chicago community where strangers crowd around a lifeless body. Yet she rejects it, as she calls for the security of a cab almost out of fear. But the cab driver "jumped out and guided her to his car" and "he helped, almost lifted her in."[33] Irene at first finds the moment perplexing—"for a minute her thoughts were nebulous"—then worthy of an opportunity as "they cleared."[34] Clearly, Irene recognizes her cab driver's misrecognition of her race. Now a white woman escaping the misfit crowd of gawkers, Irene Redfield feels empowered to "repair the damage that the heat and crowds had done to her appearance."[35]

Larsen's attention to appearance and recognition early in the novel forecasts the major themes for the remainder of the narrative. Mary Mabel Youman notes a "distaste and avid curiosity" in Irene's perceptions of sexuality later in the novel, as she hovers somewhere between awestruck and disgusted with Clare Kendry and her own repression.[36] Since her reconnection with Clare happens for readers in flashback, we can assume that Irene's between-ness informs the storytelling. In Chicago, she acknowledges both the awe and the disgust, leading her to deal with the recognition of race, sex, gender, and place all at once. These elements coalesce when she enters the Drayton Hotel, a space she would not be allowed to enter if the proprietors (or guests) thought she was black. Emboldened by her deception, Irene orders tea, and this simple act results in a crucial confluence:

> The tea, when it came, was all that she had desired and expected. In fact, so much was it what she had desired and expected that after the first deep cooling drink she was able to forget it, only now and then sipping, a little absently, from the tall green glass, while she surveyed the room about her or looked out over some lower buildings at the bright unstirred blue or the lake reaching away to an undetected horizon.[37]

Larsen uses Chicago and Lake Michigan as ever-deepening metaphors for Irene's present psyche, pitting industrialization, mechanization, and restriction against openness, nature, and freedom. That the lake reaches "away to an undetected horizon" awards Irene unfettered, yet momentary, freedom to escape her racial place. The "it" mentioned in the passage above refers to that freedom, for Irene's experience with the tea is parallel to her own experience with race in this moment. She looks down upon the lower buildings and the lake as if to dare both to out her. Deborah McDowell contends that Larsen's novels deal "simultaneously with this dialectic between pleasure and danger. In their reticence about sexuality, they look back to their nineteenth-century predecessors, but in their simultaneous flirtation with female sexual desire, they are solidly grounded in the liberation of the 1920s."[38] Larsen keenly observes Irene's power as a result of her escape from the falling man and her redemption by the cab driver. Her reward is amplified by sitting atop the great midwestern city overlooking the great midwestern lake and drinking tea from a green glass.

However, that power obstructs Irene's vision as she gazes toward "an attractive-looking woman ... with those dark, almost black, eyes and that wide mouth like a scarlet flower against the ivory of her skin. Nice clothes too, just right for the weather, thin and cool without being mussy, as summer things were apt to be."[39] Not far from being disgusted by the summer heat and the exhaustion of the sweaty crowd, Irene revels in the thin and cool clothes of a stranger. But this gaze leads to personal self-doubt as the stranger gazes back, with Irene's "unseeing eyes far away on the lake, when by some sixth sense she was acutely aware that someone was watching her."[40] Once she is seen by another, gazed upon by an outsider whom she initially gravitates toward, Irene feels "a small inner disturbance, odious and hatefully familiar."[41] That disturbance leads to recognition of her race, even though no one has publicly outed her. She lambasts white people for their stupidity and inability to recognize those that pass, since "they always took her for an Italian, a Spaniard, a Mexican, or a gipsy."[42] For Irene, "could that woman, somehow know that here before her very eyes on the roof of the Drayton sat a Negro? Absurd! Impossible! White people were so stupid about such things for all that they usually asserted that they were able to tell; and by the most ridiculous means, finger-nails, palms of hands, shapes of ears, teeth, and other equally silly rot."[43] With her eyes on the lake, Irene begins to feel the tug of her deception, but she looks to the blue waters of Lake Michigan to remind her of freedom, especially from the city: "she turned away with the firm intention of keeping her gaze on the lake, the roofs of the buildings across the sky, anywhere but on that annoying woman."[44] Carl S. Smith notes that the lake "figures in Chicago writing as an escape or relief from the city," while also functioning as "a refuge for individuals who confront certain urban dilemmas."[45] Irene looks to the lake for refuge. Will she be ejected from the Drayton? Will the other woman call attention to her deception? As Irene questions herself, the stranger moves across the room and breaks the tension. Clare Kendry moves back into Irene's life.

Because Clare recognizes Irene from afar prior to their reunion, Candace Jenkins argues, "by restricting the ability to recognize blackness, even among people who are fair enough to be taken for white, to only other blacks, Larsen's characters make it possible to delimit the boundaries of blackness on their own terms."[46] Irene notices an "intangible something, too vague to define, too remote to seize, but which was, to Irene Redfield, very familiar."[47] Jenkins reads Irene as using "the language of ambiguity" to describe her feelings toward Clare,[48] which is similar to Brian Carr's assertion that "Irene's inability to superintend the operative forms of misrecognition in this scene leads her to turn inward."[49] Irene believes that Clare stares at her solely because of her race, yet once Irene recognizes her old friend, she realizes the stare was a result of personal recognition, not racial recognition. Clare's ability to see the real Irene, coupled with Irene's rant against white misrecognition, shows Larsen empowering Clare. She can see what others cannot. That this delimiting occurs in Chicago is no mistake. Larsen carefully constructs Irene's memory to amplify the ambiguity of Chicago as much as the ambiguity of Clare. The city is energized yet constrictive, but Lake Michigan offers tranquility and freedom of motion. Irene feels free only when she deceives some of Chicago's patrons, yet an outsider (Clare) cripples that freedom by herself being free of the fear of being caught passing, a freedom Irene envies and despises.

Clare can freely move about (and live) in Chicago without detection, which both enrages and exhilarates Irene. That she had herself successfully passed through Chicago as a white woman bears her no mind, for to her Clare represents deception *par excellence*. Clare's laugh was a "trill of notes," "small and clear and the very essence of mockery."[50] Irene chooses not to formally ask Clare about her life in Chicago:

> Appearances, she knew now, had a way sometimes of not fitting facts, and if Clare hadn't—Well, if they had all been wrong, then certainly she ought to express some interest in what had happened to her. It would seem queer and rude if she didn't. But how was she to know? There was, she at last decided, no way; so she merely said again, "I must go Clare."[51]

Clare's ambiguous yet, oddly enough, well-known experience drives Irene to curiosity: "she wished to find out about this hazardous business of 'passing,' this breaking away from all that was familiar and friendly to take one's chance in another environment, not entirely strange, but certainly not entirely friendly."[52] Irene has no way of reconciling her own deception with that of Clare Kendry, her "impossibility of adequate recognition" restricting any mutual experience between the two.[53] But Irene wants it that way. As a New Yorker and Harlem resident, Irene revels in her racial identity, a player in the Harlem Renaissance scene and champion of the black community. She represents the type of identity restriction from which Clare escaped. Clare lives in Chicago, where she deceives and passes for something (not someone) else. Irene claims to have everything she wants, "except, perhaps, a little more money,"[54] to which Clare responds, "money's awfully nice to have. In fact, all things considered, I think, 'Rene, that it's even worth the price."[55] This final conversation leads Irene to conclude, "it was as if the woman sitting on the other side of the table, a girl that she had known, who had done this rather dangerous and, to Irene Redfield, abhorrent thing successfully and had announced herself well satisfied, had for her a fascination, strange and compelling."[56] Clare satisfied her initial goals in the ambiguousness of Chicago rather than submit to the apparent definiteness of Harlem. Clare seems to have escaped her past in order to both reinvent and effectively free herself. On the other hand, Irene chose an easier path. Her choice to live in a more clearly defined part of the country (Harlem) as a clearly defined black woman is at odds with Clare's more radical position. That she finds Clare's passing both strange and compelling speaks to Irene's inner struggle with definition.

At this moment, Irene recognizes Clare and Chicago as one and the same, which toys with her ability to understand her experience: "the sun had gone from overhead, but the streets were still like fiery furnaces. The languid breeze was still hot. And the scurrying people looked even more wilted than before Irene had fled from their contact."[57] She crosses "the avenue in the heat, far from the coolness of the Drayton's roof, away from the seduction of Clare Kendry's smile."[58] Lake Michigan and the tops of buildings proved most appealing to Irene atop the Drayton, but Clare fractures that reverie by representing a coolness inside the heat. Chicago once held a freedom for Irene, since she too could pass without consequence. However, once Clare breaks that confidence, Irene can no longer use Chicago as the space of freedom in her memory. Her memory is now populated with heat, sweat, and conflict. She remembers getting physically and spiritually above all those problems only to be recognized and interrupted in her brief escape by someone she once knew. Clare Kendry had her escape; she lit out confidently to deceive and she succeeded, something that terrorizes Irene for the remainder of the novel.

The coolness of the Drayton Hotel roof makes way for a "foreboding fog" on the afternoon Irene visits Clare's home.[59] She is met by Clare and Gertrude Martin, another black woman married to a white man and successfully passing in Chicago. Immediately, Irene feels "outnumbered, a sense of aloneness, in her adherence to her own class and kind; not merely in the great thing of marriage, but in the whole pattern of her life as well."[60] Larsen plays Irene against herself, as if she has completely forgotten her own desire to escape by passing earlier at the Drayton. Ironically, Irene thinks she is above certain impulses (like passing) while at the same time wanting to engage in them; she never makes public her desires, whereas Clare mindfully enacts her deception. However, once Larsen touches on Irene's confused aloneness, she shifts gears to Clare's return to Chicago after time away in Europe:

> "I simply had to. And after I once got here, I was determined to see someone I knew and find out what had happened to everybody. I didn't quite see how I was going to manage it, but I meant to. Somehow. I'd just about decided to take

a chance and go out to your house, 'Rene, or call up and arrange a meeting, when I ran into you. What luck!"[61]

In contrast to Irene's racial escape while passing at the Drayton, Clare uses Chicago to return to her race and to her home. Larsen complicates her earlier freedom metaphors by creating in Clare a new idea of escape. Instead of escaping her racial roots (which she had already done), she wishes to return to them. Meanwhile, Irene sees Lake Michigan and the Drayton Hotel as brief reprieves from the definiteness and security of Harlem. At this point Irene can only muster, "'It's the first time I've been home for five years, and now I'm about to leave. A week later and I'd have been gone.'"[62] Larsen clearly foreshadows the key conflict of the novel in this subtle exchange: Clare Kendry wishes to reintegrate into the black community without consequence, which both enrages and seduces Irene Redfield. And so, for the remainder of the novel, Irene suffers from her own duality, a duality begun while passing in Chicago.

To understand the Midwest in Nella Larsen's *Passing* is to understand Irene's fragile memory. Irene feels mortified, enraged, hurt, and humiliated once Clare's white husband—John Bellew—displays his unashamed views on African Americans to the group of women while completely oblivious to their mutual deception. As she leaves the apartment,

> Irene Redfield was trying to understand the look on Clare's face as she had said good-bye. Partly mocking, it had seemed, and partly menacing. And something else for which she could find no name. For an instant a recrudescence of that sensation of fear which she had had while looking into Clare's eyes that afternoon touched her. A slight shiver ran over her.[63]

The fear Irene feels mirrors the fear she felt for Clare as a child knitting with her "bellowing" father roaring up and down the room.[64] The bellowing father pairs with Irene's immediate description of Chicago's heat, for "what small breeze there was seemed like the breath of a flame fanned by slow bellows."[65] The slow bellows fanning the flames merge into John Bellew, a hatred of whom nests in Irene once he offers her a light for her cigarette.⁶⁶ Irene's one reaction—"a faint sense of danger brushed her, like the breath of a cold fog,"⁶⁷—responds to those three elements: Bob Kendry bellowing at his child, Chicago burning under a bellowed flame, and John Bellew offering fire for ignition. Chicago and the memories therein force Irene to oscillate between hot and cold and black and white. Before returning us to the present, Larsen shows Irene ripping apart a letter from Clare while still in Chicago: "and that, she told herself, was that. The chances were one in a million that she would ever again lay eyes on Clare Kendry. If, however, that millionth chance should turn up, she had only to turn away her eyes, to refuse her recognition."⁶⁸ We are brought back to the gaze atop the Drayton, where Irene consciously chose to stare upon a stranger and refuse that stranger's recognition.

Nella Larsen used Chicago to represent Irene's fractured memory, as well as the power the city possessed. But Irene never really returns from Chicago, even as she goes back to her husband, children, and life as a wife/mother/black community leader. And when Clare returns physically to Harlem, the resulting chaos, fluidity, anger, and frustration teem within Irene. Clare declares to Irene, "I want to see Negroes, to be with them again, to talk with them, to hear them laugh."⁶⁹ In opposition to the Chicago scene, here Clare wishes to be and see, rather than conceal and divert. But Larsen's follow-up narration solidifies the confusion deep within Irene, and the danger Clare poses to her quiet order: "And in the look she gave Irene, there was something groping, and hopeless, and yet so absolutely determined that it was like an image of the futile searching and the firm resolution in Irene's own soul, and increased the feeling of doubt and compunction that had been growing within her about Clare Kendry."⁷⁰ From the initial letter reminding her of the brief Chicago encounter with Clare, to the finale, in which Larsen writes, "One moment Clare had been there, a vital glowing thing, like a flame of red and gold. The next she was gone,"⁷¹ Irene fuses the hot bellows of Chicago with the fire of Clare's "full, red lips, and in her shining eyes."⁷² Irene, in her present state and in memory, cannot disassociate Chicago from the destructive forces represented by Clare, since the two weave together a mangled tapestry of confusion, fear, and heat.⁷³ That time in Chicago leads to Irene Redfield's ruin, a foreboding fog of an intangible something in her own confused memory.

Notes

1. Nella Larsen, *Passing,* 1929, ed. Carla Kaplan (New York: W.W. Norton & Co., 2007), 7.
2. Quoted in Mary Rennels, "Behind the Backs of Books and Authors," *The New York Telegram* (April 13, 1919): Sec. 2, pp. 1–2. Reprinted in Larsen, *Passing,* 150.
3. Larsen, *Passing,* 7.
4. Theodore Dreiser, *Sister Carrie,* 1900 (Philadelphia, PA: University of Pennsylvania Press, 1981), 4.
5. Timothy Spears, *Chicago Dreaming: Midwesterners and the City, 1871–1919* (Chicago: University of Chicago Press, 2005), xv.
6. Ibid., xvi.
7. Davarian L. Baldwin, "Chicago's New Negroes: Consumer Culture and Intellectual Life Reconsidered," *American Studies* 44, no. 1–2 (2003): 123.
8. Ibid.
9. Larsen was born April 13, 1891.
10. George Hutchinson, *In Search of Nella Larsen: A Biography of the Color Line* (Cambridge, MA: Belknap, 2006), 52.
11. Thadious Davis, *Nella Larsen: Novelist of the Harlem Renaissance* (Baton Rouge, LA: Louisiana State University Press, 1994), 21.
12. Hutchinson, *In Search of,* 14.
13. Davis, *Nella Larsen,* 21.
14. Ibid., 50.
15. Ibid., 142.
16. Hutchinson, *In Search of,* 52.
17. Davis, *Nella Larsen,* 21.
18. Hutchinson, *In Search of,* 14.
19. Larsen, *Passing,* 7.
20. Dale Kramer, *Chicago Renaissance: The Literary Life in the Midwest, 1900–1930* (New York: Appleton-Century, 1966), 8.
21. Ibid., 6.
22. Hutchinson, *In Search of,* 296.
23. Larsen, *Passing,* 7.
24. Biographers Thadious Davis and George Hutchinson lay out the history of Chicago's south side in great detail as a backdrop for Larsen's life and fiction. Carla Kaplan and others suggest that Larsen's attention to passing and racial ambiguity stemmed from growing up on the borders of the "black belt," slang for a section of the south side populated primarily by African Americans. See Kaplan's introduction and notes to her Norton critical edition of *Passing.*
25. Larsen, *Passing,* 21.
26. Ibid., 19.

27. Frank Hering, "Sneaking Around: Idealized Domesticity, Identity Politics, and Games of Friendship in Nella Larsen's *Passing*," *Arizona Quarterly* 57, no. 1 (2001): 38.
28. Larsen, *Passing*, 5.
29. Ibid., 7.
30. Ibid., 8.
31. Ibid.
32. Claudia Tate, "Nella Larsen's *Passing*: A Problem of Interpretation," *Black American Literature Forum* 14, no. 4 (1980): 142–46. Reprinted in Larsen, *Passing*, 343.
33. Larsen, *Passing*, 8.
34. Ibid.
35. Ibid.
36. Mary Mabel Youman, "Nella Larsen's *Passing*: A Study in Irony," *College Language Association Journal* 18 (1974): 235–41. Reprinted in Larsen, *Passing*, 339.
37. Larsen, *Passing*, 9.
38. Deborah E. McDowell, "Introduction to Nella Larsen," in *Quicksand and Passing*, ed. Deborah E. McDowell (New Brunswick, NJ: Rutgers University Press, 1986), ix–xxxv. Reprinted as "From [Black Female Sexuality in Passing]" in Larsen, *Passing*, 369.
39. Larsen, *Passing*, 9.
40. Ibid., 10.
41. Ibid.
42. Ibid., 11.
43. Ibid., 10–11.
44. Ibid., 11.
45. Carl S. Smith, *Chicago and the Literary Imagination, 1880–1920* (Chicago: University of Chicago Press, 1984), 178.
46. Candice M. Jenkins, "Decoding Essentialism: Cultural Authenticity and the Black Bourgeoisie in Nella Larsen's *Passing*," *MELUS* 30, no. 3 (2005): 142.
47. Larsen, *Passing*, 12.
48. Jenkins, "Decoding Essentialism," 144.
49. Brian Carr, "Paranoid Interpretation, Desire as Nonobject, and Nella Larsen's *Passing*," *PMLA* 119, no. 2 (2004): 285.
50. Larsen, *Passing*, 15.
51. Ibid.
52. Ibid., 17.
53. Carr, "Paranoid Interpretation," 285.
54. Larsen, *Passing*, 20.
55. Ibid.
56. Ibid., 20–21.
57. Ibid., 22.

58. Ibid., 23.
59. Ibid.
60. Ibid., 24–25.
61. Ibid., 25.
62. Ibid.
63. Ibid., 33.
64. Ibid., 5.
65. Ibid., 7.
66. Ibid., 29.
67. Ibid.
68. Ibid., 34.
69. Larsen, *Passing*, 51.
70. Ibid.
71. Ibid., 79.
72. Ibid.
73. Irene's sexual feelings for Clare become evident as the novel progresses, and Larsen's many heat metaphors early in the novel provide ample evidence of these desires.

Meg Gillette

The Davenport Renaissance

What Was It, and Why Does It Matter?

> "'Let's go back to Davenport, and help make it another Athens.'"
> —George Cook to Floyd Dell[1]

> "Davenport as a Literary Center is too precious a thought to be marred by a comment of mine. I pass it on to you in all its virgin beauty."
> —Susan Glaspell to Floyd Dell[2]

Hemingway, Fitzgerald, and Stein in Paris; Yeats and Joyce in Dublin; Hughes, McKay, and Larsen in Harlem; Dreiser, Millay, and Parker in Greenwich Village ... modernism is full of famous cliques romping about famous cities. As Raymond Williams has argued, the cities of modernism played a pivotal role in the practices and ideas of modernism: It was their internationalism that inspired experiment by denaturalizing language and introducing the elements of liberation and alienation, contact and strangeness that would form much of modernism's repertoire.[3] Yet, put this way, modernism seems largely out of reach of midwestern writers.

This chapter asks how a less likely city—Davenport, Iowa—participated in American modernism. Discovering that a surprising number of major American writers came from and were writing about Davenport in the early twentieth century, the chapter describes the characteristics and impact of this writing and adds yet another "s" to our understanding of America's modernism(s). Its method is inspired by historian Suzanne Lebsock's pathbreaking book *The Free Woman of Petersburg* (1985)[4], whose approach might be described as, "[C]hoose a place small enough to see whole, and read everything."[5]

For the literary historian, such a localist approach promises not only to uncover neglected bodies of literature but also, with its smaller canvas, to create new possibilities for witnessing the reciprocal relation between literature and culture—not just the ways a city shaped its literature, but ways a literature shaped its city, a relation that can be harder to witness in a larger place. This chapter asks how Davenport's writers brought forward their renaissance and what it did for their city. At a time when the Midwest was gaining a reputation as a cultural cul-de-sac, writers in Davenport were challenging stereotypes of midwestern small-minded homogeneity by fashioning Davenport as a literary center and inviting and assimilating immigrants and radicals to its neighborhoods. Far from "revolting" against their hometown villages, these writers fought to expand literary opportunities and make a home for others in the Midwest.

The Davenport Renaissance: What Was It?

As historians Andrew R.L. Cayton and Susan E. Gray explain, the story of the Midwest was undergoing radical revision during the early twentieth century. In the mid-1800s, the Midwest had been "the cutting edge of Western civilization," "a place of liberation from tradition and a source of enormous energy for change"; however, during the early twentieth century, a new image of "stifling, bourgeois, small-town conformity began to compete with and overshadow the traditional triumphal view of the region."[6] By the 1920s, so entrenched was the Midwest's reputation as a cultural cul-de-sac that vaudevillians would joke, "But will it play in Peoria?" and Harold Ross would sneer that the *New Yorker* would not be written for "the old lady in Dubuque."[7]

And yet, during the same time, not 100 miles from Dubuque and Peoria, the literary arts were flourishing in Davenport, Iowa. In the 1890s, Davenport was home to one of America's most prolific, popular, and highly paid writers—Alice French, a local colorist, who wrote about her hometown (which she called "Fairport") under the pen name Octave Thanet.[8] During the 1900s, another younger generation of Davenport writers were getting their start. George Cram Cook (later the co-founder of the Provincetown Players) had resigned his teaching position at the University of Iowa to return to his hometown of Davenport to work as a farmer/writer on the outskirts of town. There he was joined by nineteen-year-old Floyd Dell (then the editor of the *Tri-City Worker*, later the literary editor of *The Masses*), who worked as Cook's farmhand and, like Cook, used his spare time to write. Susan Glaspell (who would become one of America's foremost playwrights) was also living in Davenport, avoiding an affair with the then married Cook (she later married him) and publishing her short fiction in *Harpers* and *Black Cat* while also working on her first novel.[9] Poets Arthur Davison Ficke and Marjorie Seiffert (of nearby Moline, Illinois) were also of this set—both were frequent contributors to Harriet Monroe's *Poetry* magazine but today are better known for perpetuating the 1916 *Spectra* hoax, modernism's most famous hoax.[10] Other Davenport writers of note include muckraker and NAACP co-founder Charles Edward Russell, poet Charles Eugene Banks, and journalist and literary critic Harry Hansen. Indeed, as one journalist wrote, "At that time—the turn of the century and the following decade or two—Davenport was a literary center equaled by no other city of similar size in the country."[11]

Far from the sleepy backwoods hamlet of twentieth-century stereotypes, Davenport, Iowa, at the turn of the century, was a city in flux, undergoing the innovation, turmoil, and renewal of modernization. Its population had almost doubled (from 26,872 in 1890 to 56,727 in 1920),[12] and because steamboats and train travel introduced a large transient population, it had, as historian Sharon Woods surmises, "an urban feel characteristic of much larger cities."[13] Indeed, by 1910, the wild pigs that had once roamed Brady Street had been replaced by electric street cars, the first skyscrapers, and an electrified downtown.[14] At the crossroads of the Mississippi and numerous railroads, Davenport was the entertainment and commercial center of the trans-Mississippi region, boasting the Burtis Opera House (with seating for 2000), a modern department store (with a stained glass window brought from the Columbian exhibition), and even a red light district of saloons, dance halls, and brothels (for which Davenport earned the nickname "the wickedest city in America").[15] Early twentieth-century Davenport was also a town of immigrants. The 1910 census reported that 57% of the population were either first- or second-generation immigrants, and while the city was home to immigrants from a wide range of countries, it was the Germans, at 30% of the population, living mostly on the west side of Davenport, whose culture (including theaters, newspapers, gymnasiums, synagogues, beer gardens, parades, and shooting clubs) most inflected the town.[16] The Socialist party was another significant presence, organizing strikes of cigar markers and railroad workers, publishing a weekly newspaper (edited by Floyd Dell), and making Davenport national news at the height of the red scare when the town elected a Socialist mayor and Socialist candidates to all city offices but one.[17] As historian William Roba surmises, Davenport at this time "displayed a great deal of intellectual freedom." It touted a Carnegie library (built with the help of Alice French's fundraising), the Davenport Academy of Science (which sponsored public lectures by Jane Addams from Hull House in Chicago and Professor MacBride from the University of Iowa), and literary societies (like the Tuesday Club for women and the Contemporary Club for men). It was even the birthplace of chiropractic medicine (more controversial then than today).[18]

As Davenport transformed into a complex modern city, its writers experimented with how to represent its new urban reality. Labor strife and socialism were frequent subjects in their fiction. Alice French, daughter of a wealthy Davenport lumberer and banker, wrote against the labor movement in "Communists and Capitalists: A Sketch from Life" (1878) and *The Man of the Hour* (1905); alternatively, the working-class Dell championed socialist principles in the *Tri-City Worker* (1905–1906), while middle-class Cook and Glaspell took socialist agitators for their heroes in their novels *The Chasm* (1911) and *The Visioning* (1911).[19] Opportunities for women were another important theme in the works of Davenport writers. French, who shared her life and home with Jane Crawford, wrote frequently of the problems and possibilities faced by unmarried women, while a generation later, the New Woman featured prominently in the writings of Cook, Glaspell, and Dell.[20] An interest in pioneer and Native American history also permeates much Davenport fiction. At a time when Frederick Jackson Turner was bemoaning the closing of the American frontier and Davenport was celebrating its own historic milestones (including the 100th anniversary of the founding of Fort Armstrong on a neighboring island in the Mississippi), Davenport writers were grappling with the legacy of the town's Native American history. French wrote an introduction to a book about the Sauk Indians, Glaspell's *Inheritors*

(1921) begins in 1832 with reminiscences of the Black Hawk War, and Cook's *The Spring* (1922) takes place at the historic landmark known as Black Hawk's Spring (destroyed in 1907 by the construction of a new sewer system).[21]

Davenport's writers also made the city itself a literary subject. Picturesque descriptions of the river and town abound in their works. Alice French, for example, romanticized Davenport's electrified downtown in *Stories of a Western Town* (1893) ("lights swimming hither and thither [over the river] ... and beyond the bridge, at the point of the island, lay a glittering multitude of lights, a fairy fleet with miniature sails outlined in flame as if by jewels."),[22] and Susan Glaspell painted the neighboring army base as a pastoral landscape in *The Visioning* ("This quiet, beautiful island out in the Mississippi—large, apart, serene—seemed a great lap in which to sink. She liked the quarters: big old fashioned houses in front of which the long stretch of green sloped down to the river.").[23] As Davenport writers gave prominence to the Davenport locale, they also commemorated the customs of its people. French, for example, recorded the dialects of a multilingual Davenport in "The Besetment of Kurt Lieders" ("'[D]ost thou hear? [C]ome! But did you dare to leave him, Mrs. Lieders?' Part of the time she spoke in English, part of the time in her own tongue")[24] and chronicled the manners and pastimes of those Davenport residents most likely to be overlooked in "The Stout Miss Hopkins' Bicycle" (about two overweight old women who learn to ride bicycles).[25] A decade later, when local color was no longer in vogue, the next generation of Davenport writers turned to muckracking journalism (where many of them got their start) to describe their fellow Davenporters. The ingénue protagonist of Glaspell's *The Visioning*, for example, asks about the underpaid factory workers across the river ("'I hadn't realized,' said Katie, 'that making candy was such serious business.' ... 'How much do those girls make?'"),[26] and the outsider protagonist of Dell's *Moon-Calf* describes "with calm amusement" the courtship rituals at a popular dance pavilion ("Was it possible that *that* shabby device [mentioning the weather] would serve as an introduction to this radiant and seemingly unapproachable creature?").[27] More than just background in these stories, Davenport's geography and its people were themselves prominent themes in the works of its writers.

Dream Cities: How Do You Make Davenport "Another Athens"?

Another prominent theme in the works of the Davenport writers is the question of how to build literary communities. Arthur Davison Ficke's *Spectra* poems, for instance, go so far as to invent an imaginary Spectric group, which claimed "to push the possibilities of poetic expression into a new region."[28] As Ficke's faux movement satirizes its fantasy of literary community, other Davenport writers were more earnest in their invocation of it. In *Inheritors,* farmer Silas Morton founds a college on a Davenport hilltop, while in *The Road to the Temple* (1927), Cook builds one literary community after the next—first in Davenport, Iowa; then in Provincetown, Massachusetts; and finally in Athens, Greece. In one scene, Cook and Dell discuss America's need for more literary centers:

> So, ordering another bottle of wine, for it's Friday and they don't have to work, they begin setting out the various centers America should have. The question is not how many, but the vividness of each.... Jig makes a path from center to center, connecting all; this path is to be a live wire, it is to quiver with excitements.... Again the dream city rises on the horizon, this time as real cities vivified, dream of intense groups with common purpose.[29]

Hypothesizing "dream cities," planting new colleges, and even (in the case of *Spectra*) fabricating literary movements, Davenport writers did not so much participate in the proverbial "revolt from the village" as they explored strategies to bring modernism out from its major cities and into the Midwest.

One way they sought to multiply America's literary communities was by building their own Davenport literary network. At various times, all of the Davenport writers took turns writing about the other Davenport writers: Ficke wrote poems about French and Dell, while Dell, Hansen, and Glaspell (using Cook's diaries) all wrote memoirs in which their fellow Davenport writers played starring roles.[30] As the leaders of America's premier theater group and the literary editors of major American newspapers (Hansen at *The Chicago Daily News,* Dell and Cook at *The Friday Literary Review,* and Ficke at *The Saturday Evening Post*), Davenport's writers were well positioned to promote one another's works: Cook and Glaspell's *Provincetown Players* performed plays written by Cook, Glaspell, and Dell; Ficke wrote the book jacket blurb for Glaspell's biography of Cook; Hansen reviewed Dell's *Moon-Calf*; Dell wrote glowing reviews of Glaspell, Ficke, and Cook, and even helped Cook land a job at the *Friday Review of Literature*.[31] At a time when Paris was becoming famous for its "lost generation," New York for its bohemian Greenwich village, and Harlem and Chicago for their respective "renaissances," Davenport writers were actively promoting their own literary group and city.

"'[T]he city that shall be artist,'" says Cook in *The Road to the Temple*.[32] A place of "rare historical associations and literary promises," says Hansen in *Midwest Portraits*.[33] "[O]ne of the best possible towns to serve such an apprenticeship," says Dell in *Moon-Calf*.[34] Not only did Davenport writers promote one another, but they also promoted Davenport as a place of rare literary opportunity. In *Moon-Calf*, the rhythms of the Mississippi river inspire the protagonist's poetic experiments ("Sometimes, as he walked, rhythms rather than words came into his mind, rhythms which he could not identify with any poem he knew, and he fitted words to them"), and the people of the town nurture his literary ambitions (his classmates follow him into starting a Literary and Athletic Society, his high school history teacher helps him get his first poem published in a volume commemorating the St. Louis World's Fair, and the local librarian invites the teenage Felix to join her literary salon).[35] Glaspell's *The Road to the Temple* and *Inheritors* likewise populate Davenport with literate and eccentric freethinkers, such as the "queer fish of the town" who join Cook's and Dell's Monist Society and Silas and Madeline Morton, who seek a college for "the best that has been thought and said in the world."[36] Challenging the stereotype of small-minded Midwesterners, these characterizations advertised Davenport as a talent pool worth cultivating and an audience worth writing for.

Davenport audiences answered that call. Local news coverage suggests that Davenporters enjoyed their literary reputation. Book reviews scoured each work for local references ("Naturally, the author having done his first writing in Davenport, we do not have to look far thru his pages before we come on 'local stuff'"),[37] while feature stories boasted of the town's literary capital ("Few cities of the size of Davenport can point to a group of writers whose reputation is fairly international"),[38] and, in the case of the six-part feature titled "Environment Plays Big Part in Production of Talent and Art Works," even took a share of the credit.[39] There is also evidence that the Davenport writers engendered an active Davenport readership, spurring the town to become the kind of "city that shall be artist" that the writers foretold. Book reviews, for example, referenced Davenporters' familiarity with its writers ("Floyd Dell's easy graceful style, his naturally formed sentences, the versatility of his outlook upon life—all these are well known to Davenporters")[40] and called hungrily for the next generation of Davenport writers (the column, "Have We ... Other Writers to Succeed Them?").[41] What's more, the Tri-City Art League even credited the Davenport writers with expanding the arts in Davenport:

> As a center for literary people, [Davenport] is of course well known thru [sic] the works of Arthur Davison Ficke, Floyd Dell, Octave Thanet, Susan Keating Glaspell and George Cram Cook. There is another side to Davenport, however, which is just beginning to develop, and it is expected that in the near future more will be heard of her as an art center than ever before.[42]

While it is tempting to dismiss the Davenport writers' hometown encomiums as mere boosterism or wishful thinking (as indeed Glaspell wonders in *The Road to the Temple* when she admits, "Dream cities have advantages over real ones. You can call into them people you like, and can close gates on whomsoever you do not want."),[43] local coverage of the Davenport writers suggests the writers' "dream cities" had some effect—that Davenport audiences responded to their writers' call for literary communities by reading and discussing their literature, seeking and finding themselves in their characters, and even sharing credit and seeking to expand upon their success.

Settling Immigrants and Outsiders in *The Inheritors* and *Moon-Calf*: How Did Davenport Become "White"?

In the late nineteenth and early twentieth centuries, Davenport was coming to terms with its native and immigrant populations. The centennial of the town's founding in 1916 sparked an interest in its Native

American past, while the anti-immigrant sentiments of World War I placed new restrictions on the town's large German populations through English-only legislation and the Espionage Act.[44] Into this climate of nostalgia, remorse, and anti-immigrant sentiment came Susan Glaspell's play *Inheritors* and Floyd Dell's memoir *Moon-Calf* in 1920 and 1921.

Inheritors, the most autobiographical of Glaspell's plays, is about 120 acres of land overlooking the Mississippi that was once owned by Glaspell's great-grandfather, James.[45] While the land had long since been divided and sold by the time Susan was born, the hilltop was a popular attraction when Susan was growing up after her great-grandfather's Hungarian neighbors, the Fejérvàrys, donated their hillside to the city for the Fejérvàry park and zoo in 1902. In 1918, around the time Glaspell was writing *Inheritors*, the Fejérvàrys were back in the news again—this time because the government had confiscated all of their remaining property under the Espionage Act, and Davenport writer Alice French was leading a campaign to have it returned to them.[46] Glaspell's *Inheritors* lent its voice to French's campaign by championing the Fejérvàrys' contributions to the town: "'Twas a great thing for our family to have a family like yours next place to," Grandma Morton tells Felix Fejevary (modeled on the historical person Nicholas Fejérvàry). "They did something pretty nice for the corn belt when they drove you out of Hungary," her son Silas Morton concurs.[47]

The subject of immigrant neighbors runs throughout the play. Act 1 (set in 1879) waxes nostalgic about the inclusive diversity of the pioneer days, when Grandma Morton "never went to bed without leaving something on the stove for the new ones that might be coming" and Black Hawk "talked how the red man and the white man could live together."[48] Set 40 years later on the same Davenport hilltop, subsequent acts protest the current treatment of immigrants in the town, satirizing those who perform their Americanness by excluding others (as when a state senator congratulates Felix Fejevary for "talk[ing] like an American" when he calls two Hindu students "dirty dagoes") and making heroes of those who fight for immigrants' inclusion (as when Madeline goes to jail in protest of the deportation of the two Hindu students from the college).[49] Voicing these two versions of the Midwest, the inclusive pioneerism of 1879 and the stifling homogeneity of 1921, *Inheritors* pursues a more inclusive present by harkening to the more inclusive past.

But as the play argues on behalf of a diverse Davenport, it also assures audiences of a whitening effect. In the climax of the play, the reclusive Ira Morton rants about his corn seed blowing into his neighbor's fields, a rant his daughter interprets as an allegory on immigration:

> Plant this corn by that corn, and the pollen blows from corn to corn—the golden dust it blows, in the sunshine and of nights—blows from corn to corn like a—(*the word hurts*) gift. No, you don't understand it, but (*proudly*) corn don't stay what it is! You can make it anything—according to what you do, 'cording to the corn it's alongside. (*changing*) But that's it. I want it to stay in my field. It goes away. The prevailin' wind takes it on to the Johnsons—them Swedes.[50]

But while Ira berates the blowing wind for sharing his labors with others, his daughter Madeline sees in it a story of successful integration; not only has the contact zone improved the native stock, but in spreading to the neighbor's fields, it has also effaced the differences between native and foreign. In the final lines of the play, as Madeline commits herself to protesting the Indians' deportation, she shores up her resolve by reminding herself of the corn seed's migration and assimilation: "And you say—your corn is getting better?" she asks Emil, to which he replies, "Oh, yes—I raise better corn every year."[51] Here, Madeline takes cheer at Emil's success, and yet the play's ongoing exclusion of people of color—the American Indians in Act 1 and the Hindus in Acts 2–4, characters who are continually spoken of but never allowed on stage—reminds us of the limits of its assimilative ideal and the ways European immigrants secured their footing in the United States by excluding people of color. As Emil, described by the cast list as "an Americanized Swede," tells Madeline, the Hindu students are "nothin' to me."[52]

Like *Inheritors*, Floyd Dell's *Moon-Calf* celebrates Davenport's diversity while offering and questioning strategies of assimilation. As *Moon-Calf* presents it, Davenport is a multicultural place, far more diverse and countercultural than readers might have imagined. As Rabbi Nathan expounds, "[It] has a quality of its own. I suppose this is partly due to the pioneers from New England, who brought with them ideals and a respect for learning; but it is more due, I think, to the Germans, who left home because they loved liberty, and brought with them a taste for music, discussion, and good beer."[53] The final paragraphs of the book return to the subject of Davenport's distinction, with Felix imagining that "from the first [the town] had been a rebellious place. It had been founded so, by men who were different from others—or it was pleasant to think so."[54] In *Moon-Calf*, Davenport is a home for outsiders, a place where being different is not very different. When Felix meets Rabbi Nathan, Felix remarks, "There was something familiar about him"; when he learns the town has an Atheist group, he "imagined twenty-nine people like himself and Stephen and Margaret"; when he attends his first meeting of the local Socialist branch, he muses, "It was as if he knew this place—had always known it—as though he had frequented it in some previous existence, or in dreams. He knew that he belonged there; ... he was coming home."[55] Emphasizing the characters' familiarity, likeness, and homecoming, these passages erase differences and promise these outsiders a sense of belonging in Davenport.

But in *Moon-Calf*, as in *Inheritors*, not all outsiders are invited in. In the final chapters, Tom Alden (based on George Cram Cook) invites Felix to share his cabin on the outskirts of town, complaining of the loneliness of living there by himself. ("The only trouble is—lack of society.")[56] Yet, when Felix arrives at the cabin, he discovers that Tom does not, in fact, live there alone, but is attended by Ned, the "old negro servant who had been in the family for years" having been "left to" Tom by his aunt: "The ancient figure straightened up, with a welcoming flash of white teeth, took off his hat, and came down to the gate to meet them. 'Howdy, Mist' Tom! Howdy!'"[57] A broad racist caricature, Ned receives none of the realism characteristic of the book's treatment of other minorities, serving instead to shore up the white men's fantasies of home and belonging. When Ned leaves to kill a chicken for dinner, Felix remarks, "I don't see why you live anywhere else!" to which Tom answers, "I realize why it is I never stay here.... Loneliness."[58] As this exchange reveals, Ned's presence makes it possible for the men to live at the cabin (he performs the labor that produces their foodstuffs), while his absence, his ineligibility as a companion, gives rise and meaning to their intimacy. Though painful, Ned's caricature and exclusion register the limits of Davenport's multicultural inclusiveness.

When Floyd Dell and Susan Glaspell were living in Davenport, it was a segregated city. The Germans, who lived in the west side of town, had their own newspapers, theaters, schools, and parks, and there was a tacit agreement that their Sunday parades never crossed Harrison St. into the English side of town.[59] The town's small population of African Americans, barred from joining local unions, established a small business district on East Fifth St., two blocks from the train depot that brought black railway porters and passengers through town.[60] These ethnic and racial tensions had escalated by 1920 when Glaspell and Dell were writing *Inheritors* and *Moon-Calf*. During WWI, the German Schuetzen Park was renamed Forest Park, Davenport public schools stopped teaching German, and the Fejérvàrys' remaining property was confiscated by the government.[61] German newspapers, fearing reprisal lest they be associated with the Socialist menace, lobbied aggressively against the Socialist party.[62] In the midst of the red scare and anti-immigrant sentiment, Glaspell and Dell elected to memorialize Davenport as a place where immigrants were welcomed by their neighbors and where intellectuals and radicals enjoyed open fellowship with one another. Eager to make their outsiders at home, they assured readers of their similarities, while also contrasting their place with those Others—American Indians, Indians, and African Americans—excluded from Davenport's covenants. In *Inheritors* and *Moon-Calf*, immigrants and free-thinkers go in outsiders but come out insiders, a curious celebration of multiculturalism that ironically helped pave the way for a new story of a homogeneous Midwest.

In 1924, shortly after Cook died, Floyd Dell wrote a letter to a Davenport newspaper wondering about the next generation of Davenport writers: "I wonder what Davenport is like now, and if there are boys and girls growing up there who dream wild foolish beautiful dreams."[63] The answer, of course, is yes. Countless other writers, poets, and critics have come out of Davenport in the last 100 years. Davenport, today, is home to the Midwest Writing Center (which hosts a monthly *Spectra* poetry reading series) and numerous theater groups, one of which (as I write) is performing *Inheritors* on the very hilltop the play was written about. While today Davenport does not enjoy the literary reputation it once had, it does enjoy something the earlier generation did not: a collection at the Davenport Public Library of works by Davenport writers fashioning the town as a literary center and place where immigrants and outsiders could belong. And though a cynical Davenporter might raise an eyebrow at these writers' boastful characterizations of their town, these stories nonetheless have work they can do, for, as linguistic anthropologist Keith Basso tells us, "remembering often provides the basis for imagining."[64]

Acknowledgments

Thanks to my neighbor Dr. Nancy Hayes for introducing me to this body of literature, the librarians and volunteers in the Richardson-Sloane Special Collections at the Davenport Public Library for their assistance, and to the students in my 2014 senior seminar who researched these writers and published their work in the anthology *The Stories We Tell: Modernism Comes to the Tri-Cities* (Rock Island: East Hall Press, 2014).

Notes

1. "Floyd Dell Writes Fine Tribute to 'Jig' Cook; an 'Exile from Greece,'" *The Davenport Democrat and Leader* (January 16, 1924): 10.
2. Susan Glaspell to Floyd Dell, 17 September 1910, Floyd Dell Papers, Newberry Library.
3. Raymond Williams, "The Metropolis and the Emergence of Modernism," in *Unreal City: Urban Experience in Modern European Literature and Art*, ed. Edward Timms and David Kelley (Manchester: Manchester University Press, 1985), 13–24.
4. Suzanne Lebsock, *The Free Women of Petersburg: Status and Culture in a Southern Town, 1784–1860* (New York: W.W. Norton, 1985).
5. Sharon E. Wood, *The Freedom of the Streets: Work, Citizenship, and Sexuality in a Gilded Age City* (Chapel Hill: University of North Carolina Press, 2005), 13.
6. Andrew R.L. Cayton and Susan E. Gray, "The Story of the Midwest: An Introduction," in *The American Midwest: Essays on Regional History*, ed. Andrew R.L. Cayton and Susan E. Gray (Bloomington: Indiana University Press, 2001), 2–3.
7. Harold Ross, "Of All Things," *New Yorker* (February 21, 1925): 2.
8. George McMichael, *Journey to Obscurity: The Life of Octave Thanet* (Lincoln: University of Nebraska Press, 1965).
9. Marcia Noe, "'A Romantic and Miraculous City' Shapes Three Midwestern Writers," *Western Illinois Regional Studies* 1 (1978): 176–98.
10. Suzanne W. Churchill, "The Lying Game: Others and the Great Spectra Hoax of 1917," *American Periodicals: A Journal of History, Criticism, and Bibliography* 15, no. 1 (2005): 23–41; Audrey Russek, "'So Many Useful

Women': The Pseudonymous Poetry of Marjorie Allen Seiffert, 1916–1938," *Tulsa Studies in Women's Literature* 28, no. 1 (2009): 75–96.
11. Ralph Cram, "Former Democrat Editor, Spending Winter in Capital, Recalls Days When Davenport Was Literary Center Boasting of Seven Authors," *The Democrat and Leader* (February 21, 1949): 11.
12. "Total Population for Iowa's Incorporated Places: 1850–1920," http://www.iowadatacenter.org/archive/2011/02/citypop.pdf.
13. Wood, *The Freedom of the Streets*, 12.
14. United Light and Railway Company, *Forty Years of Development* (1925), Upper Mississippi Valley Special Collections, Augustana College; William Roba, "The Tri-Cities, 1885–1920," in *The River and the Prairie: A History of the Quad-Cities, 1812–1960* (Quad Cities: Hesperian Press, 1986), 100.
15. Wood, *The Freedom of the Streets*, 12, 237–38; Roba, "The Tri-Cities, 1885–1920," 106 (quoted in Wood).
16. Department of Commerce, Bureau of the Census. *Thirteenth Census of the United States Taken in the Year 1910.* (Washington: Government Printing Office, 1913), 636; Hildegard Binder Johnson, "German Forty-Eighters in Davenport," *Iowa Journal of History and Politics* 44, no. 1 (1946).
17. Roba, "The Tri-Cities, 1885–1920," 100, 111; "Radicals Win in Davenport," *New York Times* (April 5, 1920): 14.
18. Roba, "The Tri-Cities, 1885–1920," 109–10.
19. Alice French, "Communists and Capitalists: A Sketch from Life," *Lippincott's Magazine* 23 (October 1878): 485–93; Alice French, *The Man of the Hour* (Indianapolis: Bobbs-Merrill Company, 1905); Floyd Dell, *The Tri-City Worker Magazine* 1–11 (1905–1906); George Cram Cook, *The Chasm* (New York: Frederick A. Stokes, 1911); Susan Glaspell, *The Visioning* (New York: Frederick A. Stokes, 1911).
20. Alice French, "Max—Or His Picture" and "The Stout Miss Hopkins' Bicycle" in *Stories That End Well* (Indianapolis: Bobbs-Merrill Company, 1911); Alice French, "Mother Emeritus" in *Stories of a Western Town* (New York: Charles Scribner's Sons, 1893); Susan Glaspell and George Cram Cook, *Suppressed Desires: A Comedy in Two Episodes* (Boston: Walter H. Baker, 1916); Susan Glaspell, *The Verge* in *Plays by Susan Glaspell*, ed. C.W.E. Bigsby (Cambridge: Cambridge University Press, 1987), 57–102; Floyd Dell, *Women as World Builders: Studies in Modern Feminism* (New York: Forbes and Company, 1913); Floyd Dell, *Janet March* (New York: A.A. Knopf, 1923).
21. Alice French, Introduction to *The Saukie Indians and Their Great Chiefs Blackhawk and Keokuk* (Rock Island: The Vaile Company, 1926); Susan Glaspell, *Inheritors* in *Plays by Susan Glaspell*, ed. Bigsby, 103–67; George Cram Cook, *The Spring* (New York: Frank Shay, 1921); Roba, "The Tri-Cities, 1885–1920," 98.
22. Alice French, "The Face of Failure" in *Stories of a Western Town*, 64.
23. Susan Glaspell, *The Visioning*, 3.

24. Alice French, "The Besetment of Kurt Lieders" in *Stories of a Western Town*, 6.
25. French, "The Stout Miss Hopkins' Bicycle," 140–76.
26. Glaspell, *The Visioning*, 160.
27. Floyd Dell, *Moon-Calf* (New York: Alfred A. Knopf, Inc., 1920), 202.
28. Anne Knish and Emanuel Morgan, *Spectra: A Book of Poetic Experiments* (New York: Mitchell Kennerley, 1916), ix.
29. Susan Glaspell, *The Road to the Temple* (New York: Frederick A. Stokes Company, 1927), 90.
30. Arthur Davison Ficke, "My Princess," *Scribner's Magazine* 72 (December, 1922): 666; Arthur Davison Ficke, "An Outrageous Person," *Selected Poems* (New York: Doubleday, 1938), 177; Dell, *Moon-Calf*; Harry Hansen, *Midwest Portraits: A Book of Memories and Friendships* (New York: Harcourt, Brace and Company, 1923); Glaspell, *The Road to the Temple*.
31. Jeff Kennedy, "A History of the Provincetown Playhouse," last modified 2014, http://www.provincetownplayhouse.com/history.html; Arthur Davison Ficke, "Rev. of *The Road to the Temple*," *Saturday Review of Literature* (March 26, 1927): 675; Harry Hansen, "His First Novel—and Fame," *Chicago Daily News* (October 27, 1920): 12; Floyd Dell, "Susan Glaspell's Chicago—Chicago in Fiction: The Eighth Paper," *Friday Literary Review* (March 15, 1912): 1; Floyd Dell, "The Ficke Wing," *Measure* 42 (August, 1924): 13; Floyd Dell, "Cook, George Cram," in *Dictionary of American Biography*, ed. Allen Johnson and Dumas Malone (New York: Charles Scribner's Sons, 1930): 372–73; Rebecca J. Gildernew, "Dell, Floyd James" in *The Biographical Dictionary of Iowa*, ed. David Hudson, Marvin Bergman, and Loren Horton (Iowa City: University of Iowa Press, 2008), 123–24.
32. Glaspell, *The Road to the Temple*, 90 (quoting George Cram Cook).
33. Hansen, *Midwest Portraits*, 209.
34. Dell, *Moon-Calf*, 254.
35. Ibid., 156, 104, 170, 180.
36. Glaspell, *The Road to the Temple*, 193; Glaspell, *Inheritors*, 113.
37. "Books and Their Writers," *The Davenport Democrat and Leader* (October 14, 1923): 24.
38. "Davenport's Writing Group," *The Davenport Democrat and Leader* (April 21, 1929): 34.
39. Elizabeth Bray, "Davenport—The Background of a Writing Group," *The Davenport Democrat and Leader* (March 10, 1929): 1.
40. "Books and Their Writers," *The Davenport Democrat and Leader* (May 18, 1924): 22.
41. Elizabeth Bray, "Poet, Critic and Novelist Round Out Local Group of Which Mrs. Bray Writes," *The Davenport Democrat and Leader* (April 21, 1929): 4.

42. "Tri-City Art League Development of Idea of Local Art Student," *The Davenport Democrat and Leader* (July 17, 1924): 88.
43. Glaspell, *The Road to the Temple*, 91.
44. Johnson, "German Forty-Eighters in Davenport," 38, 33.
45. Linda Ben-Zvi, *Susan Glaspell: Her Life and Times* (Oxford: Oxford University Press, 2005), 14–16.
46. McMichael, *Journey to Obscurity*, 206, 209–10; Alice French, *Nicholas Fejérvàry; In Memoriam* (Budapest: Franklin Society, 1898).
47. Glaspell, *Inheritors*, 106, 110.
48. Ibid., 107, 105.
49. Ibid., 122.
50. Ibid., 155.
51. Ibid., 157.
52. Ibid., 103, 145.
53. Dell, *Moon-Calf*, 254.
54. Ibid., 394.
55. Ibid., 247, 150, 212.
56. Ibid., 366.
57. Ibid., 364.
58. Ibid., 365.
59. William H. Cumberland, "The Davenport Socialists of 1920," *The Annals of Iowa* 47, no. 5 (1984): 455.
60. Wood, *The Freedom of the Streets*, 96.
61. Doug Smith, *Postcard History Series: Davenport* (Charleston: Arcadia, 2017), 24; Johnson, "German Forty-Eighters in Davenport," 33; McMichael, *Journey to Obscurity*, 206.
62. Cumberland, "The Davenport Socialists of 1920," 456.
63. "Floyd Dell Writes Fine Tribute to 'Jig' Cook; an 'Exile From Greece.'"
64. Keith H. Basso, *Wisdom Sits in Places: Landscape and Language among the Western Apache* (Albuquerque: University of New Mexico Press, 1992), 5.

Marcia Noe
and
Meghan O'Dea

From Davenport to Provincetown

Floyd Dell, George Cram Cook, and Susan Glaspell Develop a Radical Theatre Aesthetic

In "The Culture of Modernism," Irving Howe enumerates the characteristics of what he calls "the spirit of modernism": literature that is difficult and inaccessible; in revolt against prevailing literary conventions and cultural assumptions; subjective; impatient with notions of cognition and rationality; skeptical about the existence of truth or genius; ahistorical; devoted to asking questions rather than finding answers; committed to the belief that human existence is inherently problematic; enamored of authenticity and sincerity; disdainful of certainties; and predisposed to experiment.[1] However, as Howe's title suggests, modernism is more than the sum of its enumerated parts and might be more insightfully conceived of as a culture.

Daniel Joseph Singal makes this case in "Towards a Definition of American Modernism," arguing that "[m]odernism should properly be seen as a culture—a constellation of related ideas, beliefs, values and modes of perception—that came into existence during the mid to late nineteenth century, and that has had a powerful influence on art and thought on both sides of the Atlantic since roughly 1900."[2] While some discussions of modernism focus on its rejection of representational modes or its evocation of inner subjectivity, in this essay we posit that broader notion of cultural modernity invoked by Howe and Singal. We argue that the theatre practice of three charter members of the Provincetown Players—Floyd Dell, George Cram (Jig) Cook, and Susan Glaspell—was shaped by their early grounding in such a culture of modernity. During the first years of the twentieth century, they interacted socially, intellectually, and politically as young adults in Davenport, Iowa, a city that journalist and author Harry Hansen called "a picturesque river town with rare historical associations and literary promises that have been richly fulfilled."³ As Timothy B. Spears observes, "In Davenport, Dell found the community, the intellectual resources, and the employment opportunities that allowed him to think of himself as a politically committed aesthete."⁴ In their introduction to *1915, the Cultural Moment*, Adele Heller and Lois Rudnick write that this generation of modernists embraced, through their radical ideas, political activities, and art, an early twentieth-century cultural style called "The New," and that they shared a "belief in the power of the individual creative effort to reshape self and society and the power of cultural expression to humanize American life."⁵ This early experience of "The New" would enable Dell, Cook, and Glaspell, in their Provincetown plays, to challenge traditional ideas about politics, gender conventions, and social organization and articulate a vision for a new social order, even as they satirized the excesses of some of its proponents.

The Aesthetic of the Provincetown Players

The aesthetic that made the Provincetown Players unique and impactful was marked by cultural critique, authenticity of voice, rebellion, and, most significantly, "an ideal of collective creation and a commitment to experimentation,"⁶ traits rooted in Cook, Glaspell, and Dell's early engagement with the "New" in Davenport. The foundational documents of the company indicate that its charter members, led by Jig Cook, had envisioned it, first and foremost, as a theater collective—as Cook put it, a "beloved community of life-givers."⁷ Active members were expected to attend meetings, vote on whether to accept a play for production, and write, act, produce, or donate labor; the author of a play slated for production was expected to participate in its staging. Glaspell, for instance, not only wrote but also acted in eight of her eleven Provincetown plays, co-directing *Tickless Time* and *Women's Honor*.⁸

This ideal of collective creation is also evident in the manifesto-like broadsides that Cook periodically issued on behalf of the Provincetown Players. "One man cannot produce drama," he asserted in one of these circulars. "True drama is born only of one feeling animating all the members of a clan—a spirit shared by all and expressed by the few for the all."⁹ In her introduction to *The Provincetown Players and the Culture of Modernity*, Brenda Murphy discusses this and other hallmarks of the troupe, noting that "all of the members of the Provincetown Players were enthusiastic participants in the culture of modernity, or what they tended to refer to as 'The New.'"[10] Glaspell would create New Woman characters who crusaded for birth control, advocated for free speech, embraced psychoanalysis, and sought the freedom to construct their own identities. Cook would engage with new theories of science and articulate a pacifist vision, and Dell would enact socialist and feminist principles on the Provincetown stage. Foundational to their world view, their aesthetic, and, ultimately, their theatre practice was the philosophical, political, and intellectual grounding of all three writers in the cultural milieu of early twentieth-century Davenport.

Davenport, Iowa: Vibrant Cultural Matrix
By the early 1900s, the city comprised thirty-five thousand inhabitants and was, according to Floyd Dell, "an extraordinarily literary and intellectual town."[11] Its citizens enjoyed a surprisingly vibrant cultural environment that included the Carnegie-funded public library, the Academy of Natural Sciences, and the Burtis Opera House.[12] Business and professional men interested in politics, science, and current events could join the Contemporary Club; working men could affiliate with the Labor Lyceum. Women with a literary bent could join the Tuesday Club.[13] Irish theatre lovers could participate in the Emerald Dramatic Club; music aficionados could belong to the Concordia Society, the Etude Club, and the Amateur Musical Club.[14]

A major cultural influence in Davenport were the German immigrants from Schleswig and Holstein, who arrived in the city in the 1840s and ultimately would come to constitute one-third of the city's population.[15] The Germans brought their love of music, athletics, and free thought to Davenport, establishing a Turngemeinde [German culture club] with sections for singing, gymnastics, and mental training; Turner Hall in downtown Davenport comprised a restaurant, bowling alleys, theatre, library, and meeting rooms. The Germans also established a rifle club, the Schuetzenverein; a singing society, the Männerchor; a German theatre society; and two German-language newspapers, *Der Demokrat* and the *Iowa Reform*.[16] Several beer gardens thrived in the German district where the Strasser brass band or the Zither Quartet might brighten the patrons' Sunday afternoons.[17] Davenporters could also enjoy concerts, lectures, and plays, both in German and in English, at Turner Hall, as well as athletic contests, movies, dancing, singing festivals, and band concerts at the Schuetzenpark: twenty-two acres of lawns, shrubs, trees, walkways, and drives that boasted a restaurant, coffee house, dance hall, music pavilion, and shooting gallery.[18]

Floyd Dell: Socialism and Feminism

The Germans also brought with them their leftist politics. Lively political discussions took place at Turner Hall, where, in 1903, sixteen-year-old Floyd Dell attended Socialist meetings after he moved to Davenport from Quincy, Illinois. Dell joined the Davenport local in 1904, participating in discussions at its meetings, giving talks on socialism around town, and leafleting at factory gates for Eugene V. Debs. Dell also served on the local's program committee and as its financial secretary; later, he represented the local as its delegate to the party's state convention.[19]

For Dell, socialism was "the greatest intellectual and imaginative stimulus which existed in the world," shaping his beliefs about pacifism and feminism for years to come.[20] Gender concerns are much in evidence in Dell's articles for *The Tri-City Workers Magazine*, a socialist periodical he edited from 1905 to 1906. Repeatedly in its pages, Dell stressed the vulnerability of working-class girls to the pitfalls of evening entertainments in Davenport's notorious Bucktown, venues that in his opinion were one step away from the brothels. His socialist analysis of the gendered politics of Bucktown is delineated in "Why People Go to Brick Munro's" (1906), his expose of James "Brick" Munro's Pavilion, a restaurant, saloon, and dance hall complex.

This article is one of the earliest published expressions of Dell's feminism, a perspective he would later employ in many books and articles.[21] A significant influence on Dell's evolving feminism was Edward Bellamy's socialist fantasy, *Looking Backward*. In that book, the protagonist, Julian West, falls asleep in 1887 and awakens in 2000 still in his native Boston, now a socialist paradise. His mentor, Dr. Leete, explains that while in capitalism women in many cases "had to sell themselves to men to get their living ... the sexes now meet with the ease of perfect equals, suitors for each other with nothing but love."[22]

Dell eagerly embraced this egalitarian ideal of male-female relations that could flower once the enslaving power of capitalist patriarchy was overcome. "Here was an atmosphere of happy comradeship between girls and men, such as did not exist for me in any American reality I had ever known," Dell wrote in his autobiography.[23] However, this happy comradeship was far from evident at Brick Munro's, where men had to pay admission but women did not, a source of consternation for Dell, who observed that the girls it attracted seemed oblivious of this particular form of patriarchal oppression:

> I knew the attitude of the young men who went hunting for girls at parks and amusement places, and boasted that a girl could be had for a glass of beer ... the fundamental sexual contempt which underlay the men's admiration ... the implicit attitude of the lords of the earth toward a slave class.... Girls were *things*. And this was an old role for girls; church and state joined in denying them rights as individuals, and employers kept them in a position of helplessness by cheap wages; when all these had done their work, Nick Bingo [Dell's pseudonym for Brick Munro] gave them a good time in his dance-hall, and so they were gathered into the houses of prostitution down the street— well trained by then to accept their destiny of being used for pleasure and profit, with no say-so of their own.[24]

Dell emphasized in this article that while male patrons of Munro's establishment were mostly businessmen and professional men, the female portion of the clientele comprised largely "department store clerks, servant girls, stenographers, tobacco and candy factory workers" who mingled there with prostitutes from the nearby red-light district.[25] In his article, Dell emphasized that when Brick Munro's closed at midnight, the brothels and saloons of that part of town were still open and available to this mixed female clientele.[26] How could this "Half-Way House to the red-light district" exist in a town dominated by churches?

Dell's materialist analysis of this phenomenon uncovers two answers to this question. Davenport tolerates Brick Munro's because the people who own and run it and the people who patronize it benefit economically: "The men go there because of Capitalism ... they go there because under Capitalism the women of the working class are the prey of the men of the business and professional classes."[27] While the need for fun is a compelling human drive that Brick Munro's satisfies, respectable church-going Davenporters turn a blind eye to this unhealthy source of fun because "[t]he ignoring of natural laws for the sake of business is a first principle of Capitalism."[28] As Sharon E. Wood asserts, "commerce in women's sexuality remained the key to Bucktown's profitability."[29] Dell closes his article with a socialist prediction that while today the amusement-seeking working class is satisfied with capitalistic institutions like Brick Munro's, "Tomorrow ... [i]t will ask a new world in which through ownership of the machinery of production and distribution, all the good things of life will flow to the producers thereof."[30]

Dell left Davenport two years after *The Tri-City Workers Magazine* folded and moved on to Chicago.[31] Relocating to Greenwich Village in 1913, he soon became, as he was in Chicago, a major player on the literary scene and joined Cook and Glaspell's nascent theatre venture three years later.[32] In an article this self-proclaimed ardent feminist published in the July 1914 issue of the *Masses*, Dell was refreshingly candid about his vested interest in gender equality: "Feminism is going to make it possible for the first time for men to be free," he wrote in "Feminism for Men."[33] Dell's rationale was that when women had their own well-paying jobs, men would finally be free from the burden of having to support them and their children. He also argued that women's freedom, and men's consequent freedom, laid the groundwork for better relationships between men and women: "When you have got a woman in a box, and you pay rent on the box, her relationship to you insensibly changes character. It loses the fine excitement of democracy. It ceases to be companionship, for companionship is only possible in a democracy. It is no longer a sharing of life together—it is a breaking of life apart."[34] This emphasis on male-female relationships is developed further in Dell's feminist tract, *The Outline of Marriage* (1926), in which he advocates using birth control to enable companionate marriage.[35]

The three one-act comedies Dell wrote and staged for the Provincetown Players reflect the feminist principles Dell articulated in the three polemical pieces discussed above, but in these plays, Dell's feminism is more complicated and nuanced; he endorses neither the bohemian view of free love and companionate marriage nor bourgeois conventions of gender relations but, rather, juxtaposes the competing claims of committed love and extramarital passion, convention and romantic impulse, and free thought and deeply felt emotions, using irony and role reversal to explore these issues. What these plays do acknowledge is that the need for sex and companionship is equally experienced by men and women, and that both men and women have an equal right to love freely where they choose. The themes that link these plays are the tenuousness of the romantic ideal, the limitations of new ideas about love and marriage, the ephemeral nature of love, the power of desire, and the equally strong pull of conventional gender mores.

The most original and well-crafted of these plays is *The Angel Intrudes* (1917), a three-hander that features a middle-aged Jimmy Pendleton, who holds modern opinions about love and romance; his much younger girlfriend, Annabelle, whose views on those subjects are more traditional; and Jimmy's cigarette-smoking, cocktail-drinking guardian angel.[36] As Jimmy and Annabelle prepare to elope to Italy, the complexities of love and romance are explored as they reverse their positions on love to comic effect after the Angel intrudes. As with Cook and Glaspell's *Suppressed Desires*, this play's set features the Washington Square arch prominently, a clear signal that Greenwich Village bohemian views will be dissected. Dell pokes gentle fun at free thinkers whose radicalism proves ephemeral when it begins to threaten deep-seated feelings and at naïve proponents of undying love whose beliefs are tested when they are confronted with their own strong sexual desires. Although the play spoofs ardent advocates of both positions, it reflects the ambivalence of Jimmy, Annabelle, and many of Dell's Greenwich Village peers in the character of the Angel, who, after eloping with Annabelle, returns to Jimmy's apartment for his wings, torn between his desire to become mortal and love a woman and his longing for the former glory of his spiritual nature.

George Cram Cook: Socialism, Monism, and the Greek Ideal

As a teenager in Davenport, Dell met George Cram (Jig) Cook, son of one of Davenport's oldest and most distinguished families.[37] When they met, Cook had already left university teaching to raise vegetables and write fiction on his family's country estate, the Cabin, near Buffalo, Iowa. He had been raised by his mother, Ellen Dodge Cook, to value literature, music, art, philosophy, and, especially, the culture of ancient Greece, and to incorporate these ideals into his life and work.[38] After he was fired from his reporter's job at the *Davenport Democrat and Leader*, Dell joined Cook at the Cabin. During their ensuing philosophical and political discussions, Dell sparked Cook's interest in socialism and radical causes, and Cook embraced these new ideas.[39]

Cook joined the Socialist Party in 1908 and would become increasingly more of an activist during the next three years, inviting workingmen and their families to picnics at the Cabin, co-founding the Monist Society—a group of free thinkers that met every Sunday afternoon for debate and discussion—and becoming involved with the local chapter of the Political Refugees Defense League, serving as the League's secretary-treasurer and working with the group to prevent the extradition of political dissidents to Russia.[40] Two years later, Cook joined with Glaspell and others to battle censorship in the Davenport Public Library.[41] In October of 1910 he lectured on socialism for the Contemporary Club; also that fall, Cook was the Socialist candidate for Congress from Iowa's Second Congressional District.[42] During this period, Cook also wrote his socialist novel *The Chasm* (1911).

Thus, the three major influences on the writing, activism, and theatre practice of George Cram Cook—socialism, monism, and the Greek ideal—were rooted in Cook's Davenport environment, and, in many ways, the Provincetown project was born of his desire to recreate the nurturing Davenport matrix in which he, Dell, and Glaspell were formed. He described his potential theater as "a whole community working together, developing unsuspected talents," much as Davenport had nurtured the embryonic talents of these three young modernist writers as they interacted with the city's collection of socialists, monists, dreamers, intellectuals, writers, and artists.[43]

One of the first plays Cook wrote for the Provincetown Players was co-authored with Glaspell, whom he married in 1913. *Suppressed Desires* (1915) pokes fun at the keen interest in psychoanalysis shown by the proponents of "The New"; it is also firmly rooted in Cook's awareness of the divide between the conservative Midwesterners of his parents' generation and the Greenwich Village crowd of which he was now a member. His main female character, Henrietta Brewster, is herself a resident of the Village, and is described as wearing "radical" clothing. Her sister Mabel, a "plump" woman visiting from Chicago, is skeptical of Freud's theories, even declaring, "I don't believe they have them [suppressed desires] in Chicago."[44] The play thus operates on the very cultural tensions that Cook and Glaspell were so familiar with from their Davenport years and even satirizes those extreme modernists who suggest that, as Henrietta puts it, "old institutions will have to be reshaped."[45]

Ironically, although it was the Midwest that inspired Cook, as with Glaspell and Dell, it was also a place he had to leave behind in search of the ever-elusive modernist ideal. As Glaspell put it in the introduction to *The Road to the Temple* (1927), "This is the romance of an American brought up on the Mississippi and buried beside the Temple of Apollo at Delphi. It is the story of a promised land that was entered ... It was not alone the past of Greece he loved. It was the past of the Mississippi upon which he was brought up; the past of his own family, entering a wilderness in their covered wagon, the past of the Indians they drove from the land, of the earth which cooled and made us and became our home."[46] Yet the question remains: Was that promised land Delphi or the Midwest itself?

Cook confronted this sense of time and history in a one-act play, co-authored with Glaspell, *Tickless Time* (1918), in which Ian and Eloise Joyce call for the return of the sundial, of "true time," in opposition to clocks and other "artificial" means of telling time. This play is essentially modernist in the way it rails against the Victorian notion of data, of precision, of railroad time, and yet paradoxically seeks a solution for the future in the past. *Tickless Time* both enacts and critiques modernist thinking, harkening back to Cook's Davenport days, as it exemplifies the monism that brought together Cook, Dell, and Glaspell. As Brenda Murphy notes, monism came to Davenport from Germany by way of Chicago, and its influence fully informs *Tickless Time*.[47] "From the last tick of the clock to that moment millions of years ago when the first particle of the oldest stratified rock sank through the sea to its place, the laws of the world have not changed. And this is Monism,"[48] wrote Glaspell, a statement Murphy cites as "a thematic principle" behind the short play.[49] This assertion echoes Glaspell's observations about Cook's preoccupation with the past, indeed, with drinking himself into a sense of timelessness and lucidity through which he could create and inspire art.[50] Ian and Eloise desire not only to live by a truer assessment of time, but also to bury false timekeepers entirely, effectively erasing the premodernist concept of time as anything but continuous and fluid.

Ian and Eloise Joyce's project is not only monistic but modernist, supporting Marxist Georg Lukacs's assertion that "modernism despairs of human history, abandons the idea of a linear historical development."[51] The precision of time is an illusion, and in freeing themselves from the tyranny of the clock and putting their faith in the sundial, the Joyces hope they can be liberated from notions of past and future in favor of what Howe characterizes as "the inescapable present."[52] Cook and Glaspell look to the far past to inform their modernist viewpoint, rejecting the more recent past in an attempt to "produce, partly as the result of unconscious process, and partly through the exercise of critical consciousness, the idioms and forms of new art."[53] Eloise and Ian look to the ancient sundial to inform their future together, a future that exists "in eternal time."[54] Their goal is a greater sense of authenticity and connection with nature, both very modernist concepts that posit individual truth as having a greater value than the religious or moral certitude of the Victorian era.

In *Tickless Time*, Cook and Glaspell also seem to respond to Einstein's theory of relativity, which ushered in a new modernist era in which synchronized time was seen as a naïve and impossible concept, contributing to the shifts in viewpoint and perspective utilized by writers such as Virginia Woolf and Cubist artists. It also seems to share a certain kinship with socialist ideals that would later blossom into Trotsky's support of a new socialist theory of how workers could relate to time pioneered by Platon Kerzhentsev in 1923, which emphasized "spontaneous self-discipline" over purely post–Industrial Revolution concepts of "rational scientific monitoring of abstract time units."[55] These revolutionary concepts of time would inspire questions within Marxist and socialist circles as Communist Party theory was developed that were answered by Eloise and Ian as they debate the merits of "true" and "standardized" time. A layer of complexity is added to the play, however, when Eloise learns that the sundial Ian has fashioned to achieve a "first-hand relation with truth" tells completely accurate time only four times a year; she then begins to dig up all of the clocks they have buried.[56]

Like *Suppressed Desires*, this play satirizes the obsession with new ideas that Cook and Glaspell witnessed in many of their Greenwich Village and Provincetown contemporaries; unlike the earlier play, however, *Tickless Time* interrogates the notion of directly achieving "true time" by demonstrating the necessity of a mediating representation of time; the sundial, like the clocks, can render time only imperfectly and is no more a means of attaining "a direct relation with the sun" than are the clocks the Joyces have earlier rejected.[57] Thus, the play also functions as a critique of modernist experiments that attempt to transcend the limitations of form, such as Imagist poetry, expressionist drama, and the stream-of-consciousness novel.[58] Howe quotes Herman Hesse, who wrote of "[a]whole generation caught ... between two ages, two modes of life, with the consequence that it loses all power to understand itself."[59] In Cook's work, however, we see him continually working toward those powers of understanding, wrestling on the page and stage with the philosophic contradictions and concerns that drove and defined his life. In the act of organizing groups like the Monist Society and, later, the Provincetown Players, Cook was attempting to "cause Athens to bring an unknown splendor into the world" or, rather, cause Davenport, Provincetown, or even the Village to exemplify modernity.[60]

Just as Cook felt himself situated in time by his modernist beliefs, so did he position himself in relation to Greece. In *The Athenian Women* (1918) Cook finds a means of expressing modernist principles and concerns by reimagining *Lysistrata*, but as Glaspell suggests in *The Road to the Temple*, for Jig Cook, Greece began in Iowa, positioning the end of Cook's life in his childhood. Cook juxtaposed the significant geographic and cultural influences of his life in balanced, almost simultaneous perspective, much as a Cubist painting balances multiple viewpoints, as the characters in *Tickless Time* carry the positions of the sun in different places, as socialists juggle productivity and the clock, as modernists must juggle the significance and influence of past and present epochs.

Susan Glaspell: Feminism and Free Speech
Susan Glaspell, the most successful and prolific of the three Davenport playwrights, was no less shaped by her experiences as a young adult in

her native city.⁶¹ Glaspell had given up a successful career in journalism in Des Moines and moved back to Davenport to become a prize-winning author of short fiction; when she began to associate with Cook and Dell, she was at work on her first novel, *The Glory of the Conquered* (1909), which she followed with a socialist novel, *The Visioning*, in 1911. After joining the Monist Society, she spent more time with Cook and Dell; Jig's father, Edward E. Cook, noted in several diary entries in 1910 that Glaspell was a frequent visitor to the Cabin.⁶² The three strengthened their bonds of intellectual and, in the case of Glaspell and Cook, romantic companionship through their participation in the Monist Society; after Dell left Davenport, Cook and Glaspell would take up the cause of free speech when they launched a letter-writing campaign and petition drive to protest the library board's refusal to purchase George Burman Foster's *The Finality of the Christian Religion*.⁶³

Glaspell's commitment to free speech and, more broadly, freedom of expression permeates her dramatic oeuvre, and in three plays set in Davenport and its environs—*Close the Book* (1917), *Inheritors* (1921), and *Chains of Dew* (1922)—free speech and feminist issues converge in New Woman protagonists who test the limits of First Amendment freedoms. Their advocacy and practice of freedom of speech and expression provide the thematic focus of these plays, which employ images that suggest confinement—walls, fences, bonds, and prison bars—representing the limitations and conventions that threaten to repress them and circumscribe their freedom of expression.

Glaspell came of age in a city where leaders such as Phoebe Sudlow, Dr. Jennie McCowen, Ella G. Bushnell-Hamlin, Annie Wittenmyer, and her own great-aunt by marriage, Martha (Mrs. Barton) Glaspell were effecting social change and opening up new possibilities for women.⁶⁴ A socialist and a proponent of women's suffrage, Glaspell joined the Lucy Stone League and Heterodoxy, a Greenwich Village feminist lunch club, after she moved East.⁶⁵ Her one-act comedy *Close the Book* features a radical New Woman character, Jhansi Mason, who would have been right at home at a Heterodoxy luncheon. In *Close the Book*, when Jhansi teams up with her professor, Peyton Root, to promote free speech, humorous consequences ensue. The three full-length plays Glaspell staged in the early 1920s further complicate the concepts of feminism and free speech.

Like *Close the Book*, *Inheritors*, staged by the Provincetown in 1921, focuses on a New Woman character and a college professor who are fighting for free speech. Like *Close the Book*, *Inheritors* is set in Iowa; the last two acts take place on a college campus where the liberal Professor Holden's support for conscientious objectors and protesters jeopardizes his job. Also, like *Close the Book*, *Inheritors* marries feminism and free speech in a female protagonist, Madeline Fejevary Morton, who supports several Indian students' right to protest British colonial policy on the Morton College campus, attacking a policeman who harasses them as they are posting handbills. But unlike Glaspell's one-act comedy, which exploits the humorous aspects of the issue when its proponents are faced with some unwelcome news that they would just as soon suppress, *Inheritors* teases out the complexities involved with the free speech question. The play's chief conflict—between the proponents of the First Amendment's guarantee of freedom of speech and assembly and the voices of financial expediency and conservatism that strive to rein them in—centers on Madeline, who must trade her carefree social life and cherished family relationships for the isolation of a prison cell if she sticks to her principles.

Giving the play depth and resonance is Silas Morton, Madeline's grandfather, who appears in act one, donating his land for a college to support the very freedoms Madeline and Professor Holden are in jeopardy for espousing. "There will one day be a college in these cornfields because long ago a great dream was fought for in Hungary," Silas promises his neighbor, Felix Fejevary, Sr.[66] However, this Hungarian revolutionary's son, Felix Jr., now president of the college and one generation removed from that dream, ironically proves to be an obstacle to its fulfillment. In this play Glaspell explores the nuances of the free speech issue through Felix Jr., who must balance the college's commitment to academic freedom with its need for continuous funding in the face of pressure from a conservative and pragmatic state legislature. "I too have made a fight, although the fight to finance never appears to be an idealistic one," he argues.[67] A further challenge to the ideals of Silas Morton is the indifference to such ideals shown by many of the school's shallow and self-involved students, including Fejevary's own son, Horace.

Another exploration of the interrelationship of feminism and freedom of expression is seen in Glaspell's comedy, *Chains of Dew*, produced by the Provincetown Players in 1922 after Cook and Glaspell had left for Greece.[68] Set mostly in Bluff City, Iowa (a fictionalized Davenport), the main plot centers on protagonist Seymore Standish, who is conflicted and frustrated because he can't reconcile his desire to write poetry with his duty to fulfill the social and business obligations he believes are imposed on him by his banking career and position in the community.[69] Although Seymore's dilemma is the focal point of the play, Glaspell examines the nexus of free speech and feminism in a subplot centering on his wife Dotty's conflicts, which revolve around a controversial topic: birth control. In this subplot two female characters each occupy opposite ends of a female socio-political continuum. At one end is New Woman Nora Powers, secretary of the Birth Control League, who journeys from New York City to Bluff City to start a Birth Control League chapter in Iowa; Dotty, situated at the other end, is a traditional woman who attempts a more difficult journey as she moves toward Nora's end of the continuum, bobbing her hair and joining the Birth Control movement.[70]

Both the main plot and the subplot explore freedom of expression; the play demonstrates that, paradoxically, free expression is sometimes better served when one doesn't feel so free to express oneself so directly. Seymore's editor, Leon Whittaker, believes that Seymore would be a better poet if he were liberated from the entanglements of his middle-western middle-class life in Bluff City, but through her discussions with Seymore's visiting New York City friends, his mother concludes that it is precisely those entanglements and Seymore's feeling of being bound by them that spark his creativity: "His soul must be the soul of an alien. It's made that way. Here—with us—longing for you, whom he cannot have. There—with you, the pull of us, to whom he must return."[71]

Motifs of communication and expression in the play reinforce this paradox. In act one, a mimeograph machine duplicating appeals to donors malfunctions, and Seymore refuses to sign a protest ad supporting an imprisoned writer whose exercise of his First Amendment rights has gotten him into trouble. In act three he balks at giving a speech for birth control in Bluff City, and Dotty's plans to hold a birth control meeting in Bluff City and put Seymore to work writing birth control hymns don't materialize. These failed efforts at free speech via traditional means—letters, ads, meetings, and speeches—contrast with less explicit and more effective modes of persuasion: Nora's ideal and not-so-ideal family posters and Seymore's mother's homemade dolls for birth control, thus emphasizing that sometimes indirection succeeds better than more overtly rhetorical approaches.

Conclusion

Although sincere in their progressive beliefs, by their Provincetown period, these writers had gained enough critical distance from their formative years in Davenport to critique with humor the excesses of "The New" and its adherents who embraced it more out of a desire to be intellectually fashionable than to live their sincere beliefs. Nevertheless, all three playwrights acknowledged the intellectual, political, and aesthetic debt they owed to their native city. Of the three, Glaspell was the most negative about Davenport; however, she set almost all of her novels and plays there and always acknowledged her feeling for the Mississippi Valley. "I live by the sea," she wrote near the end of her life, "but the body of water I have the most feeling about is the Mississippi River."[72] Dell reports that the last time he saw Jig Cook, the latter put his arm around Dell's shoulder and proposed they "gather the old Davenport crowd together, and go back there, and make it a new Athens!"[73] Dell always looked back on his Davenport days with fondness and gratitude. As *Moon-Calf*'s protagonist, Felix Fay, prepares to leave for Chicago, he reflects on his Iowa experience: "He had been happy in Port Royal [Davenport]; it had given him love, and painful wisdom, and the joy of struggle ... It had been built for young men and girls to be happy in, to adventure in, and to think strange and brave and perilous thoughts. It was not like other towns ... No—it had a history of its own. From the first it had been a rebellious town."[74] For these three playwrights, Davenport had been such a town, one that, in Felix's words, was built "for growing up in."[75] In early twentieth-century Davenport, Iowa, Floyd Dell, George Cram Cook, and Susan Glaspell served their literary apprenticeships, thoroughly engaged with the culture of "the New"; in Dell's "romantic and miraculous city," they internalized the ideals that would be formative in their lives and in their art.[76]

Notes

1. Irving Howe, "The Culture of Modernism," *Commentary* 44, no. 1 (Nov. 1967): 48–59.
2. Daniel Joseph Singal, "Towards a Definition of American Modernism," *American Quarterly* 39, no. 1 (Spring 1987): 7–26, 1.
3. Harry Hansen, *Midwest Portraits* (New York: Harcourt, Brace, and Company, 1923), 209. Notwithstanding Glaspell's comment to Dell that "Davenport as a Literary Center is too precious a thought to be marred by a comment of mine" (17 Sept. 1910, Floyd Dell Papers, Newberry Library), there is some basis for Hansen's characterization of the city. Although the earliest Davenport author on record is poet Hiram Reid, the best known of the city's writers was the prolific Alice French (Octave Thanet); her six novels and nine short story collections are shaped by nineteenth-century literary conventions. Lawyer-poet Arthur Davison Ficke, also quite prolific, was the author of seventeen volumes of verse, as well as a novel, three plays, and two books on Japanese prints. His poem, "Poetry," introduced the inaugural issue of *Poetry: A Magazine of Verse* in October of 1912. Harry Hansen's career was focused mainly on reporting, editing, and book reviewing, yet he published seven books, including a novel based on his Davenport upbringing, *Your Life Lies Before You* (1935). Before Glaspell won the 1931 Pulitzer Prize for Drama for *Alison's House* (1930), muckraker and socialist Charles Edward Russell, whose father edited the *Davenport Gazette*, won one in 1928 for his biography, *The American Orchestra and Theodore Thomas* (1927). Poet Charles Eugene Banks, editor of the *Davenport Morning Republican* and the *Davenport Weekly Outlook*, gave Glaspell her first journalism jobs and co-authored two books with Cook: *In Hampton Roads: A Dramatic Romance* (1899) and *Beautiful Homes and Social Customs of America: A Complete Guide to Correct Social Forms and Artistic Living* (1902).
4. Timothy B. Spears, *Chicago Dreaming: Midwesterners and the City, 1871–1919* (Chicago: University of Chicago Press, 2005), 216.
5. Adele Heller and Lois Rudnick, "Introduction," *1915 the Cultural Moment: The New Politics, the New Woman, the New Psychology, the New Art, and the New Theatre in America* (New Brunswick: Rutgers University Press, 1991), 1–13, 2.
6. Brenda Murphy, "Preface," *The Provincetown Players and the Culture of Modernity* (New York: Cambridge University Press, 2005), xiii–xvii, xiii.
7. Qtd. in Susan Glaspell, *The Road to the Temple* (New York: Frederick A. Stokes Company), 309.
8. Helen Deutsch and Stella Hanau, *The Provincetown: A Story of the Theatre* (New York: Farrar & Rinehart, 1931), 15–18, 34–38, 221, 226.
9. Qtd. in Glaspell, *The Road to the Temple*, 252.
10. Murphy, "Preface," xv.

11. Floyd Dell, *Homecoming: An Autobiography* (New York: Farrar & Rinehart, 1933), 170.
12. Marcia Noe, "'A Romantic and Miraculous City' Shapes Three Midwestern Writers," *Western Illinois Regional Studies* 1, no. 2 (Fall 1978): 176–98, 177–78.
13. Noe, *Susan Glaspell: Voice from the Heartland* (Macomb: Western Illinois University, 1983), 15, 22, 26; "'Romantic and Miraculous City,'" 185.
14. Marlys Svendsen, *Davenport: A Pictorial History* ([Davenport]: G. Bradley Publishing, 1985), 44, 94,100; Noe, *Heartland*, 22.
15. Hildegard Binder Johnson, *German Forty-Eighters in Davenport* (Daveport: Davenport Schutzenpark Gilde, 1998), 3–5; Bill Wundrum, *A Time We Remember: Celebrating a Century in Our Quad-Cities* (Davenport: The Quad-City Times, 1999), 169.
16. Johnson, *German Forty-Eighters*, 6–39; Wundrum, *Time We Remember*, 169.
17. Sharon E. Wood, *The Freedom of the Streets: Work, Citizenship, and Sexuality in a Gilded Age City* (Chapel Hill: The University of North Carolina Press, 2005), 227.
18. Johnson, *German Forty-Eighters*, 16–39; Kory Darnall, *Schuetzenpark: "Davenport's Lost Playland," 1870–1923* (Davenport: Davenport Schuetzenpark Gilde, 1999), 1–13.
19. Dell, *Homecoming*, 93, 118–19, 144. See also Douglas Clayton, *Floyd Dell: The Life and Times of an American Rebel* (Chicago: Ivan R. Dee, 1994), 26–37. Davenport was not unique among midwestern municipalities in its strong Socialist presence; cities that elected a Socialist government during the early twentieth century include Milwaukee, Wisconsin; Minneapolis, Minnesota; Flint and Jackson, Michigan; and Dayton, Ohio. In 1920, Davenporters elected a Socialist mayor and city council. See Donald T. Critchlow, ed., *Socialism in the Heartland: The Midwestern Experience, 1900–1925* (Notre Dame: Notre Dame University Press, 1986).
20. Dell, *Homecoming*, 146. From its inception in 1901, the American Socialist Party endorsed a platform that opposed war and advocated equal rights for men and women. See Daniel Bell, "Marxism and Socialism in the United States," *Socialism and American Life*, vol. 1, ed. Donald Drew Egbert and Stow Persons (Princeton: Princeton University Press, 1952), 265–66. Eugene V. Debs, five times the Socialist Party's candidate for President of the United States, espoused feminist principles in his pamphlet *Woman— Comrade and Equal*. See Harold W. Currie, *Eugene V. Debs* (Boston: Twayne Publishers, 1976), 104–06. Dell's wide reading in socialist texts by Edward Bellamy, Ignatius Donnelly, Peter Kropotkin, Robert Ingersoll, and others further informed Dell's opinions about war and gender issues. See George Thomas Tanselle, "Faun at the Barricades: The Life and Work of Floyd Dell" (PhD diss., Northwestern University, 1959), 18–20.
21. Although over time Dell's views about marriage and gender roles grew more conservative, in several novels, such as *The Briary-Bush* (1921),

An Unmarried Father (1927), and *Souvenir* (1929), he created New Woman characters and also celebrated female autonomy and economic independence in *Woman as World Builders* (1913), *The Outline of Marriage* (1926), and other nonfiction essays and books.

22. Edward Bellamy, *Looking Backward* (New York: Dover Publications, Inc., 1996), 128.
23. Dell, *Homecoming*, 63.
24. Ibid., 96.
25. Dell, "Why People Go to Brick Munro's," *The Tri-City Workers Magazine* 1, no. 11 (Sept. 1906): 1–4, 1–2.
26. Dell, "Brick Munro's," 1.
27. Dell, "Brick Munro's," 3.
28. Ibid.
29. Wood, *Freedom*, 214.
30. Dell, "Brick Munro's," 4.
31. Dell became a leading luminary of the Chicago Renaissance, serving first as assistant editor, then associate editor, and, finally, editor of the *Friday Literary Review* of the *Chicago Evening Post* and hosting a salon with his wife, Margery Currey. For lively discussions of Dell's Chicago years, see his autobiography, *Homecoming*; Douglas Clayton's biography; "Faun at the Barricades, part 1"; and the chapter on Dell in Dale Kramer's *Chicago Renaissance* (New York: Appleton-Century, 1966).
32. Cook and Glaspell's love affair made it difficult for them to remain in Davenport. Glaspell left in 1910, finally settling in Greenwich Village. After a brief sojourn in Chicago, where he worked with Dell on the *Friday Literary Review*, Cook joined her there after his divorce from Mollie Price Cook came through; they were married in 1913, the year Dell arrived in Greenwich Village. There Dell worked as an associate editor of the radical periodical, the *Masses*, put on plays for the Liberal Club, wrote a best-selling novel, *Moon-Calf* (1920), and instituted the "Pagan Routs," a series of costume parties that helped establish the Village's reputation as the center of wild Bohemia. Dell also joined Cook and Glaspell when they founded the Provincetown Players; the minutes of the group's inaugural meetings in September of 1916 list twenty-nine charter members; among these names is that of Floyd Dell, who would stage four one-act plays with the troupe: *King Arthur's Socks* (1916), *A Long Time Ago* (1917), *The Angel Intrudes* (1917), and *Sweet-and-Twenty* (1918). See Deutsch and Hanau, *The Provincetown*, 15–18; 202–15. Dell's *Homecoming* is a great source on these years, as are Clayton and Tanselle.
33. Dell, "Feminism for Men," *Masses* 10, no. 5 (July 1914): 19–20, 19.
34. Ibid., 20.
35. Dell, *The Outline of Marriage* (New York: The American Birth Control League, 1926).

36. Dell, "The Angel Intrudes," *The Provincetown Plays*, ed. George Cram Cook and Frank Shay (New York: D. Appleton and Company, 1921).
37. Cook was the great-grandson of Davenport pioneer settler Ira Cook, the grandson of lawyer and congressman John P. Cook, and the son of Edward Everett Cook, a prominent Davenport attorney. An aunt, Clarissa Cook, endowed a library, a church, and the Clarissa C. Cook Home for the Friendless. See Glaspell, *The Road to the Temple*, 12–14.
38. See Glaspell, *The Road to the Temple*, 16–19; Barbara Ozieblo, *Susan Glaspell: A Critical Biography* (Chapel Hill: University of North Carolina Press, 2000), 48; and Linda Ben-Zvi, *Susan Glaspell: Her Life and Times* (New York: Oxford University Press, 2005).
39. Clayton, *Floyd Dell*, 37–39; Glaspell, *The Road to the Temple*, 180–82. Although Clayton asserts that "Dell managed to convert Cook to socialism," Glaspell reports that when he was teaching at the University of Iowa, Cook was introduced to socialist ideas by a man she names only as "Jessen," a German instructor there. See Glaspell, *The Road to the Temple*, 85. Undoubtedly, though, Dell's influence a decade later was decisive in motivating Cook's involvement with the Davenport local.
40. Glaspell, *The Road to the Temple*, 190; Dell, *Homecoming*, 149–51, and "'A Romantic and Miraculous City,'" 186–87.
41. Glaspell, *The Road to the Temple*, 193.
42. Ibid., 188; George Cram Cook, "Some Modest Remarks on Socialism," *Papers of the Contemporary Club* 15 (1910–1911): 1–17.
43. Qtd. in Glaspell, *The Road to the Temple*, 251. The leftist/intellectual circle in which Cook traveled included Dell; Glaspell; Mollie Price Cook, who was married to Jig Cook from 1908 to 1911; the Rabbi William Fineshriber; and Franz (Fritz) Feuchter, a Socialist mail carrier. When the Socialists took over the Davenport City Council in 1920, Feuchter was one of the newly elected aldermen.
44. Susan Glaspell and George Cram Cook, *Suppressed Desires*, Plays (Boston: Small, Maynard and Company, 1920), 231–71, 235, 245.
45. Ibid., 244.
46. Glaspell, *The Road to the Temple*, vii.
47. Murphy, "Preface," 28.
48. Glaspell, *The Road to the Temple*, 28.
49. Murphy, "Preface," 29.
50. Glaspell, *The Road to the Temple*, 89.
51. Qtd. in Howe, "Culture of Modernism," 50
52. Ibid.
53. Qtd. in Howe, "Culture of Modernism," 49.
54. Glaspell and Cook, *Tickless Time*, Plays, 271–315, 287.
55. Stephen E. Hanson, *Time and Revolution: Marxism and the Design of Soviet Institutions* (Chapel Hill: The University of North Carolina Press, 1997), 125.

56. Glaspell and Cook, *Tickless Time*, 279.
57. Ibid., 299.
58. See Marcia Noe and Robert L. Marlowe, "Suppressed Desires and Tickless Time: An Intertextual Critique of Modernity," *American Drama* 14, no. 1 (Winter 2005): 1–14.
59. Qtd. in Howe, "Culture of Modernism," 49.
60. Cook, *The Athenian Women: A Play* (Athens: Printing House "Estia," 1926), 66. This play was originally mounted by the Provincetown Players in March 1918, which is the date given for the play in this chapter.
61. Over the course of her career, Glaspell authored nine novels, over fourteen plays, and more than 50 short stories. In 1931 she won the Pulitzer Prize for her play *Alison's House*, set, as is much of her work, in the environs of Davenport. Her seventh novel, *The Morning Is Near Us*, was a Literary Guild selection in 1940, and her most famous play, *Trifles* (1916), has been staged and filmed numerous times and reprinted in dozens of anthologies. Mary Papke's *Susan Glaspell: A Research and Production Handbook* (Westport, CT: Greenwood Press, 1993) contains primary and secondary source bibliographies that include excerpts from reviews, as does Gerhard Bach's "Susan Glaspell: A Bibliography of Dramatic Criticism," *Great Lakes Review* 3, no. 4 (1977): 1–34. Ozieblo's *Susan Glaspell* also offers a comprehensive primary and secondary source bibliography. Noe's "Susan Glaspell's Analysis of the Midwestern Character," *Books at Iowa* 27 (November 1977): 3–14, concludes with a checklist of Glaspell's work.
62. E.E. Cook, Unpublished diary, January, 1910, Cook Family Papers, MS. 109, Box 1, Special Collections, the University of Iowa Libraries, Iowa City, Iowa.
63. Noe, "'A Romantic and Miraculous City,'" 176–95.
64. In 1874, Phoebe Sudlow became Davenport's and the nation's first superintendent of schools. Dr. Jennie McCowen became the first female president of the Scott County [Iowa] Medical Society and founded the Lend-A-Hand Club for Davenport working women in 1887. Suffragist Ella G. Bushnell-Hamlin edited a weekly magazine, *Trident*, in early twentieth-century Davenport. In 1865, Annie Wittenmyer founded Davenport's Iowa Soldiers' Orphans' Home, later the Annie Wittenmyer Home. Along with Jennie McCowen and Phoebe Sudlow, Martha Glaspell, president of the local chapter of the Women's Christian Temperance Union, convinced the city of Davenport to hire a police matron. See Svendsen, Wundrum, and Wood.
65. Cheryl Black, *The Women of Provincetown, 1915–1922* (Tuscaloosa: University of Alabama Press, 2001), 13.
66. Glaspell, *Inheritors* (Boston: Small, Maynard and Company, 1921), 42.
67. Ibid., 83.
68. After seven years at the helm of the Provincetown Players, Cook grew disillusioned with the company, as several key members became more

interested in the commercial potential of their plays than in his dream of a theatre collective that embodied the spirit of ancient Greek drama. In the spring of 1922, Cook and Glaspell immigrated to Delphi, Greece, where they lived until Cook died in January 1924. Subsequently Glaspell returned to Provincetown and Truro, where she resumed writing stories, novels, and plays. Glaspell died in Provincetown in 1948. See Glaspell's *The Road to the Temple*, Noe's *Susan Glaspell: Voice from the Heartland*; Ben-Zvi's *Susan Glaspell: Her Life and Times*, Ozieblo's *Susan Glaspell: A Critical Biography*, and Robert Sarlos's *Jig Cook and the Provincetown Players: Theatre in Ferment* (Boston: University of Massachusetts Press, 1982).

69. Poet-banker Seymore Standish is most likely modeled on poet-lawyer Arthur Davison Ficke, whom Glaspell knew in Davenport and reconnected with in 1922 when the Provincetown Players put on his play *Mr. Faustus*, a few months before *Chains of Dew* was staged. Ficke's father-in-law's and son's first name, Stanhope, bears a strong resemblance to Seymore's surname, Standish, but the similarities do not end there. Like Seymore, Ficke tried to balance his obligations to his profession with his ambitions as a poet, making trips to Chicago to socialize with his literary friends. Unlike Seymore, Ficke finally walked away from his midwestern professional identity and his first marriage after World War I. See Noe's "Missed by Modernism: The Literary Friendship of Arthur Davison Ficke and Edgar Lee Masters," *Western Illinois Regional Studies* 14, no. 2 (Fall 1991): 71–79.

70. When *Chains of Dew* was staged, Section 211 of the Criminal Code of the United States made it illegal to send birth control information—considered obscene material—through the mail. The National Birth Control League, founded by Mary Ware in 1915, and the American Birth Control League, founded by Margaret Sanger in 1921, worked against this law. In 1938, a United States Circuit Court of Appeals found that disseminating birth control information did not violate the federal obscenity law if it were done under the supervision of a medical doctor. See J. Ellen Gainor, *Susan Glaspell in Context: American Theatre, Culture, and Politics, 1915–48* (Ann Arbor: University of Michigan Press, 2001), 170–98.

71. Glaspell, *Chains of Dew, The Complete Plays of Susan Glaspell*, ed. Linda Ben-Zvi and J. Ellen Gainor (Jefferson, NC: McFarland and Company, Inc., 2010), 127–78, 173–74.

72. Glaspell, "Here is the piece …," Susan Glaspell Papers, Berg Collection of English and American Literature, New York Public Library.

73. Dell, *Homecoming,* 361.

74. Dell, *Moon-Calf* (New York: Alfred A. Knopf, 1920), 394.

75. Ibid.

76. Qtd. In Tanselle, "Faun at the Barricades," 25–26.

Sara Kosiba

Breaking Binaries

Deconstructing the "Revolt" and Reassessing Midwestern Literature and Art

In 1930, Oliver M. Saylor published a book titled *Revolt in the Arts*, which comprised essays on the idea of revolt within the arts by Saylor and other notable figures. The collection reinforces the idea that some type of revolt was at work in contemporary art, architecture, drama, literature, cinema, and music, even television, of the time. This idea of an artistic revolt was not something that originated with Saylor; the analysis and commentary in his collection built upon a topic that to some degree was timeless, as many artistic efforts have been a response to or a revolt against the standards of their time. In the 1920s and 1930s, there were many artistic movements actively subverting the status quo, such as modernism or Dadaism, making Saylor's collection very relevant to its era. Saylor's text does little to define conclusively a unified reason for revolt in the arts; its value lies primarily in collecting a diverse and prominent list of voices to debate the idea of revolt, with commentary from Lillian Gish, Martha Graham, George Gershwin, Louis Bromfield, John Sloan, Frank Lloyd Wright, and many others.

The idea of artistic revolt has particular relevance to discussions of culture in the American Midwest. The region is most often characterized as inspiring a "revolt from the village," to use a phrase popularized by critic Carl Van Doren in 1921. This concept infused almost all discussion of midwestern culture in the twentieth century and has lingered in twenty-first-century discussions, as well, in essence structuring a neat binary, with one artistic side representing those who chose to stay loyal to the region or were "for" the "village" or small town (often applied more broadly to mean "for" the Midwest as a whole) and the other side consisting of those who noted flaws or inadequacies or were "against" the small town or "for" the city. A few critical and scholarly voices have begun to note the problematic nature of this ongoing revolt narrative, and I add my own analysis to that effort to show the disservice the reductive binary construction does to our understanding of midwestern art and literature. It is time to relegate the phrase "the revolt from the village" and related concepts to a historical or critical footnote in our contemporary scholarship and move beyond the limited thinking it represents. In continuing to reinforce the concept by footnoting it as anything more than a moment in a critical past that is, indeed, past, we limit our ability to view a more nuanced midwestern artistic heritage, one that is filled with cultural and individual complexity and one that more accurately reveals the region as far more than an American regional stereotype.

The "revolt from the village" label has an impressive legacy. An idea in a monthly essay on "Contemporary American Novelists," one of a series of essays Van Doren published throughout 1921 in *The Nation*, became the most significant concept in understanding midwestern literature in the almost one hundred years of criticism that followed. Section ten of his 1921 series, "The Revolt from the Village: 1920," forever linked Van Doren's name to any discussion of 1920s or 1930s midwestern literature. In that essay, Van Doren argued that prior to 1915, few authors had dared to critique the "cult of the village," instead "celebrating its delicate merits with sentimental affection."[1] Van Doren alleged that, with the publication of Edgar Lee Masters's *Spoon River Anthology* in 1915, respect and reverence for village or small-town life began to change and he highlighted several 1920 novels by authors Sherwood Anderson, E.W. Howe, Sinclair Lewis, Zona Gale, Floyd Dell, and F. Scott Fitzgerald as examples.

It is clear that subsequent students and scholars latched on to the easy binary proposed by Van Doren's idea of revolt (the idea that you are either with the village or you are against it) more than they focused on the nuance lingering within such a discussion. Even Van Doren, as he noted the village backlash or critique in the novels discussed in his essay, recognized that the overall dynamic between village life and its inhabitants was far more complex. For example, in discussing the narrator of Sherwood Anderson's *Winesburg, Ohio* (1920), Van Doren stated,

> The young man who here sets out to make his fortune has not greatly hated Winesburg, and the imminence of his departure throws a vaguely golden mist over the village, which is seen in considerable measure through his generous if inexperienced eyes. A newspaper reporter, he directs his principle curiosity toward items of life outside the commonplace and thus offers Mr. Anderson the occasion to explore the moral and spiritual hinterlands of men and women who outwardly walk paths strict enough.²

This comment, and others throughout his essay, noted that while the village is viewed in far less idyllic terms, the village itself is not always the source of the problem or the entire focus of the story. The village serves as a microcosm of humanity suitable for dissection and examination. Therefore, Van Doren is really highlighting the idea that many of these writers are engaging in a more detailed fictional analysis of the village than previous fiction writers ever had. Van Doren finished his essay with a more dynamic assessment of this movement of writers, as well, viewing their commentary as part of a "moving tide" of change and not simply overwhelming condemnation: "The traditions which may have once governed them no longer hold. They break the patterns one by one and follow their wild desires. And as they play among the ruins of the old, they reason subtly about the new, laughing."³

It is unfortunate that so many later critics read Van Doren's essay so reductively, as his observations were more nuanced than many have acknowledged. Van Doren was a Midwesterner himself, and he, like many of the authors he was critiquing, expressed both nostalgia and criticism for his upbringing in the region. He opens his 1936 autobiography, *Three Worlds*, with a recollection of his early youthful reflections on the contrast between farm and town life:

> I was born in a village then called Hope, in Illinois, and I lived there or on a farm a mile away till I was fifteen, as happy as an animal. After we had decided to leave the village for a town, I was suddenly restless. Through four or five dragging months I blamed the farm and the village, though they were the same as they had been. I resented country manners,

country clothes, country grammar. Ambition in me first took the form of snobbishness. I believe this is more general than many people will confess.[4]

That general feeling of snobbishness and the desire to cast off "country manners" in favor of city life is common in many characters found in "revolt from the village" novels. However, as Van Doren's own autobiography goes on to show, these feelings are much more nuanced than any simplistic binary tension may make them sound. In his memoir, he moves between nostalgic recollections of farm life and anecdotal stories of violence or scandal, ultimately concluding at one point that "Although the village was a bare crossroads in a cornfield, it was also the heart of a community, with the bones, flesh, blood, and nerves of any community. Any community in the world."[5] He acknowledged that these feelings shaped his discussion of the "revolt from the village" novels: "Behind the most balanced criticism there is a person as well as a critic. I was divided in this conflict between old village and new city. I remembered Hope with affection and I had not been made unhappy by anything Urbana had ever done to me. The revolt, I thought, was partly revenge for early irritations."[6]

Van Doren's terminology of a revolt among midwestern writers was picked up by critics very quickly after his article appeared, and rather than read his essay as one perspective of a changing literary tide, they read the essay as establishing clear demarcations between types of writers and their attitudes. For example, Percy Boynton, in a 1923 article discussing Booth Tarkington, was among the first to read Van Doren's assessments as drawing battle lines in perceptions of village life and the midwestern small town. He stated, "In the modern 'revolt from the village'—Mr. Van Doren's inspired phrase—Mr. Masters and all his younger successors have presented true and truly depressing pictures of life."[7] Tarkington, in contrast, according to Boynton, is a nuanced writer who sees the small town with realism, sympathy, and humor and is not engaged in revolt. In 1925, Louis Wann wrote a review essay that largely borrowed many of Van Doren's assessments (with no nod to Van Doren's earlier 1921 article) about a "revolt from the village" movement and expanded the movement's reach to encompass work published between 1920 and 1925.[8] In 1926, Dorothy Anne Dondore's *The Prairie and the Making of*

Middle America: Four Centuries of Description appeared, noting Carl Van Doren's use of the "revolt from the village" to characterize midwestern writing.[9] In 1930, Norman Eliason wrote of Sherwood Anderson, lamenting the author's inclusion in Van Doren's "revolt against the village" article, as Eliason saw that classification as limiting the depth of Anderson's work: "Anderson reveals a deep sympathetic understanding of the inhabitants of the village, an understanding which, so far as I can recall, is unparalleled in modern writing. Nor does he revolt against village institutions or customs. True, Anderson himself revolted. But it was a revolt not from the village, but from the standardization brought on by industrialism, and perhaps from life itself."[10] All of these examples show the speed with which Van Doren's essay took on a currency and value in discussing midwestern writing. More often than not, these scholars and critics viewed Van Doren's assessment as setting up battle lines requiring each side to be entrenched in defense of their perspective.

It is interesting in the longer view of defining and studying midwestern literature how an idea that may have naturally been engaged with by contemporaries becomes outright monolithic in the study of a particular region's literature for subsequent decades. While scholars and critics of the 1920s would have been reading publications and engaging with the ideas of their era, individuals throughout the rest of the twentieth century would continue to use Van Doren's assessment as a cornerstone of understanding early-twentieth-century midwestern literature (and even project that idea onto later midwestern literature as well).[11] Particularly through critical discussions, the region continued to be defined with a contrast between sentimentality and revolt. It became a constantly debated regional stereotype, but one unfortunately more often reinforced rather than deconstructed.

Anthony Channel Hilfer's *The Revolt from the Village, 1915–1930* is one example of a critical text that reinforced the concept of the "revolt from the village" long after its cultural moment. Published in 1969, Hilfer began his book by stating, "the term 'Revolt from the Village' has since become an accepted rubric of historical criticism."[12] He expanded on that commonness by observing that too often in prior critical studies, "The terms 'revolt' and 'village' have caused most of the confusion by being taken in too simplistic a matter," essentially arguing a need for deeper analysis of a widely used phrase.[13] He also confirmed the ambivalent attitudes many writers held toward their hometowns, stating that critics often co-opt that ambivalence for their own ends instead of exploring that ambivalence further: "Some critics presume that to show a writer's having ambivalent attitudes toward the village is to prove that he was not a part of the revolt."[14] However, despite noting all these lapses in nuance in the work of previous critics, Hilfer never undertakes any analysis of the phrase itself or whether it has any lasting value. Considering the phrase or the concept not to be as essential as previous scholars had argued to understanding midwestern literature is never an option. In fact, Hilfer contends that there were not one but two periods of "revolt from the village," one in the late nineteenth century and then the one more traditionally defined in the 1910s and 1920s. In addition, Hilfer expands the idea that the revolt is not just against small-town life (particularly midwestern small-town life) and what it represents but is also a critique of social class and cultural homogenization within American culture as a whole. Hilfer's analysis, therefore, becomes another rousing endorsement of a revolt within American literature of the late nineteenth and early twentieth centuries, particularly in book-length form, and further reinforces the concept's critical capital. His text is not the sole commentary on the topic in the latter half of the twentieth century, as texts by Diane Dufva Quantic, Ronald Weber, and others continued to either reinforce the trope or to argue for minor adjustments to the overall definition.[15]

One might argue that such a long history of devotion to a concept argues for some truth within the concept itself. If we, as readers and scholars, go back to Van Doren's original essay, there is clearly some truth in his assessment at that time. Many writers were critiquing small towns and midwestern social mores. Those kernels of truth, however, bloomed into a full-blown cultural critique that lasted decades and obscured a deeper discussion of the Midwest and of the texts characterized as part of the movement. In the late twentieth century, a few scholars, Barry Gross and David D. Anderson among them, dared to question the canonization of "the revolt from the village" as a critical touchstone in understanding midwestern literature. Marcia Noe observes that instead of viewing a revolt, Gross and Anderson are focused on the idea that in many of these works "the protagonist's belief in the values of the Jeffersonian dream and his departure as signaling the next phase in his search for self-fulfillment rather than a sweeping rejection of his native village" are more important.¹⁶ Indeed, scholars like Noe and Jon Lauck have been part of a small contingent of twenty-first-century critics who have continued to advocate for a more nuanced analysis of the literature associated with the classic "revolt from the village" movement and for a reconsideration of the terminology. Lauck emphatically argues at the beginning of his essay "The Myth of the Midwestern 'Revolt from the Village'" that "To find the Midwest and its lost history, this flawed interpretation—which is still embraced by many intellectuals and still exerts great power in the American cultural imagination—must be dissected and amended so that a dated and one-sided but still common interpretive construction does not block the path."¹⁷

To put this critical revision into practice, Lewis's *Main Street* is one example of a canonical "revolt from the village" novel that is far more interesting in its dynamics when we remove the idea of revolt from the equation. Van Doren critiques *Main Street* more reductively than other novels in his 1921 article, alleging that Lewis "hates such dullness—the village virus—as the saints hate sin. Indeed, it is with a sort of new Puritanism that he and his contemporaries wage against the dull a war something like that which certain of their elders once waged against the bad."¹⁸ In his autobiography, *Three Lives*, Van Doren quotes Lewis's response to his *Nation* article at great length. Lewis protested Van Doren's assertion that

> I hate all dull people, that is unintelligent people; and that therefore I am forever barred from the class of the Fieldings and Balzacs and Tolstois ... In Main Street, I certainly do love all of the following people, none of whom could be classed as anything but 'dull' (using your own sense of dull as meaning lacking in conscious intelligence): Bea, Champ and Mrs. Perry, Sam and Mrs. Clark, Will Kennicott (dull about certain things though not all), Will's mother, and almost all of the farmer patients. And I love Carol who is dull about all the male world that interests Kennicott.¹⁹

For those who have taken the time to read *Main Street* closely and who have avoided simplistically labelling it a "revolt from the village" novel, it is clear that Lewis's portrayal of Gopher Prairie was much more nuanced. As George Killough writes in an introduction to a twenty-first-century paperback edition of the novel, "Lewis tried hard to avoid oversimplification, and in so doing, he achieved a credible balance between a flawed but sympathetic observer-critic and a realistically flawed small town."[20]

For example, Carol Kennicott is the most vocal critic of the village throughout the novel, and as a primary character, her perspectives are prominent, but in many places, Lewis crafts dialogue and description that critiques Carol just as harshly as any other village inhabitant. Early in the novel, before even arriving in Gopher Prairie, Carol's potential dissatisfaction is evident through her observations of people on the train:

> She had always maintained that there is no American peasantry, and she sought now to defend her faith by seeing imagination and enterprise in the young Swedish farmers, and in a traveling man working over his order-blanks. But the older people, Yankees as well as Norwegians, Germans, Finns, Canucks, had settled into submission to poverty. They were peasants, she groaned.[21]

From the very beginning of the novel, Carol's perceptions of what she wishes things to be often color her perception of what is or what will be. As she seeks to defend her belief in an American society free of peasantry, Carol is ignoring the reality of the lives around her, as the older people are unlikely to be "submitting" to or choosing poverty as much as experiencing it through a variety of circumstances often outside of their control. Those dream-like and idealistic desires also characterize her harsh perceptions of Gopher Prairie and its inhabitants. The town does have undesirable qualities at times and has its problems, but Carol's idealism casts in it in a harsher light than it truly merits. Vida Sherwin, a character who provides a sympathetic ear to many of Carol's ambitions, rightly castigates her later in the novel for only seeing the town's failures and none of its progress: "You want perfection all at once."[22] And later, when Carol escapes Gopher Prairie for the cosmopolitanism of Washington, D.C., she happily finds some more fulfilling elements to city life; however, many of the qualities she despises about Gopher Prairie linger on: "She discovered that in the afternoon, office routine stretches to the grave. She discovered that an office is as full of cliques and scandals as a Gopher Prairie."[23] In fact, in her interaction with other "escapees" from other towns, she learns that "by comparison Gopher Prairie was a model of daring color, clever planning, and frenzied intellectuality."[24] Lewis creates Carol as the primary lens by which the reader "sees" Gopher Prairie, and while her views are critical and she continually points out flaws, he is careful to craft her character as embodying flawed qualities, as well. He is less embracing a "revolt" against the village as engaging in a portrayal of nuanced social and individual realism.

Less-canonical writer Dawn Powell was never caught up in the alleged revolt movement in quite the same way as writers like Lewis, Anderson, and Gale, but she too has suffered at the hands of reductive binary criticism. Powell's sixteen novels tend to be split between those set in Ohio and those set in New York City, with the six Ohio novels primarily representing her earlier work between 1925 and 1934.[25] While her first novel *Whither* (1925) was published five years after Van Doren's pronouncement, the fact that Powell tended to write about Ohio small towns still linked commentary about her novels to the "revolt against the village" movement. Nicholas Birns, for example, makes that connection: "The Ohio novels, though, (and for that matter the New York novels as well) show Powell as a full participant in the 'Revolt Against the Village' in American literature." Birns's perceptions of the "revolt" movement are indeed more nuanced than that of many scholars, as he clarifies that "The Revolt Against the Village is misunderstood if it is seen as just a sophomoric or unthinking rejection of small-town life in favor of the big city; there is an intense elegiac feeling that is almost apodictically part of the revolt," but his comments still place Powell within a problematic tradition.[26] Powell's novels, as with so many others often linked to the "revolt" tradition, are not just engaged in a binary battle with the small town they portray. They are engaged in a multi-layered critique of personality and place that is far richer than any possible revolt or elegiac tribute.

For example, a review of Powell's *Dance Night* (1930) in the *New York Times* noted in the first paragraph, "Miss Powell has painted in sure, even strokes the dreary boarding houses, the roisterous saloons and poolrooms, the cheap factory girls, and the gaudy dance hall which make Lamptown."[27] If a reader focused only on these details, Powell's novel would seem a perfect fit to a reductive "revolt against the village" reading. In fact, Earl Rovit declares regarding Powell's characterization of towns like this, "Reminiscent of the gnarled world of Anderson's Winesburg, Powell's factory towns seem harsher and less rural than Anderson's and, more importantly, less possible to escape."[28] Lamptown is small and indeed seems oppressive to Jen and Morry, two teenagers at the heart of the story. When asked early on if he is going to try and make something of himself in Lamptown, Morry quickly scoffs at the idea, "Not a chance. I'm going somewhere where there's something going."[29] Yet, for both these characters, Lamptown is a necessary place for them to dream and grow, even if some of the lessons they learn there are painful ones. Lamptown itself is growing, becoming more prosperous as the local factory expands and as neighborhoods grow with the influx of new workers. Where Morry's mother initially owns the only hat store in town, there is eventually enough business for her apprentice, Nettie, to move on and open her own store.

In essence, the story is more complicated than just a critique of the small town, as Jen and Morry's lives parallel in many ways the progress of the town around them. The *New York Times* review concluded with that same observation: "Miss Powell has succeeded remarkably in sustaining the adolescent note, in making them different from the town and yet part of it, linking their triumphs and disappointments with Lamptown, even while they realize its cheapness and tawdriness."[30] Jen and Morry both dream of moving beyond Lamptown, and by the end of the novel, it does seem that they might succeed in making that jump, but for both characters, the move is less a refutation of the small town and more a sign that the town has no more to teach them, and they are ready for more. The last lines of the novel read, "Now that the evening fast train roared through Lamptown, its triumphant whistle soared over the factory siren, in its vanishing echoes the beginning of a song trembled, a song that belonged to far-off and tomorrow. Yes, yes, he would come away, Morry's heart answered, now he was ready."[31] For a reader to lump all of Powell's novels dealing with the Midwest or Ohio into one generalized (elegiac or not) "revolt" category is to miss important nuances of characterization and description that are so intrinsically valuable to making Powell's work important in capturing a particular time and place.

The potential for reductive "revolt" binaries is not limited to midwestern literature. Midwestern artists, particularly of the 1920s and 1930s, are often classified in similar limiting ways.[32] For example, a line is often neatly drawn dividing Midwesterners involved in American Scene painting of that era into various camps, such as the regionalists, consisting of artists such as Thomas Hart Benton, Grant Wood, and John Steuart Curry, and the social realists, such as Joe Jones or Morris Topchevsky. The regionalists are often seen as sentimentalizing the rural Midwest, an allegation typically strengthened by the existence of a Grant Wood–attributed pamphlet, *Revolt Against the City* (1935). *Revolt Against the City* is a problematic text, as critics have noted; the text was either co-written with or ghost written by Wood's friend Frank Luther Mott, a literature professor at the University of Iowa and co-editor of the midwestern little magazine *The Midland*. Even if "[i]t seems likely that Mott wrote more of 'Revolt' than did Wood," he was still endorsing the ideas within the text by association, countering the ideas expressed by Carl Van Doren fourteen years earlier and essentially contributing to the idea of a rural/urban or an against/for binary in art as well as literature.[33]

The pamphlet clearly invokes a contrast to Van Doren's "revolt against the village" essay and critiques it for creating a short-sighted view on the Midwest (particularly through midwestern literature): "The feeling that the East, and perhaps Europe, was the true goal of the seeker after culture was greatly augmented by the literary movement which Mr. Van Doren once dubbed 'the revolt against the village.' Such books as 'Spoon River Anthology' and 'Main Street' brought contempt upon the hinterland and strengthened the cityward tendency."[34] By noting the binary established by Van Doren's essay, the pamphlet supports it by itself arguing for a perspective "against" the city and by continuing to encourage the idea that the books are to blame for the "contempt" placed on rural communities and perspectives. The impassioned case for the value of midwestern and rural perspectives in the arts at work in the pamphlet is undermined by engaging in the problematic terminology of revolt. Rather than inspire an audience to see the value of midwestern art, the pamphlet reinforced an easy categorizing binary that limited readings of Wood's work for the next several decades as clearly taking a side in this urban/rural dynamic. Most critics and scholars narrowly viewed the pamphlet as a manifesto embracing the rural, and not, for example, as Michael C. Steiner has noted, as encompassing "three progressive elements ... a critical awareness of the turmoil of the Great Depression, a disdain for hide-bound provincialism, and praise for an outward looking regionalism contributing to the greater good of the national whole."[35]

One of the more persuasive visual arguments that the revolt, whether against the village or the city, is more nuanced and less polemical than Van Doren's or Wood/Mott's commentaries endorsed lies in the nine illustrations Wood created for the 1937 Limited Editions Club republication of Lewis's *Main Street*. Created primarily in 1936 and early 1937, after publication of *Revolt Against the City*, the images are more symbolic than literal.[36] No character names are attached in the paintings, but the types of characters portrayed clearly parallel characters within the novel: *The Perfectionist*/Carol Kennicott, *Sentimental Yearner*/Raymond P. Wutherspoon, *The Radical*/Miles Bjornstam, *General Practitioner*/Dr. Will Kennicott, *The Good Influence*/Mrs. Bogart, *Practical Idealist*/Vida Sherwin, and *Booster*/"Honest Jim" Blausser. There is similar symbolism in the two other images, *Main Street Mansion* and *Village Slums*, with the house a representation of the type of house the Kennicotts might have occupied and the slums the area where Miles Bjornstam and his wife lived with the communal well. The titles were chosen by Wood and not assigned by the publisher. By focusing more on the "type" than on the actual character, Wood had room for commentary beyond the specifics detailed in Lewis's novel, and the images clearly show that he took those liberties. For example, in the *General Practitioner* image, Wood moves away from a standard definition of a portrait, which usually incorporates an individual's face, and instead portrays the doctor's hands and the hand of his patient. The image of the doctor taking the patient's pulse emphasizes the role of the doctor more than Will Kennicott the man. The blue quilt backdrop implies a house call, and the weathered hand of the patient implies the hand of a farmer or laborer. The doctor's symbolic role within the community, as the primary individual keeping all individuals within towns and communities prospering, takes center stage in Wood's image. Wood was not immune to the thematic ideas in *Main Street*, writing Lewis shortly after the novel's publication that he tried to capture the "essence" of the novel in his illustrations, but it is clear he thought about those themes and ideas for their larger symbolism and not just as a reductive reading of small-town life.[37]

Many art historians are reassessing artists such as Wood and Benton beyond their regionalist label or reassessing what regionalism really meant within the American art world of the 1920s and 1930s. As evidence of what can happen when one moves beyond rural/urban or revolt binaries, *Against the Grain: Modernism in the Midwest*, an exhibit first staged at the Massillon Museum in Massillon, Ohio, in 2010, demonstrated the value of this reassessment, particularly in examining the role of regionalism and modernism in the Midwest.[38] The exhibit was notable for both the breadth of midwestern representation (primarily focusing on the urban centers of Cleveland, Chicago, Milwaukee, Minneapolis, and St. Louis) and for its contrast, through the lens of modernism, of artists not commonly paired together. While the artists and pieces involved stretch beyond the two decades primarily discussed in this essay (the exhibit focused on modernism up until 1950), they all showed that midwestern perspectives in American art stretch beyond the canonical figures of Benton, Wood, and Curry and can be found outside the regional school of art. Christine Fowler Shearer, in her foreword to the exhibit catalog, enforced that this expanded sense of perception was the intent of the exhibit: "The goal here was to provide a broader context for modernism in all of the Midwest. It is our hope that those viewing this exhibition and catalog will see the breadth and depth of these modernists and will discover some new insights in the process."[39] The collection challenged the popular definition of midwestern art in the early twentieth century by including names both familiar and unfamiliar to most art patrons, names such as Charles Burchfield, Carl Hoeckner, Gertrude Abercrombie, Joe Jones, Lucia Stern, and Charles Biederman. As the art world tends to prioritize styles and movements in American art over regional characteristics, an exhibit like this one shows that there is much to learn in moving beyond ideas of "revolt" and labels "urban" or "rural" to delve deeper into what works of art say about where they are from and what inspire them.

Artist John Sloan's contribution to Saylor's *Revolt in the Arts*, aptly titled "Art Is, Was, and Ever Will Be," made a series of pronouncements about art while negating that any revolt in art was ever necessary: "There is undoubtedly something stirring in the spiritual life of mankind today which is bearing and will bear fruit in every branch of man's activities, and while, of course, the art of the painter will be affected, as the painter must be, by this spirit—this spirit of revolt—I can not [sic] think that there is today, nor need be, any revolt in the painter's art."[40] Arguing for a revolt in the context of a particular social or artistic problem is not, in itself, problematic, as Van Doren's and Wood's pieces were more of a commentary on a moment than an artistic manifesto. Unfortunately, scholars and critics have placed far too much importance on essays like these, ignoring the more nuanced comments of the participants themselves and limiting our critical understanding of midwestern literature and art. It is time to accept the idea that the concepts of a "revolt against the village" or "revolt against the city" are no longer effective shorthand for an entire, too often oversimplified, movement or era. By noting these concepts as merely cultural moments and not critical monoliths, we will continue to discover, as many recent readers and scholars already have, that midwestern literature and art is far richer and far more dynamic than it is often perceived.

Notes

1. Carl Van Doren, "Contemporary American Novelists: X. The Revolt from the Village: 1920," *The Nation* 113 (1921): 408.
2. Ibid., 409.
3. Ibid., 412.
4. Carl Van Doren, *Three Worlds* (New York: Harper & Brothers, 1936), 1.
5. Ibid., 2.
6. Ibid., 152.
7. Percy H. Boynton, "American Authors of Today: VI. Booth Tarkington," *The English Journal* 12, no. 2 (Feb. 1923): 123, http://www.jstor.org/stable/802199. Another 1923 article, "The American Faith as Stuart Sherman Interprets It" (*Current Opinion*, March 1, 1923: n.p.), reads Van Doren's article as highlighting pessimism in American writing. Sherman was a friend and colleague of Van Doren's at the University of Illinois in Urbana.
8. Louis Wann, "The 'Revolt from the Village' in American Fiction," *Overland Monthly and Out West Magazine* (August 1925): 298–99, 324–25.
9. Dorothy Anne Dondore, *The Prairie and the Making of Middle America: Four Centuries of Description* (1926; repr. New York: Antiquarian, 1961).
10. Norman E. Eliason, "Midwestern Writers: Sherwood Anderson," *Prairie Schooner* 4, no. 1 (1930): 59, http://www.jstor.org/stable/40622116.
11. Marcia Noe, in "The Revolt Against the Village" (in *The Dictionary of Midwestern Literature*, vol. 2, ed. Philip Greasley [Bloomington: Indiana University Press, 2016], 727–42), provides a strong overview of criticism

throughout the twentieth century that references the "revolt against the village" concept.
12. Anthony Channel Hilfer, *The Revolt from the Village, 1915–1930* (Chapel Hill: University of North Carolina Press, 1969), 3.
13. Ibid., 4.
14. Ibid.
15. Diane Dufva Quantic, "The Revolt from the Village and Middle Western Fiction 1870–1915," *Kansas Quarterly* 5, no. 4 (1973): 5–16. Ronald Weber, *The Midwestern Ascendancy in American Writing* (Bloomington: Indiana University Press, 1992). Again, Noe, in "The Revolt Against the Village," provides a comprehensive overview of later twentieth- and early twenty-first-century scholarship on the topic.
16. Noe, "Revolt from the Village," 739.
17. Jon Lauck, "The Myth of the Midwestern 'Revolt from the Village,'" *MidAmerica* 40 (2013): 39. Lauck has more recently expanded his critique of the revolt thesis in his book *From Warm Center to Ragged Edge: The Erosion of Midwestern Literary and Historical Regionalism, 1920–1965* (Iowa City: University of Iowa Press, 2017).
18. Van Doren, "Contemporary American Novelists," 410.
19. Van Doren, *Three Worlds*, 158.
20. George Killough, introduction to *Main Street* by Sinclair Lewis (New York: Signet, 2008), 10.
21. Sinclair Lewis, *Main Street* (New York: Signet, 2008), 3.
22. Ibid., 290.
23. Ibid., 445.
24. Ibid., 449.
25. The one Ohio novel that appears later is *My Home Is Far Away* (1944).
26. Nicholas Birns, "Beautiful Lamptown: The Writings of Dawn Powell," *Hollins Critic* 44, no. 5 (2007): 1–16. MLA International Bibliography, EBSCOhost.
27. "An Ohio Town," review of *Dance Night* by Dawn Powell, *New York Times* (November 16, 1930, Sunday Book Review): 9.
28. Earl Rovit, "A Memorable Reality," *Sewanee Review* 110, no. 2 (2002): 286.
29. Dawn Powell, *Dance Night* (New York: Farrar and Rinehart, 1930; New York: Library of America, 2001), 31. Citations refer to Library of America edition.
30. "An Ohio Town," 9.
31. Powell, *Dance Night*, 204.
32. A particularly interesting take on the critical oversimplification of regionally focused artists from the 1920s and 1930s and the deeper nuance that such oversimplification misses can be found in James M. Dennis's *Renegade Regionalists: The Modern Independence of Grant Wood, Thomas Hart Benton, and John Steuart Curry* (Madison: University of Wisconsin Press, 1998).

33. Brady M. Roberts, "The European Roots of Regionalism: Grant Wood's Stylistic Synthesis," in *Grant Wood: An American Master Revealed* (San Francisco: Pomegranate Art Books, 1995), 34.
34. Grant Wood, *Revolt Against the City* (1935); repr. in *America Is West: An Anthology of Life and Literature*, edited by John T. Flanagan (Minneapolis: University of Minnesota Press, 1945), 652.
35. Michael C. Steiner, "Grant Wood and the Politics of Regionalism," *Middle West Review* 3, no. 1 (2016): 86–87.
36. The composition timeline for Wood's *Main Street* images is discussed in Lea Rossen DeLong's *Grant Wood's 36. Main Street: Art, Literature, and the American Midwest* (Ames, IA: Brunnier Art Museum, 2004).
37. Grant Wood to Sinclair Lewis. 10 July 1937. Sinclair Lewis Papers, Beinecke Rare Book and Manuscript Library, Yale University.
38. The exhibit was shown at the Massillon Museum from May 15–September 12, 2010. It was also shown at the Riffe Gallery in Columbus, Ohio (November 3, 2010–January 9, 2011), the Southern Ohio Museum and Cultural Center (March 5–May 29, 2011), and the Museum of Wisconsin Art (July 20–October 2, 2011).
39. Christine Fowler Shearer, foreword to *Against the Grain: Modernism in the Midwest* (Massillon, OH: Massillon Museum, 2010), 7.
40. John Sloan, "Art Is, Was, and Ever Will Be," in *Revolt in the Arts*, ed. Oliver M. Saylor (New York: Brentano's, 1930), 318.

Harmony Jankowski

Dance Pioneering

Ted Shawn and His Men Dancers Tour the Midwest

In 1926, dancer, choreographer, and impresario Ted Shawn expressed what he saw as an impulse bred into and cultivated in American men—the desire for conquest—in terms of his chosen art. He writes, "There is no frontier left.... There is nothing left for us to conquer so far as the natural wildernesses of this continent are concerned, but the wilderness of our national art consciousness is producing just now its great pioneers."[1] The mid-1920s saw a surge of formal experimentation in painting, literature, music, architecture, and Shawn's own field, modern dance. The work of Mary Wigman, Doris Humphrey, and Martha Graham, among others, garnered accolades as audiences and dancers alike began to consider how their art might adapt in order to reflect and critique their present. Shawn's desire to become one of these pioneers emerged through an itinerant career that began after an overdose of diphtheria antitoxin paralyzed him and a doctor recommended dance as physical therapy. He took to it quickly, picking up training in ballet and ballroom before devoting himself to "'classic and interpretive dancing.'"[2] This new vocation drew Shawn away from his course of study at the University of Denver, where an unwitting fraternity brother provided the germ of an idea that would become the locus of Shawn's innovations in modern dance. The insolent youth "closed an impassioned harangue with the flat statement, 'But, Ted, *men* don't dance.'"[3]

Ted Shawn's career, spanning nearly sixty years between his first tour in 1914 and his death in 1972, involved countless coast-to-coast expeditions as he sought to blaze his own pioneering trail. That first tour, as part of the Shawn-Gould Company of Interpretive Dancers, ran along the Santa Fe railroad line, where the company played employee recreation centers in return for passage to New York.[4] This journey led him to Ruth St. Denis, already famous for her Orientalist dances, whom he married in 1914 and with whom he directed the famed Denishawn

Company from 1915 to 1931.[5] In the mid-1920s, while expanding his repertoire as dancer and choreographer, Shawn returned to his fraternity brother's assertion and was drawn to fight for men's place at the forefront of modern dance. Though he already believed that the "creative genius" of modern dance was "entirely masculine," audiences and critics alike associated the art more readily with women. Shawn called for the necessity of "an entire change of the public consciousness … before we will find parents aiding and abetting a son to become a dancer."[6] This idea, articulated in 1926, would shape the next fifteen years of Shawn's career as he attempted to change the views of "the average man of our country," who likened artistic beauty to "weakness, effeminacy, prettiness,"[7] by reframing dance as a virile, masculine, athletic activity integral to the health of the modern man.

In keeping with his mission, after Denishawn disbanded and he separated from St. Denis, Shawn began teaching modern dance in the early 1930s at Springfield College, which, at the time, graduated nearly half the gym and athletic coaches in the country.[8] Although, as George Chauncey reports, "rough sports" had gained favor on college campuses decades earlier, "endorsed by educators and students alike as the optimal way to build character,"[9] Shawn held fast to his belief that dance could build the same musculature and stamina while also providing an outlet for artistic expression. At Springfield, students began the course "sorely lacking in their knowledge of dance and in the rudimentary rhythmic and motor skills prerequisite to technical performance on a beginning level." They also "harbored the usual prejudices of the day concerning dance as an effeminate, light, and inappropriate activity for men."[10] By the end of the 1932–1933 academic year, he had convinced his five hundred students of the art's merits and had a pool of dancers from which to draw for his all-male company, Ted Shawn and His Men Dancers. He chose men specifically for their visually arresting athleticism and virility, and, with the exception of company star Barton Mumaw, for their lack of previous dance training so that he could mold their movement in keeping with his rigid ideas of dance appropriate to men.

The company toured the United States, with sojourns to London and Havana, during the winters of 1933–1940 and spent their summers living a spartan life at Jacob's Pillow in Becket, Massachusetts. Shawn's mission for the company was to show concert dance was a viable occupation for American men; essential to this was the troupe of men whom he trained and nurtured. Perhaps more important to Shawn's conquest, however, were the twin notions of Ted Shawn and His Men Dancers as pioneers and of the middle of the country as the frontier they sought to conquer. Frequent references to the choreographer and company as pioneers—in press materials, program notes, and pre-performance lectures—paint a picture of the Men Dancers that sought to make their art more palatable to the "average American male" by invoking a nigh-inviolable masculine archetype in the traditionally feminine context of concert dance. Shawn's argument for dance pioneering required the construction of a new frontier, one that he located conveniently in the same geographic locale as the original, gauging his success on the company's reception in the Midwest while constructing its inhabitants as at once dangerous and in dire need of aesthetic education.

Even as he gestured forward through his innovations in modern dance, Shawn believed that expanding the literal geography of his audience necessitated a gesture back to the familiar. Thus, as the company toured the country tacitly arguing for dance as a respectable profession for men, the choreographer offered, through the archetypal pioneer, a recognizable image that opened minds to the idea of men dancing. The company's first evening-length program, called *O, Libertad!* after Walt Whitman's poem, premiered during the 1937–1938 season. The collection of dances positions the company at once within this familiar trope and on the frontier of modern dance through its breadth of style, its stylized masculinity, and its deliberate invocations of temporality in its three sections: "The Past," "The Present," and "The Future." "The Past" moved from America's brutal colonial history to the California Gold Rush, dramatizing and performing the work of manifest destiny as the company zigzagged through the Midwest. "The Present" entrenched the Men Dancers firmly within the masculine territories of military and athletic miseries and victories, maintaining the pantomimic movement qualities of "The Past." "The Future," though, broke from the easily interpretable narratives of the previous temporalities in favor of a formally innovative presentation of eleven common human experiences and emotions in a piece called "Kinetic Molpai." As the program moved through Shawn's vision of the United

States' history and future, *O, Libertad!* offered the illusory lure of a familiar story told anew by an all-male dance company, while bringing their innovative dance forms and gender norms to Shawn's imagined frontier, the Midwest.

"Frontiersman of an Art-Form for Athletes"

Throughout his career, Ted Shawn carefully framed the public's reception of both his choreography and his mission, directing his critics' interpretations and ensuring through extravagant prose that his dances, dancers, and aims were understood. In order to make a strong case for Ted Shawn and His Men Dancers as capable, virile, modern-day pioneers, the company began by constructing Ted Shawn as a red-blooded, all-American man. An undated press release from the Men Dancers era calls Shawn's career "as traditional to American dance as Maple sugar is to Vermont—and as indigenous to the portrait of America." The release designates his biography as a "chapter in the story of Cultural Americana," calling his early life a beginning that could not have been "purer U.S.A.," citing his birth in Kansas City and studies in Denver, before assuring readers that "his consequent career and entire personality is of the flavor of the hardy and staunchly patriotic early American pioneer."[11] Similarly, a souvenir program from the 1934–1935 season introduces Shawn on its first page with a photo in profile, captioned, "Mr. Shawn: Frontiersman of an Art-Form for Athletes" and links this athleticism to his pioneering, compounding images of traditional masculinity in order to undermine dance's feminine associations. It explains the choreographer's work in terms of "pioneering for years to restore dancing for men to its rightful standing" and assures audiences that they will soon see "a program of dances essentially masculine in principle and performance."[12] The image of Shawn as pioneer persisted throughout the company's active years and worked in tandem with notions of the choreographer as America's own "native son": "Ted Shawn is no Petersburg prancer in disguise, but a native son of these free and independent states."[13] These press materials attempt to forestall familiar criticisms about the mutual exclusivity of dance and masculinity through an over-the-top portrait of Shawn that borders on camp patriotism.

The midwestern region emerges in Shawn's writings and the company's press materials as the premiere object of conquest and the geographical manifestation of middle-America values. The company's early reception prompted this assessment. In letters to Lucien Price, Boston-based journalist and company booster since the troupe's inception, Shawn called the segment of the tour they covered between Iowa and Ohio in 1934 "front line trench fighting."[14] A few months later, another letter to Price related an incident in Cleveland, Ohio, in which an audience "remained noisy all through the program. The [sic] laughed, talked out loud, whistled and threw pennies on the stage. Nothing like it had ever happened in my whole career."[15] Such incidents reinforce a view of the region Edward Watts describes as an "undifferentiated hinterland that might be either populated by harmless laughingstocks or dangerous psychopaths, or both."[16] Lucien Price wrote a paean to Shawn and the dancers called "All-Man Performance" (1936) in which he situates their work within the greater scope of masculine activity: "Your average American male is comically gun-shy of the arts. He blames it on his pioneering origins; but pioneers are not timorous. Neither are ten men who have driven across the Great American Desert for the past three years."[17] His references both to pioneers and to the Great American Desert are telling, the first for the image of westward-bound men battling elements and living off the land, and the second for its projection of an image of the area between the coasts as a vast cultural, and literal, No Man's Land. Both Shawn and Price operated within what Richard Lyle Power called "Yankee Cultural Imperialism," which rested on notions of the Midwest as belated regarding style and culture.[18]

Pioneering and frontiering, as metaphorical activities, function to highlight the "newness" of an idea or action as well as physical and geographical movement away from the old and into the new. Because these images also reference a time long since past by the 1930s, however, they provided a comforting nostalgia for Shawn's largely white audiences in the Midwest. Thus, these images infuse the activity they describe with a sense of time that invokes both impalpable past and limitless futurity. In both Shawn's dance works and his ways of framing his company, the Janus-faced choreographer looked back in order to invoke the familiar while looking forward toward an as-yet-unimagined future that was objectionable within his present.

"Pioneering with a Vengeance"

Ted Shawn and His Men Dancers toured extensively from early autumn through late spring in the years 1933–1940. The company's financial records log close to 580 performances during their first six tours, with nearly 170 of those taking place within the midwestern and Great Plains states.[19] The tours played to audiences in state capitals and cities that housed large universities like Chicago, Cleveland, and Lincoln; they also played to smaller audiences in towns of only a few thousand citizens, such as Ada, Ohio, Carthage, Illinois, and Hibbing, Minnesota. Their belief in themselves as crusaders moving into dangerous territory was bolstered by reports from local house managers around the country who "met the dancers with lamentations: the public was indifferent to men's dancing, or frankly hostile."[20] When the company began touring, Shawn reports, "A friend warned me that I was setting out to turn upside down an established national habit of thought. I expected a fight; I got one."[21] The Men Dancers were, as Shawn reported to Price, "pioneering with a vengeance," as they brought their work to audiences on what they saw as the frontier of modern art and culture.

The 1930s were ripe for modern dance to extend its reach beyond coastal cities. Emerging out of summer workshops at Bennington College in Vermont, "a network of dedicated teachers created centers of modern dance education in the Midwest and South as well as the Far West."[22] As Julia Foulkes explains, Bennington was also instrumental in creating the "'gymnasium circuit,' the label given for the touring routes of modern dancers in the mid- and late 1930s. University and college gymnasiums housed many of the first modern dance concerts around the country."[23] In its early days, the Men Dancers' management company, Willmore and Powers of New York City, "just threw [the company] a few dates if and when they could." The rest was shored up by Margerie Lyon and George Gloss. Lyon, according to Shawn, "had never booked but believed so fanatically in the value of my proposed project that she was eager to try while she drove across country" from the east coast to the west. Gloss, a member of one of Shawn's companies, held a master's degree in physical education and compensated for his lack of marketing experience with "his wide knowledge of the educational field and his close friendships with many phys. ed. directors who were potential buyers for the show."[24] These provided Shawn's ideal audience: young people ripe for exposure to new arts, ideas, and professions. Though it took time to develop strong bookings, Shawn reports, "those who did come were converted,"[25] an assertion borne out by increased exposure and ever-growing audiences.

Shawn assumed that the prevailing opinion in the United States, especially in the hinterlands, held male dancers to be "sissies," a stereotype he sought to dismantle. When founding his troupe, he reported having chosen "'top athletes ... the type that even the Keokuk [Iowa] Rotary Club would describe as the ideal of strong American manhood.'"[26] The pool of students he trained at Springfield College provided men whose technique he could mold to reflect the strength, athleticism, and rigidity he believed would play throughout the country. Shawn highlighted the Men Dancers' athleticism by associating them explicitly with traditionally masculine actions like battle, sport, and labor in his choreography, a discursive strategy still used by dance companies and critics.[27]

Though Shawn's restrictive ideas about the kind of movement suitable to male and female dancers, respectively, traffic in retrograde sexism, his choreography and the manner in which he framed it were meant to be both legible and appealing. Julia Foulkes locates a political impulse in choreographers' desire to broaden their art's appeal: "In the 1930s modern dancers shaped their art form within the democratic, pluralist Popular Front thrust of the times and attempted to appeal to a large audience, from workers in labor unions to townspeople in rural areas of the Midwest."[28] This was particularly the case for Shawn, ever-vigilant about making his work accessible to audiences who might not have encountered concert dance as either performers or spectators. Thus, the company's performances were often part lecture, and their programs tended to include extensive explanatory notes.

O, Libertad! played to the audiences Shawn desired through its depictions of military and athletic prowess punctuated by abstract movement in its final section. Billed as "An American Saga in Three Acts," the program attempted a narrative arc tracing American history from colonial conquest in "The Past," through World War I, the Great Depression, and the Olympics in "The Present," and into imagined conflicts and their resolution in "The Future."[29] John Martin, a much-lauded dance critic for the *New York Times,* queried whether Shawn's work remained fresh in his review of *O, Libertad!,* calling the choreography "extremely explicit" and occasionally "well over on the side of banality."[30]

Shawn's perception of his audience in the Midwest and Great American Desert as lacking sophistication in matters of dance and perceptions of masculinity directed him to keep his choreography unambiguous, though the program's final section saw Shawn moving in a more strictly movement-oriented direction.

"The Past" dramatized the violent conquest of the southern United States and California. The souvenir program offered the choreographer's rationale: "Choosing this episode as the crucial moment of the impact of the European civilization upon the indigenous one, Mr. Shawn has created a dance scene of barbaric splendor and bitter tragedy." The rest of the segment offered a violent picture of self-flagellating monks, slave labor on sugar plantations, and a celebration of Forty-Niners who struck gold. This section attempted "a rhythmic biography of the country" and offered the principle of selection: "Mr. Shawn has chosen significant periods in the past of one of the many colorful sections of the country, suitable to rhythmic treatment, in one single line of development, believing that this line was to a great degree parallel to the stages of history in other regions."[31] This section garnered little discussion in reviews of the Men Dancers' performances and in contemporary dance criticism. Its primary interest lay in its thematic link to Shawn's "pioneering" activity and to the notions of masculinity it implied. The *New York Herald Tribune* described "The Past" as "end[ing] on a truly American note with the dance of the forty-niners, a superb theatrical folk dance which captures the lusty spirit, the rough good humor of the pioneer forefathers."[32]

"The Present" depicted the years 1914–1937 and began with a scene of athletic victory on a college campus, which was quickly interrupted by a World War I soldier who transported the dance to No Man's Land. The program notes continued to lead the audience through dances depicting Jazz Age decadence and satirizing the high-modernist dance of Shawn's contemporaries before moving into a series of sports dances. In this way, "The Present" ran the gamut of masculine activity from sports victory to war and back again. The sports dances, often grouped as "Olympiad," are referenced frequently for their pantomimic athleticism and as salient examples of how Shawn believed men should dance. Maura Keefe explains how these dances function within "an equation: athletes plus dance subtracts effeminacy from the standard stereotype, leaving as a remainder an aura of authentic masculinity."[33]

"The Future" consisted of the eleven-part "Kinetic Molpai."[34] Program notes acknowledged Gilbert Murray's study of "the Molpo," "the ancient [Greek] art form which included rhythmic movement, instrumental music, singing, poetry, and drama." They also cited Murray's explanation of the form as "only the yearning of the whole dumb body to express that emotion for which words, and harps and singing were not enough."[35] The program explained, "These eleven Molpai of Shawn's are an evocation of experience as universal to modern life as it was to primitive, experience at once sacred and poetic,"[36] creating a rationale for the program's formal shift from the explicitly pantomimic, narrative-based choreography of the dance's first two sections. The Molpai sought to "utter in dance that for which no other language exists"[37] and asked audiences to move beyond seeing the dances as entertainment and to engage with them affectively in order for each spectator "to make his own poem of every dance."[38] "Kinetic Molpai" as a whole ranged in movement quality from strong stomps of the feet and dynamic weight shifts to smooth undulations of toned torsos, with the Men Dancers poised and posed throughout the piece until Apotheosis, in which the dancers showcased not only their athleticism, but also their classical technique. In this final section, a series of solos took the men through cabrioles and jetés, through fouettés and leaps ending with balances, all before a canon of hitch-kicks took the dancers onto their knees at center stage, with a triumphant Shawn standing, arms outstretched, above them.

This final gesture at once signaled the end of the dance and functioned as Shawn's acknowledgment that he had shown the audience what he meant for it to see, which is ultimately what contemporary dance critic Deborah Jowitt called "a pictorialization of masculine energy" in her review of Alvin Ailey's 1972 revival of the dance. Jowitt marveled at the emphatic masculinity of the whole production: "The nine bare-chested dancers thrust their heels forward into big purposeful strides; they clench their fists, assume heroic, broadbased stances." She noted that, for much of the piece, Shawn "wanted to show what real American men dancing ought to look like: strong, assertive, brave, forward-looking, kinda plain, able to flourish under discipline," but then turned to more balletic passages, as if by "having proved their virility by a lot of somber posturing, the men [could] show the audience that dancing is not for sissies."[39]

"Enthusiastic Endorsement"

By the 1937–1938 season, Ted Shawn and His Men Dancers had given over five hundred performances throughout the United States. During this, their penultimate season on the road, audiences were not only prepared for the company's offerings; they were, by and large, excited for and enticed by them. *O, Libertad!* earned accolades from critics and, more importantly, from the audiences Shawn sought to engage throughout the Midwest. Reviews of *O, Libertad!* show that the company won its audiences over, with an Ohio reporter calling the company "absolutely unique in ballet today" for its "intensely masculine" choreography.[40] In Iowa, the same program "held the audience of 11,500 spellbound through one hour of interpretive dancing" until members were "breathless and stunned at the marvelous performance."[41] A Wisconsin reviewer noted the degree to which Shawn played to his audience:

> It was a good show for three reasons: Shawn understands alternating seriousness with good humor and leaves the crowd wanting just a bit more; the dancing, except for the last section, was a literal translation of what was in the men's heads, intelligible to everybody in the theater. And taken for what it was—simply a series of rhythmic movements—that final, futuristic chapter was enjoyable, too.... Hit of the show, though, was the Olympiad—a humor-packed proceeding which had the audience practically cheering.[42]

These reviews echoed Shawn's own writing where he reported of audiences entranced by entertaining, humorous, intelligible dances. After several years of touring, Shawn also asserted that the company was accomplishing its goals: "[T]he progress toward restoring the art of the dance to men has been beyond my wildest dreams.... The idea has met with enthusiastic endorsement from the leading men in the field of physical education, and endorsement of men's organizations of all kinds."[43] Like pioneers in any movement, and like the travelers who sought the frontier, Shawn recognized the importance of converting others to his mission and did so primarily by emphasizing how dance, rather than detracting from the men dancers' masculinity, played up their manly qualities. In this light, the company succeeded in its professed mission of making dance an acceptable endeavor for men.

As the 1930s drew to a close and the United States' entry into World War II approached, a pamphlet on the history of Jacob's Pillow explains, "Shawn felt the battle had been won—he had convinced the public, press, and educators that Dance is a legitimate and honorable profession for men.... A significant chapter in the history of American Dance had been written."[44] Ted Shawn's place in the history of modern dance is secure; in fact, he is commonly lauded as the Father of Modern Dance. However, these reviews and conclusions, along with his heteronormative title, reveal the limitations of Shawn's intervention in modern dance. He brought a version of modern dance to the Midwest that extended the horizons of men's participation in the art, but did so by reinforcing cultural norms around acceptable activities for men and women. Frequent invocations of the pioneer myth throughout his writings, lectures, and the company's press materials align with the modernist obsession with innovation, but do so through a traditional and restrictive trope of masculinity.

"The Future" section of *O, Libertad!* issued a potential challenge to the rigid notions of manhood Shawn avowed throughout his career, and especially during the tenure of Ted Shawn and His Men Dancers. "Kinetic Molpai" invoked the kinds of movement Shawn saw as masculine, athletic, and strong, with "very little bending of the knee," "locked and straight" hips, and "very little use of the elbow or the wrist."[45] This piece was unique among the other temporalities depicted in *O, Libertad!*, however, for its lack of narrative or over-written interpretive program notes, leaving audience members' minds open to any and all affective resonance that the dance might call up. This performance highlighted the manner in which Ted Shawn and His Men Dancers simultaneously invoked and challenged traditional notions of masculinity by privileging strength, muscle development, and virility through an art form still associated primarily with women during this historical moment. In this way, the piece's stylized but uncomplicated movement performed a no-frills masculinity within a typically feminine milieu that modeled how men might inhabit spheres that were not traditionally "manly," like the concert dance stage, without explicitly avowing their innovations.

Notes

1. Ted Shawn, *The American Ballet* (New York: Henry Holt and Company, 1926), 9.
2. Ted Shawn, *One Thousand and One Night Stands* (New York: Doubleday & Company, 1960), 11.
3. Ibid.
4. Ibid., 15–16.
5. For a more detailed narrative of Ted Shawn's biography and the inception of Denishawn, see Olga Maynard, *American Modern Dancers* (New York: Little, Brown, and Co., 1965) and Shawn's autobiography, *One Thousand and One Night Stands*.
6. Shawn, *The American Ballet*, 93, 87.
7. Ibid., 95.
8. Maynard, *American Modern Dancers*, 92.
9. George Chauncey, *Gay New York: Gender, Urban Culture, and the Makings of the Gay Male World, 1890–1940* (New York: Perseus Books Group, 1994), 113.
10. Betty Poindexter, "Ted Shawn: His Personal Life, His Professional Career, and His Contributions to the Development of Dance in the United States of America from 1891 to 1963" (PhD diss., Texas Woman's University, Denton, TX). Jacob's Pillow Archive, Becket, MA.
11. "Ted Shawn: His Career as a Dancer," c. 1930s, Box 31, Folder 628, The Ted Shawn Collection, Jerome Robbins Dance Division, New York Public Library, New York, NY.
12. Souvenir Program, 1934–1935, Box 50, Folder 9, Ted Shawn Papers, Additions 1833–1980, Jerome Robbins Dance Division, New York Public Library, New York, NY.
13. Transcript of radio address by Irving Deakin, WQXR, Thursday 10 March 1938 9:00–9:30, Box 11, Folder 11, Fern Helscher Papers, Jerome Robbins Dance Division, New York Public Library, New York, NY.
14. Ted Shawn to Lucien Price, 13 April 1934, Unpublished Manuscript: Shawn's Autobiography. Part V draft April 1933–1934, Ted Shawn Collection, Jerome Robbins Dance Division, New York Public Library, New York, NY.
15. Ted Shawn to Lucien Price, 21 April 1934, Unpublished Manuscript: Shawn's Autobiography. Part V draft April 1933–1934, Ted Shawn Collection, Jerome Robbins Dance Division, New York Public Library, New York, NY.
16. Edward Watts, "The Midwest as Colony: *Transnational Regionalism*," in *Regionalism and the Humanities*, ed. Timothy R. Mahoney & Wendy J. Katz (Lincoln: Bison Books, 2009), 182.
17. Lucien Price, "All-Man Performance," *The Atlantic Monthly* 158, no. 5 (1936).

18. Richard Lyle Power, *Planting Cornbelt Culture* (Indianapolis: Indiana Historical Society, 1953), 5–19.
19. These numbers were tallied using the company's financial records. Financial Records, Ted Shawn and His Men Dancers 1933–1939, VII: Denishawn Company; Shawn and His Men Dancers, Folder 684A, Ted Shawn Collection 1903–1971, Jerome Robbins Dance Division, New York Public Library, New York, NY. Shawn's own figures differ slightly. For instance, the financial records show the company was paid for 96 performances during its first season; Shawn, however, writes in a letter to Lucien Price (Apr. 13, 1934) of 111 performances.
20. Ted Shawn to Lucien Price, 13 April 1934, Unpublished Manuscript: Shawn's Autobiography. Part V draft April 1933–1934, Ted Shawn Collection, Jerome Robbins Dance Division, New York Public Library, New York, NY.
21. Ted Shawn, "Dancing Originally Limited to Men Alone," Series IV: Ted Shawn. Box 11, Folder 11, Fern Helscher Papers, Jerome Robbins Dance Division, New York Public Library, New York, NY.
22. Ellen Graff, *Stepping Left: Dance and Politics in New York City, 1928–1942* (Durham: Duke University Press, 1997), 169. According to Graff, an unfortunate byproduct of this geographic expansion was that "as modern dance spread beyond its urban origins and became established within the academic community, the populist and working-class elements that had helped define early modern dance declined."
23. Julia Foulkes, *Modern Bodies: Dance and American Modernism from Martha Graham to Alvin Ailey* (Chapel Hill: University of North Carolina Press, 2003), 115–16. In addition to Ted Shawn and His Men Dancers' extensive tours on this circuit, modern dance troupes and soloists such as Humphrey-Weidman, Helen Tamiris, Hanya Holm, and Martha Graham toured the United States in the mid-1930s.
24. Shawn, *One Thousand and One Night Stands*, 249.
25. "Ted Shawn: His Career as a Dancer," c. 1930s, Writings about Ted Shawn, Folder 628, Ted Shawn Collection, Jerome Robbins Dance Division, New York Public Library, New York, NY.
26. Ibid.
27. For a more cogent discussion of this tendency in dance training and criticism, see Michael Gard, *Men Who Dance: Aesthetics, Athletics & the Art of Masculinity* (New York: Peter Lang, 2006).
28. Foulkes, *Modern Bodies*, 5.
29. Souvenir Program, 1937–1938, Box 50, Folder 9, Ted Shawn Papers, Additions 1833–1980, Jerome Robbins Dance Division, New York Public Library, New York, NY. The program reprinted Walt Whitman's poem "Turn, O, Libertad" from *Leaves of Grass*.
30. John Martin, "Audience Cheers Shawn Dancers," *New York Times*, Feb. 28, 1938.

31. Souvenir Program, 1937–1938, Box 50, Folder 9, Ted Shawn Papers, Additions 1833–1980, Jerome Robbins Dance Division, New York Public Library, New York, NY.
32. "Shawn Dancers Open Farewell Series in New York," *New York Herald Tribune*, Feb. 21, 1940.
33. Maura Keefe, "Is Dance a Man's Sport Too? The Performance of Athletic-Coded Masculinity on the Concert Dance Stage," in *When Men Dance: Choreographing Masculinities Across Borders*, ed. Jennifer Fisher and Anthony Shay (Oxford: Oxford University Press, 2008), 98.
34. "Kinetic Molpai" was first performed in 1935 as a stand-alone piece to music composed by Jess Meeker, the company's signature accompanist.
35. Program, *O, Libertad!*, Box 84, Folder 2, Programs—Dance, 1930–1939, Ted Shawn Papers, Jerome Robbins Dance Division, New York Public Library, New York, NY.
36. Souvenir Program, 1937–1938, Box 50, Folder 9, Ted Shawn Papers, Additions 1833–1980, Jerome Robbins Dance Division, New York Public Library, New York, NY. The program lists the eleven actions as follows: Strife, Oppositions, Solvent, Dynamic Contrasts, Resilience, Successions, Unfolding and Folding, Dirge, Limbo, Surge, and Apotheosis.
37. "Your card came telling me about Gilbert Murray's book The Classical Tradition in Poetry and the chapter on 'Molpe.' It is the exact word I wanted—and as usual the Greek's [sic] had it." Ted Shawn to Lucien Price, 9 July 1935, Unpublished Manuscript: Shawn's Autobiography, Part V draft July 1934–February 1938, Ted Shawn Collection, Jerome Robbins Dance Division, New York Public Library, New York, NY.
38. Shawn, *One Thousand and One Night Stands*, 273.
39. Deborah Jowitt, "Visionaries and Visions," *The Village Voice* (New York, NY), Nov. 30, 1972. http://sarma.be/docs/562.
40. Review, *Daily Call* (Piqua, OH), Mar. 9, 1939.
41. Review, *Hawarden Independent* (Hawarden, IA), Nov. 11, 1937.
42. Review, *State Journal* (Madison, WI), Nov. 15, 1939.
43. Shawn, "Dancing Originally Limited to Men Alone," Series IV: Ted Shawn. Box 11, Folder 11, Fern Helscher Papers, Jerome Robbins Dance Division, New York Public Library, New York, NY.
44. *Jacob's Pillow History*, Writings, Box 67, Folder 8, Ted Shawn Papers, Jerome Robbins Dance Division, New York Public Library, New York, NY.
45. Specifics about "Subject Matter and Themes," "Movement," and "Space Consciousness" are outlined in Ted Shawn, "Dancing for Men," undated transcription, Box 65, Folder 28, Ted Shawn Papers 1913–1982, Jerome Robbins Dance Division, New York Public Library, New York, NY.

Dustin Gann | The Unrepentant Outsider

Emanuel Haldeman-Julius
and the Creation of a
Nationwide Audience

In 1939, Raymond Lawrence travelled to Girard, Kansas, to profile Emanuel Haldeman-Julius for *Public Opinion Quarterly*. He observed firsthand the frigid relationship between local residents and the radical publisher. Lawrence reported that Girard residents valued "religion, strict 'family life,' nationalism, patriotism, the profit system, and largely the Republican Party. Intellectual and cultural life is bankrupt except for the small group of Haldeman-Julius's [sic] friends." Consequently, he noted that "in his newspaper, Mr. Haldeman-Julius ignores local affairs, because they bore him, and devotes his attention to national and international subjects."[1]

Over the previous two-and-a-half decades, Haldeman-Julius had emerged as both a prominent proponent of radical free-thought and a prolific publisher. Through mail order and mass marketing, he distributed materials nationwide that addressed all aspects of modern life. His numerous publications allowed for interaction between readers and authors and assured anonymity for anyone purchasing texts on self-improvement or sexuality. Consequently, his array of periodical and book offerings created an ideologically unified readership that transcended geographic boundaries. His success, in fact, came despite the absence of a sizeable regional audience or sympathetic local community. Lawrence concluded his profile of Haldeman-Julius by noting that "toward his immediate environment he [Haldeman-Julius] is aloof and scornful. Horrified Kansans might be more inclined to focus their aggressions on him if it were not for the fact that he is the owner of the largest business in town."[2]

Community Context

Kansas, primarily known for agrarian production and pre–Civil War bloodshed, grew exponentially during the early twentieth century. As the state's population expanded it also shifted away from the farm: "between 1900 and 1910 the population of the state defined by the census as urban increased 49%, from 330,000 to 492,000. By 1920, it increased by another 120,000, or 25%."[3] The state's growth mirrored national trends, yet slowed during subsequent decades averaging around 4–6% per year.[4] Kansas publishers were delighted to find their local audiences expanding and the demand for news growing. Despite increasing urbanization, however, Kansas did not develop a sizeable urban center on par with New York or Chicago, both of which were well known for supporting successful socialist and radical publications.

On a regional level, a sizeable audience was also not to be found within southeast Kansas. In 1920, the town of Girard, county seat of Crawford County, boasted a population of 3161 while nearby Pittsburg had 18,052 residents. Crawford County's total population numbered 61,800. Further, growth in the region did not center in Girard. The town had grown by only 688 residents since 1900, while Pittsburg had added 7940 and Crawford County had attracted almost 23,000 additional residents.[5] The 1920 census noted that within Crawford County's population, however, were approximately 14.7% foreign-born whites.[6] Craig Miner notes the concentration of immigrants earned the region the moniker "Little Balkans."[7] During subsequent decades the region experienced significant population decline. By 1950, Pittsburg remained relatively steady at 19,341, while Girard had shrunk to 2426 and Crawford County fell to 40,231 total residents. Geographic proximity also played a factor in limiting the local audience. Girard is located approximately 14.59 miles south of Pittsburg, Kansas, 123.58 miles south of Kansas City, and 167.95 miles east of Wichita. Joplin, Missouri, the town other than Pittsburg most frequently mentioned as a destination for Haldeman-Julius and his family, is located 49.33 miles west of Girard.[8]

The *Appeal to Reason*

Born Emanuel Julius in Philadelphia to Russian immigrant parents in 1889, Emanuel Haldeman-Julius's life embodied core American values of social mobility, self-reliance, and the fulfillment of childhood dreams through perseverance and hard work. He became enthralled with books at an early age and pursued intellectual stimulation wherever he could find it.[9] An early thirst for knowledge led Emanuel quickly into journalism and publishing. Before turning thirty he completed successful stints with the *Philadelphia Daily, Milwaukee Leader, Chicago Daily World, Los Angeles Citizen,* and the *New York Call.*

In 1915 Emanuel Julius joined J.A. Wayland's *Appeal to Reason* in Kansas City. He left a paper based in an established and diverse metropolitan area that boasted 40,000 readers to join a midwestern publication surrounded by a primarily conservative and native white population. Yet, he did not leave behind the action and influence of national publishing when he fled the East Coast. During the early twentieth century, the *Appeal to Reason* stood as the most widely distributed socialist publication in the United States and boasted almost a million readers.[10] In 1916, he explained to Jane Addams that "after a year or more in N.Y. I was offered the position of editorial writer for the *Appeal to Reason*. I accepted because I wanted the experience of working on a successful weekly of huge circulation."[11]

Soon after Emanuel Julius joined the publication, the *Appeal to Reason* relocated to Girard, Kansas. J.A. Wayland believed southeast Kansas's largely immigrant population and heavy reliance on industrial production, specifically coal mining, created an ideal environment for his publication. He envisioned a symbiotic relationship with the local community that would lead to expanded influence and new readers. The *Appeal to Reason* would become an advocate for residents, and the region's economy and diversity would reinvigorate the publication's socialist perspective.

Emanuel cemented his place in Girard when he married Marcet Haldeman. The couple's decision to adopt the hyphenated last name Haldeman-Julius symbolized their intellectual partnership and shared enthusiasm for pushing social boundaries.[12] Over the next several decades Marcet—a member of a prominent Girard banking family, activist, and niece of Jane Addams—injected personal capital into her husband's burgeoning publishing efforts and enhanced the success of his publications through effective reporting. During the early years of their marriage this intertwining of personal and professional roles proved wholly successful.[13]

The move to Girard and the *Appeal* proved a transformative opportunity for Haldeman-Julius. His early years at the paper, however, coincided with a downturn in the paper's fortune. In 1917, editor Louis Kopelin asserted, "something radically different will have to be accomplished by the Appeal to survive these unfavorable times. If the injection of a new idea and new blood will not come up to our expectations the paper is doomed."[14] A year later, Emanuel and Marcet, who loaned him more than half the cost of his share, along with Louis Kopelin, purchased a controlling interest in the *Appeal to Reason*.[15] Under their leadership and with a streamlined staff, the paper managed to pull itself back from the brink of financial ruin.

Yet, challenges remained. Governmental officials eager to quell radical publications' influence and deprive them of an ability to foment domestic unrest used access to mail distribution as a hammer to ensure compliance. To maintain acceptance, Kopelin and Haldeman-Julius de-emphasized radical political rhetoric and moved toward more general "free-thought." Moreover, though "at first they supported the Socialist party's antiwar position ... when the United States entered the war, they switched sides and supported the Wilson administration."[16]

Haldeman-Julius had been lured to Girard by the prospect of working for a widely read radical socialist paper. He had married and started a family in southeast Kansas. Unfortunately, soon after the *Appeal to Reason* relocated to Girard a shift in the national mood imperiled editorial freedom and the region entered a prolonged period of decline. As mining activity decreased so too did the arrival of new immigrants. Both factors contributed to a weakening regional economy and made southeast Kansas less hospitable to a radical publication. Far from the expanding readership and growing influence envisioned by Wayland, as regional growth slowed the paper lost readers and experienced diminishing financial returns. Over the next several years these events forced Haldeman-Julius to shrewdly transform himself and the publication. He turned his attention toward other distribution methods, such as books, that ultimately proved more profitable and popular. He refashioned the content of the *Appeal*, renamed it *Haldeman-Julius Weekly*, and began to advocate an agenda of free-thought and rationalism that appealed to a much larger readership.[17]

A New Direction: Little Blue Books

Due to the diminishing appeal of radical newspapers and lingering wartime tension, Haldeman-Julius sought a more stable and lucrative economic venture. He explained to Louis Kopelin, "The Appeal is a tremendous thing in itself. We have gone ahead and put a tremendous amount of ability into a new venture which has been an enormous success—book publishing."[18] Eric Schocket argues that Haldeman-Julius's move to Little Blue Books came as a result of increased scrutiny shown to radical writing following World War I. He asserts, "the Little Blue Books emerged then, quite literally, into the space left by the Espionage Act's suppression of the radical press."[19] The Espionage Act stifled criticism of government policies, especially those relating to U.S. involvement in World War I, by threatening publications that promoted alternative political and social agendas with criminal prosecution and economic penalty, including the curtailment of mail distribution. Consequently, Haldeman-Julius increasingly emphasized free-thought rather than overt socialism or governmental criticism within his publications.

The sales of the new book series quickly dwarfed the success of the *Appeal to Reason*. Emanuel reported to Marcet in 1919, contrasting his success with Kopelin's, "that in nine months and 13 days I had sold $28,000 worth of books, breaking all records. I beat Louis' 1915 (his last year) by $7000. That is to say in 9 months and 13 days I sold more by $7000 than Louis sold in 12 months."[20] The success that Emanuel first enjoyed continued throughout the next several decades as Little Blue Books were embraced by millions. Schocket notes that "pamphlet publishing [was] safer and more profitable in the conservative political climate of the post-war years" and as a result "Haldeman-Julius turned over more and more of his press to the less explicitly political Little Blue Books."[21]

Ultimately, Haldeman-Julius's book business furthered his dual goals of widespread influence and personal profit. In the *First Hundred Million: How to Skyrocket Book Sales with Slam Dunk Titles*, Haldeman-Julius proclaimed, "I am a business man and not a philanthropist." He explained on one hand Little Blue Books "from the beginning emphasized education in their policy. That series is known far and wide as the University in Print."[22] Yet, on the other hand, he insisted, "I invested my capital in the Little Blue Book because I thought it was a sound business venture."[23]

Reprints of classic works, such as *Rubaiyat of Omar Khayyam* and Oscar Wilde's *Ballad of Reading Gaol*, available within the public domain provided the first 250 titles published as Little Blue Books. In order to expand his operation, however, Haldeman-Julius needed to make contact with active authors and gain access to new titles. Writers such as Joseph McCabe, William Fielding, and D.O. Cauldwell provided a plethora of volumes centered on topics ranging from Catholicism to sexuality. Clarence Darrow, W.E.B. DuBois, and Margaret Sanger provided fewer, but better known, volumes. Many other authors provided works on topics within their area of expertise.[24] The sheer volume of titles available to the public formed the backbone of Haldeman-Julius's marketing strategy. He revealed to a potential business partner that he had a "policy of keeping the public supplied with an ever-growing list ... It keeps the receipts up and fights off real competition. There will always be publishers with a few titles to challenge us, but our immense list swamps them out in the end."[25]

The Little Blue Book series featured a wide array of authors and topics ranging from intellectual and practical to entertaining and comical. Haldeman-Julius distributed information on all aspects of American life: workplace conduct, scientific discoveries, sexual habits, human interaction, and current political events. Readers could find titles that provided practical skills and useful information for modern living. The extensive catalog compiled by Haldeman-Julius allowed readers to find information on virtually any subject and, combined with his periodical publications, fostered a sense of community for many Americans isolated from familial ties or cultural bonds.[26] Raymond Lawrence analyzed the type of information Haldeman-Julius readers found most attractive. He wrote that

> circulation figures show that the most popular categories of books are: (a) sex, which includes love, marriage, passion, men, women, birth control, etc; (b) self-improvement, which includes better English, 'education' in particular subjects such as psychology, philosophy, etc; (c) free thought, which according to the publisher, means for the

readers "releasing themselves from the fetters of superstition, religious bigotry, and theological dogmatism."[27]

Within nine years of publication, Haldeman-Julius compiled a catalogue of 1250 titles with "fully three-fourths of the list protected by copyright."[28] By the time of his death in 1951, Haldeman-Julius had "almost unbelievably quintupled his 100,000,000 sale figure and had published nearly 2000 different titles" through his Blue Book series.[29]

By using a myriad of writers across numerous platforms Haldeman-Julius allowed consumers to pick and choose which they read, while the rest remained insulated from controversy. This strategy also allowed him to offer targeted book lists to specific consumers. For example, he targeted catalogues to medical professionals, educators, and school children. Subsections within his advertisements also divided titles by subject to direct readers to their preferred selections. This practice allowed Haldeman-Julius to segregate his radical political views from works focused on more benign subjects and reach a much larger reading audience through targeted marketing. Ultimately, Haldeman-Julius positioned himself within the book business as a purveyor of knowledge rather than an all-knowing opinion maker. When readers criticized one of his authors, Haldeman-Julius assumed the neutral role of editor and defended both his publication and his author without fully endorsing the problematic positions. As a result, he simultaneously marketed his products to the largest possible audience while tailoring his message to suit particular groups.

The Connection between Little Blue Books and Haldeman-Julius's Periodicals

Despite the financial success of Little Blue Books, Haldeman-Julius continued to publish numerous periodicals. He criticized the often salacious stories covered by local media and assured his readers that his papers provided "more critical and more extensive" coverage of important issues.[30] These offerings provided Haldeman-Julius a direct link to his readership and were filled with editorials, investigative reports, and random musings on daily life. In his 1939 profile of Haldeman-Julius, Raymond Lawrence described Haldeman-Julius's newspaper publications as "the most direct diffusion of his ideas." Lawrence further argued that the "national circulation of the *American Freeman*" essentially constituted "a personal journal with a circulation of 55,000."[31]

Once a customer placed a single order for one of Haldeman-Julius's periodicals, his or her name went onto a mailing list for future publications. Within the first decade of business, Emanuel Haldeman-Julius compiled a list "exceeding half a million names and addresses the world over."[32] In *First Hundred Million* he argued, "it is better, I have found, to list some of the more attractive books in the original advertisement, and solicit orders directly on the merit of the product itself."[33] After establishing a mailing list, Haldeman-Julius then distributed both book catalogues and contribution cards for his periodical publications. For example, a fundraising draft letter began "Dear Friend," and continued with, "There is one peculiar fact about my writing. Critics agree that it is of high quality, yet commercial editors won't print it because I insist on expressing ideas that are unpopular with the more bigoted portion of the population." As a result, "my literary work must be published without regard to the commercial side. How can this be done? By letting my readers send such donations as they can afford."[34] The link between subscriptions, direct contributions, and profit gave Haldeman-Julius almost immediate feedback in terms of his ability to connect with his readers. Crucially, his personal publishing also allowed him complete freedom to report on issues he individually deemed important.

Newspaper publications not only allowed Haldeman-Julius to offer supplemental editorial content, but they also helped generate new interest in his book business. In *First Hundred Million*, Haldeman-Julius stated, "these publications of mine, especially the *Monthly* and *Quarterly*—are not only valuable to me as advertising mediums for the Little Blue Books and for each other, but their editorial requirements constantly complement the editorial needs of the Little Blue Books."[35] Haldeman-Julius operated under the philosophy that "wherever there are readers—there is a place for the Little Blue Books."[36] He believed that just as he had sought inexpensive and reliable information, there were others like him with a thirst for knowledge that far exceeded their financial means. Widespread distribution, however, depended on demand and, importantly, on direct orders rather than subscriptions. Thus, despite the fact that the combined subscriptions to his periodicals had created a mailing list he described as "that most essential of tools," Haldeman-Julius recognized that "there was a limit to what could be done with about 175,000 readers." Without access to a large number of retail locations, Haldeman-Julius turned his attention to advertisements, catalogues, and mail order.[37] He gambled that reaching out directly to downtrodden but industrious Americans represented sound business strategy.

Haldeman-Julius placed advertisements in national newspapers and his own periodical publications that highlighted not only the editorial perspective of the book, but also the potential benefit for the reader. These advertisements grabbed a reader's attention with provocative claims and touted the intellectual and social benefits available from Little Blue Books. For example, in the *Critic and Guide*, an advertisement for a manual on sexuality by D.O. Cauldwell asked, "Is Anyone Sexually Normal?" The advertisement explained that the work "is a study of humanity, refined and in the raw, and of the vagaries the human animal recognizes under the labels of normality and abnormality." It promised that Cauldwell's text "will help you explain to yourself the oddities of your own behavior, showing whether or not they are harmful, anti-social, self-destructive, perverted, and the like."[38] Another advertisement that promoted Joseph McCabe's *The Foundation of Science* urged readers to "be sure to get this great popularization of the latest discoveries in the world of science." The text of the advertisement explained, "here we have Joseph McCabe at his best. The author and scholar is a great authority on science and he has the literary ability to make science an exciting and interesting study." Readers were promised that McCabe's work provided "a wonderful knowledge of present scientific thinking."[39]

The symbiotic relationship between Haldeman-Julius's periodical offerings and book list helped him establish a nationwide readership. It gave him complete editorial freedom and an ability to communicate directly with his readers. Moreover, from a marketing perspective, Haldeman-Julius's advertising efforts exemplified sound business practice: Convince the consumer the product signifies a necessity and will lead to great potential benefit. More importantly, perhaps, in terms of ideological propaganda, his strategy also made sense from an intellectual perspective: Persuade the consumer that others around him or her already have the information and their social advancement depends on an ability to acquire it.

Had he chosen to market his businesses within Girard, or even southeast Kansas more generally, opposition to his political views and public persona may well have grown stronger and diminished sales or forced further changes within his editorial perspective. By embracing mass marketing techniques, especially direct-mail catalogs, Haldeman-Julius used the breadth of his offerings to greatly expand his number of potential readers and to target an audience that had largely been forgotten by dominant media outlets.

Prolific correspondence reflects the deep bond between Haldeman-Julius and his readers. In fact, he billed the *American Freeman* as "The question and answer magazine" and prominently featured reader questions followed by his own answers. Topics ran the gamut from questions concerning specific political figures, gender relations, organized religion, and current events. Moreover, readers expressed a keen desire to know more personal information about Emanuel and Marcet and often wrote to suggest future publications.

Frequently, published reader correspondence sought advice from Haldeman-Julius or other authors regarding personal problems. Just as frequently, the advice Haldeman-Julius dished out came with comments and corrections from other readers. Reader Myrtle E. Croyall took Haldeman-Julius to task for the way he had answered a lovelorn woman. She wrote, "Your article in the last Weekly about the Lewisville woman wanting your advice about how to keep her husband, has invited from me a reply." She chastised Haldeman-Julius for his flippant and sarcastic remarks, writing "I know that you were only joking in what you replied to her question. But that you meant exactly the opposite, unless I am very much mistaken in your knowledge of human psychology."[40] Croyall's letter went on to explain she overcame a similar situation by befriending her husband's target and flirting with his friends. This plan, she concluded, implemented effectively with "pretty, fresh gingham house dresses and little nighties and everything," resulted in a husband who realized that he still loved his wife and a potential mistress who "having learned to like you, will see how things are going and will say to herself, 'Well as they seem so well satisfied, guess I better beat it.'"[41]

Rather than limiting reader letters to timely comments on news stories or local issues, as a traditional community-based newspaper editorial page might, Haldeman-Julius expanded reader participation in his publications and fostered a sense of interactive involvement among his audience. The pages of his publications became a community forum where readers not only interacted directly with the editor, but also spoke among themselves at a time when widespread access to mass communication did not exist.[42]

Personal Advocacy and Controversy

Haldeman-Julius used his publications not only to create and educate a captive audience, but also to draw attention toward progressive causes and the issues he deemed important. His support of and involvement with the Tom Mooney legal defense effort demonstrates how his publications juxtaposed journalistic fact finding and political considerations. In 1917, Tom Mooney and Warren Billings were convicted of bombing a public rally in San Francisco. Many believed the two had been framed by politicians who opposed their radical politics and involvement with organized labor.[43] As evidence trickled out about the circumstances surrounding both men's convictions, supporters of labor rallied to their side. Haldeman-Julius asserted in 1929 that "Tom Mooney's only 'crime' was in being a labor leader ... today there is only one reason that can be seen for Mooney's continuance in jail—namely, the persistent cruel effort of the capitalistic terrorizers of California public life to keep him unjustly imprisoned."[44]

Haldeman-Julius believed that his publications could shine a bright light upon the case and increase attention and pressure on public officials in California. Haldeman-Julius told readers on May 10, 1930, that "if the full story of the Mooney case can be carried to the American people they cannot resist the forcible, honest conclusion that simple justice demands the immediate release of Mooney and Billings."[45] Moreover, he urged them to support efforts to free Tom Mooney and provided several methods for readers to send monetary contributions.

The May 31 edition, which became the "Mooney edition," featured Marcet's on-scene reporting, an overview of the case by John Gunn, and a petition for readers to sign and return to Haldeman-Julius. Throughout the case, Emanuel and Marcet Haldeman-Julius became repositories of information regarding the Mooney case and interested parties across the country sought access to their research materials and personal opinions. The couple also personally campaigned among friends and acquaintances for the defense of Tom Mooney and sought publicity for the case. Haldeman-Julius's efforts in the Mooney case, along with those of other influential Americans, achieved success when Mooney received a pardon in 1939.

Beyond the Mooney case, Marcet tackled regional, national, and international issues. Her reporting provided vital contributions to Haldeman-Julius's editorial perspective. For example, she produced a scathing call for integration on Kansas college campuses in 1927.[46] Published initially in the *Haldeman-Julius Weekly* and later as a Little Blue Book, "What Negro Students Endure in Kansas" drew upon extensive correspondence with university leaders, current and former students, and community activists. She argued that university officials willingly catered to local populations who demanded segregation, denied African American students academic opportunity, and generally practiced policies in violation of the open-minded ideals of higher education.[47] Marcet also contributed numerous independently authored pieces for *Haldeman-Julius Weekly* and *The American Freeman*.[48] On a national level she reported on issues including the Scopes trial, lynching, and changing gender roles.[49] Their shared sympathies for socialism led to Marcet's 1931 tour of the Soviet Union. Haldeman-Julius published multiple *Freeman* columns based on her firsthand observations, and the trip epitomizes the symbiotic relationship between the couple's personal activism and his professional interests.

Haldeman-Julius's personal activism repeatedly jeopardized his ability to distribute periodicals using federal postage. In 1932, in response to ongoing criticism of Herbert Hoover, government officials insisted the *Appeal to Reason* could be mailed only to paying customers. This vastly limited distribution and threatened the paper's financial stability. Haldeman-Julius's standard practice was to sell a bundle of fifty papers for a dollar and encourage readers to distribute them among themselves; often, the company could distribute fifty copies with a single stamp.

Haldeman-Julius galvanized his readers against the "censorship" through the *American Freeman* and urged their increased financial contributions during the period of diminished sales. This campaign resulted in "more than 100,000 signatures of responsible men and women in every state of the union that affirm they had paid for the paper [*The Appeal*] with their own money." Additionally, Haldeman-Julius cleverly procured rival papers and "when bundles arrived in Girard, the postmaster observed the stamps were not affixed, as required under the new rule and held the papers for postage." When the proprietors learned their publications were held up, Haldeman-Julius reported, "their Washington representatives raised a mighty objection to the action of the postmaster at Girard. The rule was immediately rescinded."[50] Subsequently, postal officials begrudgingly acquiesced and restored access to second-class shipping of both individual copies and bundles. Though he had restored mail access for *The Appeal*, the controversy again demonstrated the perilous nature of subscription-based publishing and the importance of multiple publication outlets. Moreover, it reinforced the inherent advantages of Little Blue Books, which could be purchased individually rather than via subscription. Finally, the rapid mobilization of Haldeman-Julius's readers illustrates their loyalty to him personally and his publications in time of crisis.

In addition to ideological controversies, Haldeman-Julius's draft status during World War I also caused tension within Girard. The local draft board initially granted but then revoked Haldeman-Julius's protected status. Haldeman-Julius had sought an exemption because Marcet had moved back to Illinois to care for an aging relative and oversee a recently inherited family farm. Within his appeal to the draft board Haldeman-Julius explained that he had remained in Kansas to care for his young daughter and manage their financial holdings in southeast Kansas. Moreover, he argued that "my status has changed inasmuch as I have become an owner of the New Appeal (published here in Girard)."[51] Newton D. Baker, Secretary of War, wrote to J.I. Shepperd, Haldeman-Julius's attorney, explaining the "Local Board ... found that his wife and child were independent" and though Haldeman-Julius played a significant role managing the family's agricultural interests in Kansas, he "was not indispensable to its successful operation."[52]

At the core of the controversy was the issue of influence. Many in Pittsburg and Girard believed Haldeman-Julius, whose patriotism they already questioned since the *Appeal* had initially opposed the war, was trying to use his reputation to escape the draft. To combat this notion, Shepperd detailed Haldeman-Julius's desire to accept the local board's reversal in a letter to the editor published by the *Pittsburg Sun* on July 20, 1918.[53] It seems to have worked, since Marcet wrote a friend, "after reading this statement practically everyone calmed down as they had been angry chiefly because they thought we had made misrepresentations." Yet, she lamented, "there is a little group here who for personal and political reasons have made up their minds that Manuel is a go. They will leave no stone unturned."[54]

Political controversies plagued the *Appeal to Reason* in the years prior to Haldeman-Julius's purchase of the paper and demonstrated the perilous nature of newspaper publishing. The dustup with the local draft board further revealed the fickle nature of local residents. Collectively, these events influenced Haldeman-Julius's decision to pursue other forms of publishing and a readership outside of the Midwest.

Conclusion

Emanuel Haldeman-Julius, in pursuit of both profit and societal reform, followed the socialist *Appeal to Reason* to Girard, Kansas, in 1916. Over the next several decades, in response to changing social and economic circumstances, he transformed himself into the publisher of multiple periodicals and a book catalog that boasted over 3000 titles. The small local audience and conservative regional politics in southeast Kansas led Haldeman-Julius to eschew local issues in favor of national and international events. His broad focus earned a widespread following, and direct distribution via mass marketing and mail-order allowed him the freedom to focus on issues of individual concern. Haldeman-Julius's publications provided intellectual sustenance to everyday Americans and expanded their access to knowledge and information. They also became a clearinghouse for political and social problems. Direct communication with readers allowed Haldeman-Julius to share an intensely personal political perspective and replicate the bonds of community for many Americans on the margins of society.[55] As a result, his career reveals the increasing ability of publishers during the early twentieth century to create and reach an audience unified by ideology and personality rather than geography.

Notes

1. Raymond D. Lawrence, "Haldeman-Julius Has Made Propaganda Profitable," *The Public Opinion Quarterly* 3, no. 1 (1939): 79. This does not mean, however, that Haldeman-Julius was especially bitter toward local residents or totally aloof from community concerns. See *America: The Greatest Show on Earth* (Girard, KS: Haldeman-Julius Publications, 1928). Also, see Mark Scott, "The Little Blue Books in the War on Bigotry and Bunk," *Kansas History* 1 (autumn 1978): 174.
2. Lawrence, "Haldeman-Julius," 79. For information regarding the political views of Kansans at the time of the 1950 census, see George L. Anderson and Terry H. Harmon, eds., *History of Kansas: Selected Readings* (Lawrence, KS: University of Kansas Press, 1974).
3. Craig Miner, *Kansas: The History of the Sunflower State, 1854–2000* (Lawrence, KS: University of Kansas Press, 2002), 226.
4. Ibid., 405. Miner notes that in the 1950s Kansas again approached 15% growth as it had been between 1900 and 1910.
5. "Statistics of Population, Occupations, and Agriculture," *State of Kansas Census Compendium*, K 312 un. 3 (1950). Kansas State Historical Society, Topeka, Kansas.
6. Ibid.
7. John G. Clark, "A Study in Regional Industrialization: Southeastern Kansas, 1890–1930," in *History of Kansas: Selected Readings*, ed. George L. Anderson and Terry H. Harmon (Lawrence, KS: University of Kansas Press, 1974), 332–48. See also, Miner, 240–41.
8. Distance information was obtained using www.mapquest.com. I have provided raw mileage statistics instead of travel time due to the difficulty determining what roads would have been available in 1920 and the approximate speed of automobile travel. In several letters Marcet Haldeman-Julius mentions car rides to Kansas City.
9. Dale Herder, "Education for the Masses: The Haldeman-Julius Little Blue Books as Popular Culture During the 1920s" (PhD diss., Michigan State University, 1975), 2. Also, see Scott, 156–58.
10. Herder, "Education," 15.
11. Emanuel Haldeman-Julius to Jane Addams. March 8, 1916. Haldeman-Julius Family Papers, Daley Library, University of Illinois-Chicago. Emanuel's wife, Marcet, was Jane Addams's niece.
12. Marcet Haldeman-Julius, *Why I Believe in Companionate Marriage*, Little Blue Book no. 1258, ed. E. Haldeman-Julius (Girard, KS: Haldeman-Julius Publications, 1927).
13. Haldeman-Julius Family Papers, Daley Library, University of Illinois-Chicago. There are several separate loan documents in this file that demonstrate the new *Appeal* benefited from a continual line of credit drawn on the Pittsburg State Bank in 1922. They also show that Marcet

Haldeman-Julius provided bonds as collateral for these loans. Also, see Jason Barrett-Fox, "Feminism, Socialism, and Pragmatism in the Life of Marcet Haldeman-Julius, 1887–1941" (master's thesis, University of Kansas, 2008), 33–34. Barrett-Fox asserts Marcet transferred funds to Emanuel to cement the marital bond and details her ongoing influence on Emanuel's work. The couple separated in the early 1930s, though they remained living in the same Girard home and collaborating professionally. Also, see Scott, "Little Blue Books," 159–60. Finally, see Herder, "Education," 14.

14. Louis Kopelin to Allan Benson, January 19, 1917. Haldeman-Julius Family Papers, Daley Library, University of Illinois-Chicago.
15. Scott, "Little Blue Books," 160.
16. Elliot Shore, *Talkin' Socialism: J.A. Wayland and the Role of the Press in American Radicalism* (Lawrence, KS: University of Kansas Press, 1988), 220–21. See also, Miner, *Kansas*, 240–42. Finally, see Regin Schmidt, *Red Scare: FBI and the Origins of Anticommunism in the United States, 1919–1943* (Copenhagen: Museum Tusculanum Press, 2000).
17. Shore, *Talkin' Socialism*, 225.
18. Emanuel Haldeman-Julius to Louis Kopelin. Undated. Haldeman-Julius Family Papers, Daley Library, University of Illinois-Chicago.
19. Eric Schocket, "Proletarian Paperbacks: The Little Blue Books and Working-Class Culture," *College Literature* 29 (Fall 2002): 4.
20. Emanuel Haldeman-Julius to Marcet Haldeman-Julius. August 23, 1919. Haldeman-Julius Family Papers, Daley Library, University of Illinois-Chicago.
21. Schocket, "Proletarian Paperbacks," 4.
22. Emanuel Haldeman-Julius, *The First Hundred Million* (New York: Simon and Schuster, 1928), 21.
23. Ibid., 136.
24. Ibid., 108–19. Haldeman-Julius discusses, in general, his relationship with authors in a section titled "An Editor and His Writers: Peculiar Editorial Problems of the Little Blue Books."
25. Emanuel Haldeman-Julius to Mr. Harold O. Woolever. October 6, 1945. E. Haldeman-Julius Collection, Axe Library, Pittsburg State University, Pittsburg, KS.
26. Schocket, "Proletarian Paperbacks," 71. He argues that Haldeman-Julius "brought a heterogeneous mixture of literary culture, self-help, indigenous socialism, and freethought into the homes and lives of farmers and workers who as often as not found themselves on the margins of modernity."
27. Lawrence, "Haldeman-Julius," 79–80.
28. Haldeman-Julius, *First Hundred Million*, 109.
29. Herder, "Education," 4.
30. Emanuel Haldeman-Julius, *American Freeman* (December 1928).
31. Lawrence, "Haldeman-Julius," 79.
32. Haldeman-Julius, *First Hundred Million*, 149.

33. Ibid., 152.
34. Undated fundraising letter for *The American Freeman*. E. Haldeman-Julius Collection, Axe Library, Pittsburg State University.
35. Haldeman-Julius, *First Hundred Million*, 151.
36. Ibid., 149.
37. Scott, "Little Blue Books," 164. Haldeman-Julius experimented briefly with establishing Little Blue Book outlets and granting exclusive geographic rights to individuals in exchange for their maintaining a store presence. This, however, proved unsuccessful in the long term and the vast majority of readers obtained books based on catalog and mail-orders. In addition, Haldeman-Julius helped "coach" retailers on the best way to market his books. See, Mr. Harold O. Woolever to Emanuel Haldeman-Julius, May 28, 1945 and Emanuel Haldeman-Julius to Mr. Harold O. Woolever, October 6, 1945. The E. Haldeman-Julius Collection, Axe Library, Pittsburg State University. Woolever represented a group of servicemen who were interested in the rights to publish and distribute Haldeman-Julius's work in Hawaii.
38. Haldeman-Julius, *Critic and Guide* (August 1950).
39. Marcet Haldeman-Julius, *Spurts from an Interrupted Pen* (Girard, KS: Haldeman-Julius Publications, 1931). Advertisement appears on the final unnumbered page.
40. Myrtle E. Croyall to Emanuel Haldeman-Julius, September 25, 1924. Haldeman-Julius Family Papers, Daley Library, University of Illinois-Chicago.
41. Ibid.
42. Emanuel Haldeman-Julius, *American Freeman* (June 1940): 1.
43. Virginia L. Close. "The Mooney Case." Dartmouth College Library Bulletin. http://www.dartmouth.edu/~library/Library_Bulletin/Nov1989/LB-N89-VClose2.html last accessed August 30, 2017.
44. Emanuel Haldeman-Julius, *American Freeman* (December 14, 1929).
45. Ibid.
46. James Wheldon Johnson to Marcet Haldeman-Julius, October 19, 1927. E. Haldeman-Julius Collection, Axe Library, Pittsburg State University. Johnson stated, "I am going to refer your letter to Dr. Du Bois for the answers to your questions. He has been for two years making a study of education conditions as they concern colored students and I am sure he will be a better source of information than anybody else in our office."
47. Marcet Haldeman-Julius, "What the Negro Students in Kansas Endure," *The Haldeman-Julius Monthly* (July 1927). Also see Barrett-Fox, "Feminism, Socialism, and Pragmatism," 79–84. He notes that both children of Emanuel and Marcet, Alice and Henry, attended the University of Kansas. Also see correspondence between University of Kansas Chancellor E.H. Lindley and Marcet Haldeman-Julius in 1927. E. Haldeman-Julius Collection, Axe Library, Pittsburg State University.

48. Barrett-Fox, "Feminism, Socialism, and Pragmatism." Barrett-Fox illuminates Marcet's personal literary contributions and influence on Emanuel's work. Also see Scott, "Little Blue Books," 160.
49. For example: Marcet Haldeman-Julius, *The Story of a Lynching: An Exploration of Southern Psychology* (Girard, KS: Haldeman-Julius Publications, 1927); Marcet Haldeman-Julius, *Judge Ben B. Lindsey on Companionate Marriage* (Girard, KS: Haldeman-Julius Publications, 1927); and Marcet Haldeman-Julius, *The Girl in the Snappy Roadster* (Girard, KS: Haldeman-Julius Publications, 1931). See also Scott, "Little Blue Books," 159–60.
50. Emanuel Haldeman-Julius, "Post Office Denies the Mails," *American Freeman* (March 19, 1932).
51. Emanuel Haldeman-Julius to Newton D. Baker. August 2, 1918. E. Haldeman-Julius Collection, Axe Library, Pittsburg State University, Pittsburg, Kansas.
52. Newton D. Baker to Mr. J.I. Sheppard, July 27, 1918. E. Haldeman-Julius Collection, Axe Library, Pittsburg State University, Pittsburg, Kansas.
53. In contrast, Louis Kopelin, prior editor of the *Appeal to Reason*, did get drafted. See "Kopelin Mission to Italy and France," *Pittsburg Sun* (June 18, 1918). Kopelin's absence paved the way for Haldeman-Julius to assume increased authority over the *Appeal*.
54. Marcet Haldeman-Julius to Mr. Klein, July 27, 1918. Haldeman, Mrs. SA MSS. Collection, Lilly Library, University of Indiana.
55. Emanuel Haldeman-Julius to Isaac Goldberg, June 22, 1935, E. Haldeman-Julius Collection, Axe Library, Pittsburg State University.

Gregory S. Rose | The Midwest as a National and International Economic Powerhouse by 1920

The author of the introductory text for Part 1 of the 1900 *Census of Manufactures* wrote, "The most striking phenomenon of the manufacturing development of the United States in the half century has been the rapid advance of the Central states from a comparatively insignificant position to second place among the geographic groups" and responsible for 30.7% of the nation's total value of manufactured products, exceeded only by the Middle states region of New York, Pennsylvania, and New Jersey with 38.0%.[1] Compared to the Midwest, "nowhere else in the world has there been so rapid a transformation of the occupations of the population" toward industry because "The agricultural resources of the Central states are unsurpassed, their mineral deposits are hardly inferior to those of any other section, their transportation facilities by rivers, by the Great Lakes, and more recently by railroads have rapidly developed."[2] Fifty years later, the preface of a regional geography stated, "Only within the present century has the significance of the Midwest become apparent, for it is within this time that the continent has completed its growth, an unparalleled technology has developed, and the whole world order has changed drastically."[3] The Midwest "is a gigantic center of agriculture, manufacturing, and transportation unexcelled or perhaps unequaled anywhere. As such it exerts a dominating influence on the affairs of the nation and indirectly of the world."[4]

By the first decades of the twentieth century, the Midwest had become a national and international economic powerhouse. It dominated corn and wheat production. It processed more agricultural goods and livestock than any other region. Its industry led in production of steel, agricultural machinery, and motor vehicles. While the Northeast might have been considered the nation's premier economic region, containing the financial capital of New York, the intellectual capital of Boston, and leading manufacturing areas including southern New England where American industrialization began, the Northeast could not match the breadth and depth of the Midwest's production-based economy. By the early 1920s, the Midwest, with Chicago as its physically and economically linked capital, represented the complete package.[5]

Data from the U.S. census is relied upon in this paper to reveal the Midwest's economic achievements in this era. The Midwest is defined using the "North Central" census region, which consisted of two parts: the East North Central district (Ohio, Indiana, Illinois, Michigan, and Wisconsin) and the West North Central district (Minnesota, North Dakota, South Dakota, Iowa, Nebraska, Kansas, and Missouri). Key categories of development measures—transportation, agriculture, population growth and urbanization, and industry—are examined as the basis of argument for the Midwest's position of economic dominance.

Transportation

By 1920, the Midwest's natural and constructed transportation network supported easy movement of raw materials, agricultural products, and manufactured goods within the region and around the world. The earliest white settlers ascribed great importance to accessibility and connectivity in their quest to build a commercial economy. Fortunately, the Midwest is surrounded and crossed by major waterways: the Great Lakes and the Ohio, Missouri, and Mississippi rivers. But in their natural state, these waterways had limitations. Droughts, floods, snags, and shallows along the rivers slowed or endangered navigation. Ice limited travel to the warmer months. Two major constrictions—rapids on the St. Marys River between Lakes Superior and Huron and Niagara Falls between Lakes Erie and Ontario—required portages.

To overcome confinement of waterborne transport to the continent's interior, connecting the Midwest's great water assets of lakes and rivers to each other and beyond required construction of canals and locks. By the Civil War, early versions of the St. Marys River Canal and the Welland Canal tied the Great Lakes together.[6] Three major canal systems—Ohio and Erie, Miami and Ohio, and Wabash and Erie—crossed Ohio and Indiana to join Lake Erie with the Ohio River, and the Illinois and Michigan Canal connected Lake Michigan to the Mississippi

River.[7] Very soon after the initial phase of canal construction, the new transportation technology of railroads attracted even greater interest.[8]

By 1840, the United States had about 3000 miles of track, mostly in the Northeast, but during the 1850s the "most striking advance" in mileage occurred in the Midwest: "Ohio, Illinois, and Indiana experienced a railroad boom such that by 1860 Ohio and Illinois were the leading states in railroad mileage and Indiana was not far behind."[9] The heavy web of rails across those three states extended into Michigan, Wisconsin, Iowa, and Missouri by the Civil War, and "Chicago, with eleven major railroads, had assumed her place as the greatest railroad center in the world," becoming "the Great Trader, as well as the Great Junction" for moving raw materials and agricultural and manufactured products between East and West and beyond.[10] By 1900, the nation's rail network had expanded westward and filled in considerably, with trackage still heavily concentrated in the Midwest, Chicago as the primary focal point, and secondary nodes in Cincinnati, Minneapolis, St. Louis, and Kansas City.[11]

National railroad mileage and density statistics ranked the Midwest highly in 1918.[12] The region composed 25.4% of the area of the 48 contiguous states but accounted for 38.4% of its miles of track. Illinois contained the second-longest mileage of railroads (12,126) and Michigan was eighth (8888 miles); between them were Iowa fourth, Kansas fifth, Minnesota sixth, and Ohio seventh. Nationally, 8.5 miles of track were laid per 100 square miles of territory, but the North Central region averaged 13.9 miles of track: 18.7 in East North Central states and 10.5 in West North Central states.

Agriculture

A globally unique combination of climate, vegetation, topography, and soil supported the agricultural bounty generated by the Midwest. Warm air and moisture from the Gulf of Mexico colliding with cool air from Canada generated sufficient precipitation and growing season lengths sufficient for corn.[13] A glaciated topography of generally flat to gently rolling plains (ideal for mechanized equipment) characterized much of the Midwest and yielded high proportions of arable land.[14] Deep, rich, loamy soils—the nation's largest concentration of Class I and Class II types—developed under original forest cover or prairie vegetation.[15] Even in early times, grain surpluses were produced and, within a few decades of pioneer settlement, this abundance quickly moved the Midwest's agricultural activities from subsistence to commercial and demanded agricultural equipment and machinery to more effectively exploit the region's potential.[16]

The first two decades of the 1900s have been described as the "Gold-Plated Age of Midwest Farming."[17] Already underway were efficiencies in planting and harvesting resulting from mechanization and application of steam and other power sources, as well as practical hybridization of corn and selective breeding of livestock conducted by farmers, changing agriculture "to such an extent that [these developments] should be considered precursors of the twentieth-century American agricultural revolution."[18] Demand for American products spiked during World War I, increasing the total value of agricultural output in the North Central region from $2.3 billion in 1899 to $9.6 billion in 1919 and lifting the average price of a bushel of corn from about 60 cents to $1.44.[19] Between recovery from the Panic of 1893 in the late 1890s and the "economic depression, which began for farmers in 1920," high demand and prices for crops and acreage and increasing productivity made it "seem that nothing could go wrong for the farming community."[20]

Midwestern agriculture was the nation's most productive and valuable by the early 1900s. Seven of the ten leading states according to agricultural product value in 1899 were in the North Central region, with Iowa first, Illinois second, and Ohio third.[21] In 1909, the region again contained seven of the ten leading states, with Illinois and Iowa at the top and Ohio fourth; by 1919, although Texas was first, Iowa, Illinois, and Ohio were next in order and six of the ten top states were midwestern.[22] Another measure of the Midwest's agricultural leadership appears in census assessments of the nation's total farm property value, including land, buildings, implements, machinery, and livestock. Consistently from 1900 through 1920, the North Central region accounted for over half of all farm property value, increasing from 56.1% in 1900 to 58.0% in 1920.[23]

Today, modifying the traditional notion of the Corn Belt, soybeans are as important as corn in the Midwest. But soybeans were "a minor forage and soil enrichment crop until the early 1920s" and still produced in "relatively insignificant" amounts in the Midwest throughout that decade: In 1916 only one thousand acres were planted in Illinois.[24] When corn alone was king, the Midwest dominated its production. In 1899, all seven of the leading corn-producing states were midwestern, accounting for 65.8% of the nation's total bushels; including all midwestern states lifted the region's production to 72.8% of corn grown, compared to 37.5% in 1850 (Table 1).[25] Deep, fertile prairie soils, flat to gently rolling topography, and sufficient precipitation provided an ideal growing environment in Illinois and Iowa. Illinois was the top producer of corn in 1899, raising nearly 15% of the nation's total, closely followed by Iowa with 14.4% and Kansas in third place. Nebraska and Missouri came in fourth and fifth respectively, with Indiana sixth. Again in 1909, the top two states were Illinois and Indiana, and the Midwest grew 73.9% of the nation's corn. In 1919, Iowa ranked first, Illinois second, and Nebraska third, in both production and acreage; Indiana was the fourth producer and Ohio fifth. Seven of the ten leading corn growing states (producing nearly 60% of the total) were midwestern as were seven of the ten leading states in corn acreage (over 46% of the total).[26]

The center of the Wheat Belt occurred farther west and north than the Corn Belt in locations where precipitation was somewhat lower,

Table 1. Corn Production in the Midwest, 1899, 1909, 1919: U.S. Rank and Percent of Total

	1899			1909			1919	
Rank	State	%	Rank	State	%	Rank	State	%
1	IL	14.6	1	IL	15.3	1	IA	15.8
2	IA	14.4	2	IA	13.4	2	IL	12.2
3	KS	8.8	3	IN	7.7	3	NE	6.8
4	NE	7.9	4	MO	7.5	4	IN	6.8
5	MO	7.8	5	NE	7.1	5	OH	6.4

Source: Twelfth Census, VI, Agriculture, Part II, Plate 3, 20–21; *Thirteenth Census, V, Agriculture,* Table 12, 581; *Fourteenth Census, V, Agriculture,* Table 9, 736.

although some East North Central states were significant producers. Six of the seven leading wheat-raising states in 1899—all midwestern—produced 48.5% of the nation's bushels, and together the Midwest accounted for 67.0% of all wheat (Table 2).[27] Minnesota ranked first, North Dakota second, and Ohio third. In 1909, North Dakota, Kansas, and Minnesota led all producers in bushels raised; in 1919, Kansas was first, Illinois second, Missouri fourth, and North Dakota fifth. Eight of the ten leading wheat-producing states were midwestern in 1919, together accounting for nearly 58% of all wheat grown.[28] In all three census years, midwestern states also dominated among the top growers of oats (horses still provided farmers' primary motive force), barley, and rye, representing between six and nine of the top producers for each small grain.[29]

Meat and grain processing, outgrowths and facilitators of the massive farm economy, were important agricultural "manufacturing" activities in the Midwest. Animal processing came early to the region (Cincinnati was "Porkopolis" by the mid-1800s), but by 1900 Chicago, as the cattle and "Hog Butcher for the World," was the new "Porkopolis."[30] Illinois generated 40.1% of the nation's value of slaughtering and meatpacking products in 1900; Chicago alone produced 35.6% of the total.[31] Kansas was the next leading state, at 11.0% and Nebraska was third with 10.2%. The same states led animal processing production value in 1919, although Illinois's proportion declined to 30.2% (and Chicago's to 25.5%) with Kansas and Nebraska also losing ground.[32] With 18.6% of

Table 2. Wheat Production in the Midwest, 1899, 1909, 1919: U.S. Rank and Percent of Total

	1899			1909			1919	
Rank	State	%	Rank	State	%	Rank	State	%
1	MN	14.4	1	ND	15.3	1	KS	15.7
2	ND	8.9	2	KS	13.4	2	IL	7.5
3	OH	7.6	3	MN	7.7	3	OK	7.0
4	SD	6.4	4	NE	7.5	4	MO	6.9
5	KS	5.9	5	SD	7.1	5	ND	6.5

Source: *Twelfth Census, VI, Agriculture, Part II*, Table 21, 90; *Thirteenth Census, V, Agriculture*, Table 19, 590; *Fourteenth Census, V, Agriculture*, Table 15, 741.

the total, Minnesota's value of flour and grist mill production topped the nation's in 1919; it also led all producers in 1900.[33] Kansas ranked second in 1919, and six of the top ten flour and grist mill producing states were midwestern.

Population Growth and Urbanization

By the early 1900s, the Midwest and the Northeast (the Middle Atlantic states plus New England) were the country's two most heavily populated regions. The Midwest accounted for about one-third of the nation's population in 1900 and 1920, a slightly larger proportion than the Northeast's 28%. The most populated portions—the East North Central region and the Middle Atlantic region—each contained about 20% of the U.S. population.

The eastern Midwest underwent rapid population increase following the arrival of predominantly white immigrants after 1800. Growing to over 900,000 inhabitants in 1830, Ohio became the nation's fourth-most-populous state and third in 1840; its 1.5 million people were exceeded in number only by New York and Pennsylvania.[34] Ohio remained third until surpassed by the 3.8 million residents of Illinois in 1890, and Illinois maintained second place until after World War II. Other midwestern states were among the nation's most populous by 1900. Over three million were counted in Missouri and two to three million each lived in Indiana, Michigan, Iowa, and Wisconsin. Between one and two million people resided in every other midwestern state except the Dakotas, with fewer than half a million inhabitants each.

For most of the nineteenth century, the Midwest's primary lure was its agricultural lands, although some immigrants found urban employment. Cincinnati became the nation's eighth-largest city in 1830 and peaked at sixth in 1850; St. Louis was the nation's eighth-largest city in 1850 and ranked between fourth and sixth from 1870 through 1920.[35] Toward the century's end, industrialization fueled nearly explosive growth of other urban centers, drawing in excess agricultural labor, younger generations from small towns, and newly arrived European immigrants. By 1890, Cleveland was the nation's tenth-largest city, and it continued to move upward in size to seventh in 1900, sixth in 1910, and fifth in 1920; it also ranked fifth in manufacturing that year.[36]

Chicago's growth in the second half of the 1800s was remarkable. It was the twenty-fourth-largest city in 1850, jumping to ninth in 1860 and fifth in 1870. Recovering quickly from the Great Fire of 1871, Chicago became fourth-largest in 1880 and second in 1890 through 1920, also ranking second in 1920 behind New York according to value of manufactured products.[37] The rise of Detroit, particularly after the automobile industry concentrated there, was truly amazing. It was the thirteenth-largest city in 1900, ninth in 1910, and fourth in 1920, doubling its population between 1910 and 1920; Detroit also ranked fourth in value of manufacturing in 1920.[38] Other midwestern urban centers such as Milwaukee and Minneapolis experienced notable population and industrial growth in the late 1800s and early 1900s, and in 1920, four of the top six cities in population and value of manufacturing were midwestern.[39]

Industry

Forest products were among the first natural resources exploited in the Midwest. As late as 1900, upper midwestern hardwoods and softwoods remained nationally significant resources: Wisconsin led production of lumber and timber products, Michigan was second, and Minnesota third.[40] Abundant natural resources to feed the iron- and steel-based industrialization dominating the post–Civil War era were located in the Midwest. Major reserves of coal existed in southern Ohio, southern Indiana, and southern Illinois. Huge quantities of readily accessible and high-quality iron ore dotted the southern shores of Lake Superior in Michigan, Wisconsin, and Minnesota.[41] Oil and natural gas, present in modest amounts, provided raw materials, supported refineries, and fueled the region's industries.

Midwestern industrial dominance was built on the foundation of agricultural implement and machine manufacturing, which, in turn, rose from the foundation of agricultural productivity. Manufacturing, initially of agricultural implements, appeared early in the 1800s. Briefly existing manufacturers utilized the inventions of local mechanics and tinkerers, while other major producers with greater longevity appeared. Some began with locally invented plows developed to turn the prairie soil (Deere, Oliver, and Moline), while others transplanted to the Midwest to exploit the demand for agricultural machinery (McCormick's reaper and J.I. Case's thresher) or combined existing companies into larger units (Allis-Chalmers and International Harvester).[42]

Illinois led the nation in manufacture of agricultural implements according to the 1890, 1900, 1910, and 1920 censuses, averaging 38.3% of the total value of these products across that period.[43] Ohio's contribution, 12.5%, was next highest during those years. Wisconsin ranked third, Indiana fourth, and Michigan fifth. These five states accounted for nearly two-thirds of agricultural implement value in 1890; by 1919, they generated almost 80% of it.[44]

The expansion of steelmaking also contributed to the Midwest's rise to industrial prominence. The historical association of iron and steel with Pennsylvania is strong, and for good reason. In 1899, it housed the largest number of steelworks such as blast furnaces and rolling mills, and produced the greatest value of steel.[45] Machinations by industry leaders assisted Pennsylvania (especially Pittsburgh) in retaining leading producer status during the first two decades of the 1900s, slowing but unable to halt the industry's inevitable westward shift.[46]

Pittsburgh mills serviced some of midwestern industry's booming demand, including the needs of automobile manufacturers (by World War I they "became the steel industry's leading consumers"), but the Midwest offered irresistible natural resources and attractions for steelmakers.[47] The industry increasingly relied upon the vast iron ore reserves near the southern shore of Lake Superior, fluxing limestone from the northern Lower Peninsula of Michigan, and advanced furnace technology to free it from Pennsylvania coke. Commodious sites for new, larger, more technologically advanced facilities and future expansion beckoned along the southern shores of Lake Michigan and Lake Erie. Shoreline break-in-bulk points made unloading iron ore from lake freighters more efficient, and concentrations of rail lines brought coal northward and distributed finished products.

Three measures of iron and steel production—facilities, production, and value—confirm the eastern Midwest's rise during the twentieth century's first decades. While the output of iron and steel increased in support of the nation's rapid industrialization, proportions produced by each state changed. Pennsylvania had the largest number of blast furnaces, steelworks and rolling mills, and iron and steel forges

Table 3. U.S. Rank and Percent of Total Steel Production by Selected States

	1904 Rank	1904 %	1909 Rank	1909 %	1914 Rank	1914 %	1919 Rank	1919 %
PA	1	56.6	1	51.9	1	50.6	1	44.9
OH	2	18.5	2	20.0	2	23.3	2	24.0
IN	5	0.6	5	3.3	4	7.1	3	9.2
IL	3	11.4	3	11.4	3	7.6	4	7.7

Source: Fourteenth Census, X, Table 55, 340.

in 1909 and 1919, while Ohio ranked second in both years and Indiana or Illinois either third or fourth, although the Midwest's totals did not exceed Pennsylvania's.[48] From 1904 to 1919, as steel rather than iron became the dominant product, Pennsylvania's proportion of national steel production declined to less than half while Ohio's grew to nearly a quarter and Indiana's increased to over 9% (Table 3).[49] The Midwest's total portion of steel production rose from less than one-third in 1904 to over 40% in 1919, nearly equaling Pennsylvania's.[50] And the proportional value of Pennsylvania steel also declined, falling from close to 60% of the nation's total in 1890 to just over 42% by 1919 (Table 4). Ohio's steel production value grew by over 40% in that same period, and the midwestern proportion rose by a third.[51]

Table 4. Percent of Value for Total Steel Production by Selected States

	1890	1900	1909	1919
Pennsylvania	57.7	54.0	47.4	42.3
Ohio	13.3	17.3	19.9	22.6
Illinois	8.7	7.5	8.7	6.5
Indiana	0.7	2.4	2.7	5.3
Total Midwest	22.7	29.2	31.3	34.4

Source: Twelfth Census, Manufactures, Part I, Table CV, cxcviii; Fourteenth Census, VIII, Table 49, 199–200.

Automobile production exemplified the nation's industrialization during first decades of the twentieth century, and Detroit became its symbol. The shift of automobile manufacturing from New England and New York to the eastern Midwest occurred in concert with two transformative and interrelated trends in automobile history: key manufacturers conceiving the car as a general consumer item, not a luxury, and huge increases in output and declining prices resulting from assembly line and mass production techniques. The concept of a cheap car for the masses, brought to fruition by Ransom E. Olds with the Curved Dash Oldsmobile of 1901 ("the first low-priced car to be produced in quantity" with over 5000 made in 1904 and 6500 in 1905) and launched on an even greater climb in 1908 by Henry Ford through his Model T, reoriented the hub of automobile manufacturing to southeastern Michigan, which was "unquestionably the most important aspect in the history of the American automobile industry."[52] Existing advantages helped concentrate automobile manufacturing in the Midwest: a long history of carriage and wagon manufacturing (in 1900, Ohio was the nation's leading producer, Indiana third, Michigan fourth); capable engineers, machinists, and machine shops designing and supplying components for assembly; a history of manufacturing gasoline engines for stationary and marine power (the internal combustion engine quickly became the preferred motive force); a plethora of mechanics and tinkerers, often self-trained on midwestern farms; and financiers willing to invest in the automobile's potential.[53]

Midwestern automobile production leapt forward significantly in the early 1900s. Although industry statistics from 1899 were considered of "no great significance" because "the industry was largely in the experimental stage," that year fifty-seven manufacturers produced 3723 automobiles, bodies, and parts valued at $4.7 million.[54] Seventeen Massachusetts manufacturers led all states, accounting for 16.2% of product value, and New Jersey and New York each generated around 10% of value while Ohio, the only Midwest state listed, produced 3.1%. Ohio housed eight "motorcar" manufacturing firms and Illinois and Wisconsin each contained six, but Michigan had fewer than four.[55] Change came quickly in the next few years: By 1903 Cleveland had eleven firms and Detroit nine; by 1905, Detroit had thirteen, with eight each in Cleveland and Chicago.[56]

According to the 1910 census, more reliable "statistics for 1904 and 1909 ... indicate a remarkable growth of the industry during the intervening period," with automobiles and automobile bodies and parts manufacturing rising from seventy-seventh among the nation's industries in 1904 to twenty-first in 1909.[57] In 1904, more than 21,600 automobiles, bodies, and parts were manufactured by over 13,000 employees and the product value exceeded thirty million dollars. Michigan, not among the top five states in either category in 1899, jumped to the national leader in employment and value of production in 1904, with Ohio claiming second place and New York third (Table 5). Four Midwest states—Michigan, Ohio, Indiana, and Wisconsin—accounted for 55.4% of the industry's employment and 59.5% of its production value in 1904. In 1909 nearly 126,600 automobiles, bodies, and parts were manufactured by 34,500 employees whose output was valued at nearly 250 million dollars.[58] As Michigan had twice the employment and product value of any state and Ohio was second, "by 1910, it was obvious that automobile manufacturing was going to be concentrated in the Middle West, with its focus in Detroit."[59]

Concentration of automobile manufacturing in the eastern Midwest only intensified by 1920, with Michigan "preeminently the leading state in the industry in 1919, as it was in 1914, 1909, and 1904."[60] Passenger vehicle production skyrocketed from 544,000 units in 1914 to 1.56 million in 1919, and "automobiles advanced in rank among the

Table 5. Percent of Automobile Industry Employees and Percent of Product Value for Automobiles, Bodies, and Parts

	Employees			Product value		
	1904	1909	1919	1904	1909	1919
Michigan	22.1	32.9	50.0	26.6	38.8	52.6
Ohio	22.0	15.8	13.5	21.1	15.6	12.3
New York	15.8	13.6	9.2	14.2	12.4	6.9
Indiana	6.9	9.4	7.5	3.5	9.4	5.8
Wisconsin	4.4	5.4	4.1	6.2	4.6	3.9

Source: Thirteenth Census, X, Manufactures, Table 22, 819; Fourteenth Census, VIII, Manufactures, Table 54, 304, 306.

manufacturing industries from eighth place to third place with respect to the value of products," now exceeding three billion dollars.[61] In 1919, Michigan accounted for half the employment and over half the production value of automobiles, bodies, and parts. Ohio filled second place, followed by New York (declining), Indiana, and Wisconsin. Together, East North Central states accounted for 78.0% of the total value of automobile production; adding Missouri lifted the Midwest's contribution to over 80%.

Midwestern dominance in automobile manufacturing significantly impacted numerous ancillary industries. Despite New England's long tradition of precision manufacturing, Ohio had achieved first position among the states in 1919 according to the value of machine tools produced, accounting for nearly 30% of the total.[62] New England states occupied the next three places, but Illinois (sixth) and Michigan (seventh) were not far behind. Together, Ohio, Illinois, and Michigan produced 42.5% of the total worth of machine tools. Automobile production fostered the Midwest's rising rubber and tire industry, making Ohio by 1920 "preeminently the leading state in the manufacture of rubber goods."[63] Ohio generated 48.5% of the total value of rubber products in 1919 (it was fourth in 1900); Massachusetts led rubber goods production in 1900 but fell to a distant second in 1919 (13.3% of value).[64] Tires and related products such as inner tubes represented just under half the total worth of rubber products in 1914 but claimed nearly two-thirds in 1919, and that year Ohio produced 59.0% of the value of pneumatic tires and inner tubes specifically for automobiles.[65]

The overall significance of manufacturing in the Midwest is confirmed by its steadily increasing value of products from 1880 to 1899 to 1919.[66] According to the 1900 census, Illinois experienced "the most notable and rapid advance in position which has occurred in our industrial history."[67] In 1840, Illinois ranked sixteenth in production, jumping to eighth in 1860, fourth in 1880, and third in 1900, where it remained in 1920, exceeded only by New York and Pennsylvania. Other midwestern states experienced similar increases. Ohio was in fifth place in 1880 and 1900 and fourth in 1920, followed by Massachusetts. On the strength of its automobile industry, Michigan leapt from tenth place in 1900 to seventh in 1920, with Indiana and Wisconsin also in the top ten that year. In 1880, five Midwest states ranked among the top ten according to value of production, six were included in 1900, and seven made the list in 1920. The Middle Atlantic region accounted for 31.8% of manufacturing value in 1920 compared to 28.4% in the East North Central district, but adding the West North Central district increases the Midwest's total to 36.7% and places the region first. It also housed more manufacturing establishments than the Middle Atlantic region.[68]

Conclusion

Transportation, agriculture, population growth and urbanization, and industry—activities intertwined and mutually supporting—fueled the Midwest's rapid economic development by the early twentieth century. At the region's center, Chicago symbolized the Midwest's achievements. Drawing upon "its symbiotic relationship with its rich hinterland" of surrounding agricultural and natural resources and leveraging its position as the transportation hub, Chicago experienced explosive growth in population, trade, food and meat processing, and industrial might.[69] In his 1914 poem, Carl Sandburg famously described Chicago as "Hog Butcher for the World, Tool Maker, Stacker of Wheat, Player with Railroads and the Nation's Freight Handler."[70] Somewhat less lyrically, a lengthy 1919 article in *National Geographic* described Chicago as "Situated in the very heart of the world's most fertile and prosperous valley," serving as the "natural crossroads of the industrial East and the agricultural West," and possessing "the cheapest water transportation on earth and the finest railway facilities in the world."[71] Echoing Sandberg, the *National Geographic* article's author wrote that compared to Chicago and its hinterland, "No other place butchers as much meat, makes so much machinery, builds as many cars, manufactures as much furniture, sells as much grain, or handles as much lumber."[72] By 1920, the Midwest was clearly established as the national and, in many ways, international economic powerhouse.

Bibliography

Cavalier, Jacqueline M. "Immigration's Impact." In *The Industrial Revolution in America. Volume 1: Iron and Steel,* edited by Kevin Hillstrom and Laurie Collier Hillstrom, 183–209. Santa Barbara, CA: ABC-CLIO, 2005.

Cochrane, Willard W. *The Development of American Agriculture: A Historical Analysis,* 2nd ed. Minneapolis: University of Minnesota Press, 1993.

Conzen, Michael P. "The Maturing Urban System in the United States, 1840–1910." *Annals of the Association of American Geographers* 67, 1 (March 1977): 88–108.
Cutler, Irving. *Chicago: Metropolis of the Mid-Continent*, 4th ed. Carbondale: The Southern Illinois University Press, 2006.
Department of Commerce. *Statistical Abstract of the United States, 1920*. Washington, Government Printing Office, 1921.
Flink, James J. *America Adopts the Automobile, 1895–1910*. Cambridge, MA: The MIT Press, 1970.
———. *The Automobile Age*. Cambridge, MA: The MIT Press, 1988.
Fourteenth Census of the United States Taken in the Year 1920, Vol. V, Agriculture, General Reports and Analytical Tables. New York: Norman Ross Publishers, 2000.
Fourteenth Census of the United States Taken in the Year 1920, Vol. VIII, Manufactures, 1919. General Report and Analytical Tables. New York: Norman Ross Publishers, 2000.
Fourteenth Census of the United States Taken in the Year 1920, Vol. X, Manufactures, 1919. Reports for Selected Industries. New York: Norman Ross Publishers, 2000.
Garland, John H. "The Heart of a Continent." In *The North American Midwest: A Regional Geography*, edited by John H. Garland, 3–18. New York: John Wiley and Sons, 1955.
———. "Preface." In *The North American Midwest: A Regional Geography*, edited by John H. Garland, vii–viii. New York: John Wiley and Sons, 1955.
Gennaro, Stephen. "Major Entrepreneurs and Companies." In *The Industrial Revolution in America. Volume 4: Automobiles*, edited by Kevin Hillstrom and Laurie Collier Hillstrom, 51–80. Santa Barbara, CA: ABC-CLIO, 2006.
Hart, John Fraser. "The Middle West." In *Regions of the United States*, edited by John Fraser Hart, 258–82. New York: Harper and Row, 1972.
Hillstrom, Kevin. "Origins and Development." In *The Industrial Revolution in America. Volume 1: Iron and Steel*, edited by Kevin Hillstrom and Laurie Collier Hillstrom, 1–25. Santa Barbara, CA: ABC-CLIO, 2005.
———. "Origins and Development." In *The Industrial Revolution in America. Volume 2: Railroads*, edited by Kevin Hillstrom and Laurie Collier Hillstrom, 1–38. Santa Barbara, CA: ABC-CLIO, 2005.
———. "Origins and Development." In *The Industrial Revolution in America. Volume 4: Automobiles*, edited by Kevin Hillstrom and Laurie Collier Hillstrom, 1–30. Santa Barbara, CA: ABC-CLIO, 2006.
Hillstrom, Laurie Collier. "Innovations and Inventions." In *The Industrial Revolution in America. Volume 4: Automobiles*, edited by Kevin Hillstrom and Laurie Collier Hillstrom, 31–50. Santa Barbara, CA: ABC-CLIO, 2006.
Lewis, Robert. *Chicago Made: Factory Networks in the Industrial Metropolis*. Chicago: The University of Chicago Press, 2008.

May, George S. *A Most Unique Machine: The Michigan Origins of the American Automobile Industry.* Grand Rapids: Wm. B. Eerdmans Publishing Company, 1975.

McCallum, E.D. *The Iron and Steel Industry in the United States: A Study in Industrial Organisation.* London: P.S. King and Son, Ltd., 1931.

Misa, Thomas J. *A Nation of Steel: The Making of Modern America, 1865–1925.* Baltimore: The Johns Hopkins University Press, 1995.

Nordin, Dennis S. and Roy V. Scott. *From Prairie Farmer to Entrepreneur: The Transformation of American Agriculture.* Bloomington: Indiana University Press, 2005.

Oxford Regional Economic Atlas: The United States and Canada, 2nd ed. Oxford, England: Oxford University Press, 1975.

"Population of States and Counties of the United States: 1790–1990," last modified July 14, 2016, https://www.census.gov/population/www/censusdata/PopulationofStatesandCountiesoftheUnitedStates1790-1990.pdf.

Rae, John B. *American Automobile Manufacturers: The First Forty Years.* Philadelphia: Chilton Company – Book Division, 1959.

Sandburg, Carl. "Chicago." *Poetry: A Magazine of Verse* 3, 4 (March 1914): 191–92.

Segal, Harvey H. "Cycles of Canal Construction." In *Canals and American Development,* edited by Carter Goodrich, 169–215. New York: Columbia University Press, 1961.

Showalter, William Joseph. "Chicago Today and Tomorrow." *National Geographic* 35, 1 (January 1919): 1–49.

Smith, Philip Hillyer. *Wheels within Wheels: A Short History of American Motorcar Manufacturing.* New York: Funk and Wagnalls, 1968.

Stover, John F. *American Railroads.* Chicago: University of Chicago Press, 1997.

Taylor, George Rogers. *The Transportation Revolution, 1815–1860. Volume IV of The Economic History of the United States,* edited by Henry David, Harold U. Faulkner, et. al. New York: Holt, Rinehart, and Winston, 1951.

Telgen, Diane. "Major Entrepreneurs and Companies." In *The Industrial Revolution in America. Volume 1: Iron and Steel,* edited by Kevin Hillstrom and Laurie Collier Hillstrom, 45–96. Santa Barbara, CA: ABC-CLIO, 2005.

Thirteenth Census of the United States Taken in the Year 1910, Vol. V, Agriculture, 1909 and 1910. New York: Norman Ross Publishers, 1999.

Thirteenth Census of the United States Taken in the Year 1910, Vol. X, Manufactures, 1909. New York: Norman Ross Publishers, 1999.

"Top 20 Cities, Highest Ranking Cities, 1790 to 2010," last modified July 14, 2016, http://www.census.gov/dataviz/visualizations/007/508.php.

Twelfth Census of the United States Taken in the Year 1900, Vol. V, Agriculture, Part I, Farms, Live Stock, and Animal Products. New York: Norman Ross Publishers, 1997.

Twelfth Census of the United States Taken in the Year 1900, Vol. VI, Agriculture, Part II, Crops and Irrigation. New York: Norman Ross Publishers, 1997.

Twelfth Census of the United States Taken in the Year 1900, Vol. VII, Manufactures, Part I, United States by Industries. New York: Norman Ross Publishers, 1997.

Twelfth Census of the United States Taken in the Year 1900, Vol. X, Manufactures, Part IV, Special Reports on Selected Industries. New York: Norman Ross Publishers, 1997.

Vance, James E., Jr. *The North American Railroad: Its Origin, Evolution, and Geography.* Baltimore: The Johns Hopkins University Press, 1995.

Visher, Stephen S. "Weather and Climate." In *The North American Midwest: A Regional Geography,* edited by John H. Garland, 19–27. New York: John Wiley and Sons, 1955.

Walker, David A. *Iron Frontier: The Discovery and Early Development of Minnesota's Three Ranges.* Minneapolis: Minnesota Historical Society, 1979.

Warren, Kenneth. *The American Steel Industry, 1850–1970: A Geographical Interpretation.* London: Oxford University Press, 1973.

Williams, Charles E. "Environmental Impact." In *The Industrial Revolution in America. Volume 1: Iron and Steel,* edited by Kevin Hillstrom and Laurie Collier Hillstrom, 157–182. Santa Barbara, CA: ABC-CLIO, 2005.

Notes

1. *Twelfth Census of the United States Taken in the Year 1900, Vol. VII, Manufactures, Part I, United States by Industries* (New York: Norman Ross Publishers, 1997), clxxvi.
2. Ibid.
3. John H. Garland, "Preface," in *The North American Midwest: A Regional Geography,* ed. John H. Garland (New York: John Wiley and Sons, 1955), vii.
4. Ibid.
5. Michael P. Conzen, "The Maturing Urban System in the United States, 1840–1910," *Annals of the Association of American Geographers* 67, no. 1 (March 1977): 88–108.
6. George Rogers Taylor, *The Transportation Revolution, 1815–1860* (New York: Holt, Rinehart, and Winston, 1951), 52, 61–62, 162–63.
7. Harvey H. Segal, "Cycles of Canal Construction," in *Canals and American Development,* ed. Carter Goodrich (New York: Columbia University Press, 1961), 184–85; Taylor, *Transportation Revolution,* 46–48; James E. Vance, Jr., *The North American Railroad: Its Origin, Evolution, and Geography* (Baltimore: The Johns Hopkins University Press, 1995), 17.
8. Segal, "Cycles of Canal Construction," 171–73; John F. Stover, *American Railroads* (Chicago: University of Chicago Press, 1997), 35; Taylor, *Transportation Revolution,* 52–55, 74; Vance, *North American Railroad,* 13–124.
9. Taylor, *Transportation Revolution,* 85; Vance, *North American Railroad,* 102.

10. Taylor, *Transportation Revolution*, 86, 74–103; Vance, *North American Railroad*, 139–40; Kevin Hillstrom, "Origins and Development," in *The Industrial Revolution in America. Volume 2: Railroads*, ed. Kevin Hillstrom and Laurie Collier Hillstrom (Santa Barbara, CA: ABC-CLIO, 2005), 8, 13.
11. Vance, *North American Railroad*, front end papers, 144.
12. Department of Commerce, *Statistical Abstract of the United States, 1920* (Washington, Government Printing Office, 1921), 333, No. 226.
13. Dennis S. Nordin and Roy V. Scott, *From Prairie Farmer to Entrepreneur: The Transformation of American Agriculture* (Bloomington: Indiana University Press, 2005), 3; *Oxford Regional Economic Atlas: The United States and Canada*, 2nd ed. (Oxford, England: Oxford University Press, 1975), 64–69; Stephen S. Visher, "Weather and Climate," in *The North American Midwest: A Regional Geography*, ed. John H. Garland (New York: John Wiley and Sons, 1955), 19–27.
14. John Fraser Hart, "The Middle West," in *Regions of the United States*, ed. John Fraser Hart (New York: Harper and Row, 1972), 262, 263; Nordin and Scott, *From Prairie Farmer to Entrepreneur*, 3; *Oxford Regional Economic Atlas*, 58–59.
15. Garland, John H., "The Heart of a Continent," in *The North American Midwest: A Regional Geography*, ed. John H. Garland (New York: John Wiley and Sons, 1955), 6–7; Hart, "The Middle West," 259; Nordin and Scott, *From Prairie Farmer to Entrepreneur*, 2–3, 71; *Oxford Regional Economic Atlas*, 52–55.
16. Willard W. Cochrane, *The Development of American Agriculture: A Historical Analysis*, 2nd ed. (Minneapolis: University of Minnesota Press, 1993), 71–73.
17. Nordin and Scott, *From Prairie Farmer to Entrepreneur*, 25.
18. Nordin and Scott, *From Prairie Farmer to Entrepreneur*, 12; Cochrane, *The Development of American Agriculture*, 100.
19. Nordin and Scott, *From Prairie Farmer to Entrepreneur*, 26, 27.
20. Cochrane, *The Development of American Agriculture*, 101.
21. *Twelfth Census of the United States Taken in the Year 1900, Vol. V, Agriculture, Part I, Farms, Live Stock, and Animal Products* (New York: Norman Ross Publishers, 1997), cxxiii.
22. *Fourteenth Census of the United States Taken in the Year 1920, Vol. V, Agriculture, General Reports and Analytical Tables* (New York: Norman Ross Publishers, 2000), 699.
23. *Twelfth Census of the United States Taken in the Year 1900, Vol. VI, Agriculture, Part II, Crops and Irrigation* (New York: Norman Ross Publishers, 1997), xxiii–xxiv; *Fourteenth Census, Vol. V, Agriculture*, Table 13, 88–93.
24. Nordin and Scott, *From Prairie Farmer to Entrepreneur*, 71.
25. *Twelfth Census of the United States Taken in the Year 1900, Vol. V, Agriculture, Part I*, Plates 3 and 12; Table VII, 23.

26. *Fourteenth Census, Vol. V, Agriculture,* Tables 8 and 9, 736.
27. *Twelfth Census of the United States Taken in the Year 1900, Vol. VI, Agriculture, Part II,* Table XX, 31.
28. *Fourteenth Census, Vol. V, Agriculture,* Table 15, 741.
29. *Twelfth Census of the United States Taken in the Year 1900, Vol. VI, Agriculture, Part II,* Plates 2 and 12; *Thirteenth Census of the United States Taken in the Year 1910, Vol. V, Agriculture, 1909 and 1910* (New York: Norman Ross Publishers, 1999), 596–97, 604, 609; *Fourteenth Census, Vol. V, Agriculture,* Table 24, 749; Table 30, 754; Table 36, 758.
30. Robert Lewis, *Chicago Made: Factory Networks in the Industrial Metropolis* (Chicago: The University of Chicago Press, 2008), 26–27.
31. *Twelfth Census of the United States Taken in the Year 1900, Vol. X, Manufactures, Part IV, Special Reports on Selected Industries* (New York: Norman Ross Publishers, 1997), Table CXXXIII, ccvi; Table CXXXIV, ccvii.
32. *Fourteenth Census of the United States Taken in the Year 1920, Vol. X, Manufactures, 1919. Reports for Selected Industries* (New York: Norman Ross Publishers, 2000), Table 4, 47; Table 5, 47.
33. *Fourteenth Census of the United States Taken in the Year 1920, Vol. X, Manufactures, 1919,* Table 3, 105; *Twelfth Census of the United States Taken in the Year 1900, Vol. VII, Manufactures, Part I,* Table LXXVI, clxxxix.
34. "Population of States and Counties of the United States: 1790–1990," last modified July 14, 2016, https://www.census.gov/population/www/censusdata/PopulationofStatesandCountiesoftheUnitedStates1790-1990.pdf.
35. "Top 20 Cities, Highest Ranking Cities, 1790 to 2010," last modified July 14, 2016, http://www.census.gov/dataviz/visualizations/007/508.php.
36. "Top 20 Cities, Highest Ranking Cities," *Fourteenth Census of the United States Taken in the Year 1920, Vol. VIII, Manufactures. General Report and Analytical Tables* (New York: Norman Ross Publishers, 2000), Table 12, 19.
37. "Top 20 Cities, Highest Ranking Cities," *Fourteenth Census of the United States Taken in the Year 1920, Vol. VIII, Manufactures,* Table 12, 19; Lewis, *Chicago Made,* 21, 23.
38. "Top 20 Cities, Highest Ranking Cities," *Fourteenth Census of the United States Taken in the Year 1920, Vol. VIII, Manufactures,* Table 12, 19.
39. Ibid.
40. *Twelfth Census of the United States Taken in the Year 1900, Vol. VII, Manufactures, Part I,* Table LXXVI, clxxxiv–clxxxvii.
41. David A. Walker, *Iron Frontier: The Discovery and Early Development of Minnesota's Three Ranges* (Minneapolis: Minnesota Historical Society, 1979).
42. Cochrane, *The Development of American Agriculture,* 67–110, 189–208; Nordin and Scott, *From Prairie Farmer to Entrepreneur,* 122–26.

43. *Twelfth Census of the United States Taken in the Year 1900, Vol. VII, Manufactures, Part I,* Table LXXVII, cxc–ccxiv; *Fourteenth Census of the United States Taken in the Year 1920, Vol. VIII, Manufactures,* Table 49, 174.
44. *Twelfth Census of the United States Taken in the Year 1900, Vol. VII, Manufactures, Part I,* Table LXXVII, cxc–ccxiv; *Fourteenth Census of the United States Taken in the Year 1920, Vol. VIII, Manufactures,* Table 49, 174.
45. *Twelfth Census of the United States Taken in the Year 1900, Vol. VII, Manufactures, Part I,* Table CV, cxcviii.
46. E.D. McCallum, *The Iron and Steel Industry in the United States: A Study in Industrial Organisation* (London: P.S. King and Son, Ltd., 1931), 51–52; Kenneth Warren, *The American Steel Industry, 1850–1970: A Geographical Interpretation* (London: Oxford University Press, 1973), 195–98.
47. Thomas J. Misa, *A Nation of Steel: The Making of Modern America, 1865–1925* (Baltimore: The Johns Hopkins University Press, 1995), 212, 159–79, 212–47; Kevin Hillstrom, "Origins and Development," in *The Industrial Revolution in America. Volume 1: Iron and Steel,* ed. Kevin Hillstrom and Laurie Collier Hillstrom (Santa Barbara, CA: ABC-CLIO, 2005), 13–15; McCallum, *The Iron and Steel Industry,* 50–51, 59, 64–65; Diane Telgen, "Major Entrepreneurs and Companies," in *The Industrial Revolution in America. Volume 1: Iron and Steel,* ed. Kevin Hillstrom and Laurie Collier Hillstrom (Santa Barbara, CA: ABC-CLIO, 2005), 67–69, 89, 92; Warren, *The American Steel Industry,* 41–205; Charles E. Williams, "Environmental Impact," in *The Industrial Revolution in America. Volume 1: Iron and Steel,* ed. Kevin Hillstrom and Laurie Collier Hillstrom (Santa Barbara, CA: ABC-CLIO, 2005), 179.
48. *Fourteenth Census of the United States Taken in the Year 1920, Vol. X, Manufactures, 1919,* Table 5, 312; *Fourteenth Census of the United States Taken in the Year 1920, Vol. VIII, Manufactures,* Table 49, 199–200.
49. Jacqueline M. Cavalier, "Immigration's Impact" in *The Industrial Revolution in America. Volume 1: Iron and Steel,* ed. Kevin Hillstrom and Laurie Collier Hillstrom (Santa Barbara, CA: ABC-CLIO, 2005), 196.
50. *Fourteenth Census of the United States Taken in the Year 1920, Vol. X, Manufactures, 1919,* Table 55, 340.
51. *Twelfth Census of the United States Taken in the Year 1900, Vol. VII, Manufactures, Part I,* Table CV, cxcviii; *Fourteenth Census of the United States Taken in the Year 1920, Vol. X, Manufactures, 1919,* Table 55, 340.
52. John B. Rae, *American Automobile Manufacturers: The First Forty Years* (Philadelphia: Chilton Company – Book Division, 1959), 31, 50; George S. May, *A Most Unique Machine: The Michigan Origins of the American Automobile Industry* (Grand Rapids: Wm. B. Eerdmans Publishing Company, 1975), 11; Stephen Gennaro, "Major Entrepreneurs and Companies," in *The Industrial Revolution in America. Volume 4: Automobiles,* ed. Kevin Hillstrom and Laurie Collier Hillstrom (Santa Barbara, CA: ABC-CLIO, 2006), 67.

53. *Twelfth Census of the United States Taken in the Year 1900, Vol. VII, Manufactures, Part I*, Table LXXVI, clxxxviii–clxxxix; James J. Flink, *America Adopts the Automobile, 1895–1910* (Cambridge, MA: The MIT Press, 1970), 308–09; James J. Flink, *The Automobile Age* (Cambridge, MA: The MIT Press, 1988), 10–11, 24–25; Kevin Hillstrom, "Origins and Development," in *The Industrial Revolution in America. Volume 4: Automobiles*, ed. Kevin Hillstrom and Laurie Collier Hillstrom (Santa Barbara, CA: ABC-CLIO, 2006), 5–8; Rae, *American Automobile Manufacturers*, 18–29.
54. *Thirteenth Census of the United States Taken in the Year 1910, Vol. X, Manufactures, 1909* (New York: Norman Ross Publishers, 1999), Table 2, 808; Table 22, 819.
55. *Twelfth Census of the United States Taken in the Year 1900, Vol. X, Manufactures, Part IV*, Table 7, 256.
56. Philip Hillyer Smith, *Wheels within Wheels: A Short History of American Motorcar Manufacturing* (New York: Funk and Wagnalls, 1968), 16.
57. *Thirteenth Census of the United States Taken in the Year 1910, Vol. X, Manufactures, 1909*, Table 2, 808.
58. *Fourteenth Census of the United States Taken in the Year 1920, Vol. X, Manufactures, 1919*, Table 13, 873.
59. Rae, *American Automobile Manufacturers*, 48.
60. *Fourteenth Census of the United States Taken in the Year 1920, Vol. VIII, Manufactures*, 866.
61. *Fourteenth Census of the United States Taken in the Year 1920, Vol. VIII, Manufactures*, 866; Table 13, 873; Table 49, 174–75.
62. *Fourteenth Census of the United States Taken in the Year 1920, Vol. VIII, Manufactures*, Table 16, 382; Laurie Collier Hillstrom, "Innovations and Inventions," in *The Industrial Revolution in America. Volume 4: Automobiles*, ed. Kevin Hillstrom and Laurie Collier Hillstrom (Santa Barbara, CA: ABC-CLIO, 2006), 36.
63. *Fourteenth Census of the United States Taken in the Year 1920, Vol. VIII, Manufactures*, 993.
64. *Twelfth Census of the United States Taken in the Year 1900, Vol. VII, Manufactures, Part I*, Table LXXVI, clxxxiv–clxxxvii.
65. *Fourteenth Census of the United States Taken in the Year 1920, Vol. VIII, Manufactures*, Table 11, 1001; Table 12, 1002.
66. *Twelfth Census of the United States Taken in the Year 1900, Vol. VII, Manufactures, Part I*, clxxxi; *Fourteenth Census of the United States Taken in the Year 1920, Vol. VIII, Manufactures*, Table 10, 18.
67. *Twelfth Census of the United States Taken in the Year 1900, Vol. VII, Manufactures, Part I*, clxxxi.
68. *Fourteenth Census of the United States Taken in the Year 1920, Vol. VIII, Manufactures*, Table 10, 18.

69. Irving Cutler, *Chicago: Metropolis of the Mid-Continent*, 4th ed. (Carbondale: The Southern Illinois University Press, 2006), 225.
70. Carl Sandburg, "Chicago," *Poetry: A Magazine of Verse* 3 no. 4 (March 1914): 191–92.
71. William Joseph Showalter, "Chicago Today and Tomorrow," *National Geographic* 35, no. 1 (January 1919): 3.
72. Ibid.

Paula Wisotzki | Revolt in the City
Labor and Art in
the Urban Midwest

As a cultural symbol, labor is bound up with its locale. An orderly image of farmers tilling fields carries with it connotations of people in tune with nature or even a divinely ordained world. Similarly, laborers in an industrial setting may communicate a harmonious relationship between human beings and machinery, but as a product of man the environment is by definition unnatural. The power of place to mark a fundamental difference between peasants (even yeoman farmers) and industrial workers is, of course, as old as the first stirrings of the Industrial Revolution, and when it comes to analyzing 1930s American art, the polarity between rural life and urban existence emerges time and again as a framework for examining social issues of the period. Crucial as this oppositional pairing was, any contrast between the two primarily was expressed implicitly rather than explicitly; visual artists who embraced the countryside as their subject usually celebrated it as the locus of a meaningful way of life that harmonized with nature without representing the city, and artists whose concerns were with urban centers saw the city as a marker of modernity while ignoring the countryside. Through a close examination of a select body of Depression Era images, the nuances of artists' responses to city and country emerge. Similar elements of modernist styles influenced those who rendered each location, but the underlying assumptions—about the meaning of labor in one place or the other—remained separate and distinct. Ultimately, each site served as the locus for discrete solutions for contemporary social and economic travails.

Any investigation of 1930s subject matter of this sort must contend with artistic camps that were themselves often neatly, if problematically, distilled into opposite ends of the political spectrum represented by social realism and regionalism. Here, too, reality was more complex, with boundaries between subjects as well as styles blurred by a variety of factors—not the least of which was contested territory over what it meant to be American. As they had done since colonial times, American artists struggled to define themselves in relationship to their European counterparts. Yet, by the turn of the twentieth century, the ability to identify the "American-ness" of American art was further complicated by the addition of European avant-garde practices to a long history of traditional art making. Consequently, in the 1930s, artists' stylistic choices became an important if potentially confusing marker for American cultural identities, enmeshed as they were with questions of the appropriate content to convey a meaningful response to the upheavals of a troubled decade. This problem has, of course, been recognized before, but its centrality to understanding modernism's impact on the Midwest makes it worthy of additional examination. As a result, the interdependence of these supposed oppositions between subject and style, realist and modernist, and even rural and urban, emerges more clearly.

These concerns with style and content were evident across a full range of American art in the 1930s. For social realists, the varied, intense experience of the city was something worth exploring for its restive changeability, although primarily these artists offered a negative critique of industrialization and its consequences for city dwellers. Their art identified social ills and celebrated the power of the oppressed to advocate for positive change in their lives. Their messages were often rendered with a realist visual language in order to guarantee the legibility of their positions, but the boldness of their statements was often countered by loose and casual mark making to suggest circumstances that were in flux rather than intransigent. Regionalist paintings, however, tended to be executed with careful detail and more than a nod to traditional ways of art making, and thus could be seen as conservative both in execution and in message, although for some time scholars have recognized the impact of modernism on these seeming idyllic images.[1]

Grant Wood's plowing scenes exemplify the intersection of traditionalism and modernist elements in regionalist painting. On one hand, they depicted the efforts of hard-working men taming their fields with implements farmers had used for centuries and thus marking the land with a powerful rhythm that harmonized with nature, as can be seen in *Young Corn* (1931) (Figure 1). Yet, as James Dennis has pointed

Figure 1. Grant Wood, *Young Corn* (1931). Oil on Masonite panel, 24 x 29 ⅞ in. Collection of the Cedar Rapids Community School District, on loan to the Cedar Rapids Museum of Art.

out, in reality the scale and regularity of the contoured furrows Wood captured were only possible with the steam-powered farm machinery that, by the 1930s, had been widely available for several decades.[2] Not only was modern industry ultimately responsible for the look of Wood's plowed fields, but it has now been well established that the appearance of his paintings was also significantly influenced by an abstraction rooted in the European modernism Wood observed during his extensive 1920s travels abroad.[3]

This interweaving of old and new in both subject and style serves as another reminder of the complex ways modernism functioned for American visual artists in the era. If modernism was primarily associated with avant-garde, European-influenced styles, it had additional implications for artistic subject matter. In this way, modernism could reference both experimental artistic styles—the formalism usually associated with artists from Edouard Manet forward—and modern life subjects closely linked to urban culture as they evolved in the wake of the Industrial Revolution. Although much of 1930s American art is associated with a conventional sort of realism, new devices such as flattened planes, repeated forms, and abstracted shapes—in other words the influence of modernist stylistic developments—were evident in the vast majority of these works, whatever the political inclinations of the artists or the subjects they chose.

While an overt visual contrast between city and country was generally absent in the work of artists in this decade, Grant Wood's 1935 essay *Revolt Against the City* famously articulated the regionalists' rejection of the city and all it represented. In this manifesto, Wood asserted in terms redolent of Jeffersonian Democracy the necessity of spurning urban centers in favor of the rural United States, claiming that "the cities were far less typically American than the frontier areas."[4] For Wood, "frontier virtues" were to be found in the center of the country and in the "rugged individualism" of the "self-supporting" midwestern farmer.[5] Positing the city as "other" to the regionalist world that Wood celebrated in his paintings, his essay specifically juxtaposes the purity and strength of rural life against the sullied, over-indulged ways of urban life. To revolt against the city was, for Wood, to reject the many negative qualities of urban spaces enumerated in his text and summed up with his quotation of Thomas Jefferson's characterization of cities as "ulcers on the body politic."[6]

Despite Wood's vociferous rejection of urban life in *Revolt Against the City*, he had left the rural Midwest to travel to Europe's capitals.[7] And if he addressed all American cities as one undifferentiated, offensive blot on civilization in his essay, he had an extensive history of engagement with Chicago, that "Paris of the Prairie," which in this period was truly the nation's Second City. As a young man, Wood studied at the School of the Art Institute of Chicago and lived and worked in the suburb of Park Ridge. Later, he would further his professional reputation by submitting paintings to the Art Institute of Chicago's Annual Exhibition of American Painting and Sculpture.

Whatever Wood's conflicted relationship with cities, the urban centers of the United States—in the Midwest, notably Chicago—were a magnet for many in the 1930s. The attractions of the midwestern city were celebrated by the 1933 Century of Progress International Exposition in Chicago, which offered a shining example of urban life's promise with its colorful, streamlined buildings. The general orientation of the fair was to embrace new, modern ideas, and this conception was specifically embodied in the experimental architecture of its exposition halls. Chief among them was the Travel and Transport Building designed by Edward H. Bennett, John Holabird, and Hubert Burnham.[8] Suspension cables attached to its twelve towers supported a dome and provided clear, unobstructed space for exhibitions on the interior of the building. One of several dramatic structures on the fairgrounds, the exposition hall became an icon for the exposition—frequently reproduced in the fair's publicity and often standing in for the entire grounds.

Although the Travel and Transport Building was intended as a manifestation of progress, at the same time viewers with a more critical perspective might have seen it as a powerful reminder of the gulf between the illusion of advances and the harsh reality of the 1930s. It was this sort of message about the city that attracted the social realists. Chicago artist Morris Topchevsky (1899–1947) used this very structure in his *A Century of Progress* (c. 1933) (Figure 2) to call attention to the illusory nature of that progress for some of the city's inhabitants. In this painting, the exhibition hall gleams in the distance beyond a shanty town constructed of drab, improvised materials—making a powerful contrast between two sets of temporary structures. Sarah Kelly Oehler has called Topchevsky's painting a "deliberate provocation, intended to highlight the distance between the ideals of progress espoused by the fair and the economic problems" facing the Depression's dispossessed.[9] In the foreground, six men while away their time in the open air. An African American figure at the left of this group reads an issue of the *Daily Worker*, the official organ of the Communist Party USA (CPUSA), suggesting that he and his colleagues are not merely lazy or mindlessly idle, but—given the right information—capable of changing their situation. An outspoken leftist, Topchevsky was himself a member of the CPUSA and a leading member of the Chicago branch of the John Reed Club (an artists' organization closely aligned with the left).[10] His social ideals, in a manner consistent with those of many American political leftists of the 1930s, led him to be equally committed to racial equality; this is shown by the diversity of figures in his painting, resulting in a population very different from the people exclusively of European descent typically depicted in regionalist works.

Figure 2. Morris Topchevsky, *A Century of Progress* (1933). Oil on canvas, 35 ½ x 29 ½ in. Collection of Clifford Law Offices (Chicago). Photo: Kenneth Oakes.

A Century of Progress is an easel-sized painting, but Topchevsky, like many artists of the period, no matter their political orientation, painted murals under the sponsorship of the Works Progress Administration-Federal Art Project or WPA.[11] Such government-sponsored murals were, of course, one important avenue for American artists to both pursue their craft and reach out to a mass audience in the 1930s. The WPA has, in practice, become an umbrella term for a variety of government-sponsored public art projects that operated in the 1930s and into the 1940s. Founded in 1934, it was an outgrowth of several different "seed" projects, often local in sponsorship, which emerged to support public art in the early 1930s. Although primarily associated with towns, these programs were by no means limited to the big cities such as Chicago where Topchevsky worked. Grant Wood, as a populist, was supportive of certain aims of these projects and, in 1934, he became the supervisor of the Iowa Section of the Public Works of Art Project (PWAP, one of the early incarnations of such projects for artists that gave rise to the WPA).

Under Wood's leadership, the Iowa PWAP program operated with federal money under the auspices of the University of Iowa campus in Iowa City. Among its projects was a set of murals for the Iowa State University Library in Ames.[12] Wood designed the library murals and directed their execution but recruited other artists to paint them. He derived the project's unifying theme from Daniel Webster's 1840 assertion that "When tillage begins, other arts follow," which offered ample opportunity for imagery that celebrated Iowa's pioneer past, most notably a large, centrally positioned image of the breaking of the prairie (Figure 3). This portion of the mural was typical of regionalist aesthetics: orderly in its composition, cleanly rendered, and depicting solemn workers in spacious surroundings. It dominated the multipartite mural and functioned as the metaphorical stimulus for subsequent intellectual and cultural accomplishments codified in peripheral panels. Those addressed engineering, agriculture and home economics, in keeping with the university's leading academic departments in the 1930s.

Wood's mural complex, with its emphasis on agriculture as the fountainhead of civilization, can be usefully contrasted with another mural project undertaken about the same time in nearby Cedar Rapids, Iowa. There, in 1934, Francis Robert White formed the Cooperative Mural Painters of Iowa with three other artists, and together they devoted two years to a government-funded commission for murals to decorate a courtroom in the Linn County Federal Courthouse.[13] White, a younger artist who had been a student at Wood's experimental Stone City, Iowa, artists' colony in the summers of 1932 and 1933, was responsible for supervising the Cedar Rapids project and worked collectively with the other artists to determine the mural's subject matter. The artists then divided the labor of executing the four panels that together ran entirely around the walls of the large courtroom.

Figure 3. Designed by Grant Wood (American, 1885–1942), *Breaking the Prairie* (1936–37). Oil on canvas. Located in the Parks Library, Iowa State University, Ames, Iowa. Commissioned by Iowa State College as a joint project of the federal Works Projects Administration (WPA) and the National Youth Administration (NYA) and Iowa State College for the Iowa State Library. In the Art on Campus Collection, University Museums, Iowa State University, Ames, Iowa. Image © University Museums, Iowa State University, 2017.

In the section titled *Opening of the Midwest,* White's themes reveal his very different perspective on the sweep of history from that of his one-time mentor Wood. Reading from left to right, *Opening of the Midwest* follows the march of time from nomadic peoples to contemporary urban life. In the first scene, a Native American woman is seated before a village of teepees. Then Europeans arrive, first as violent conquerors and then as pioneers. Toward the center of the wall, white workers intermix with people of African and Asian descent as they labor on a waterfront and build a railroad. This segment of the mural is followed by an image of a farm where the fields show evidence of an abundant harvest. At this point, the sequence of images might suggest an approach that paralleled Wood's treatment of the region's history, but White's mural moves beyond agriculture to a final scene of urban industry, bringing history along to contemporary times instead of establishing settlers as the source of civilization's advancements (Figure 4). In general, this dynamic view of history owed something to the Mexican muralists with whose work White and his colleagues were familiar. Even the powerful visual language of the courthouse murals with their bold shifts in scale and angular brushwork was influenced by Mexican examples—a model that at the time seemed a significant and notably American alternative to European modernism, despite the fact that it, too, had roots in the Parisian avant-garde.

While the Grant Wood–led Iowa State University mural project mythologized pioneer life and the taming of the prairie, the Lynn County Courthouse mural presented the arc of civilization as a series of struggles where change occurred but was not necessarily to be equated with a conventional definition of progress. There are stark differences in the messages of these two projects, and there can be no question that Wood and White had divergent perspectives on the roles of the rural farmer and urban worker. Wood focused on the farmer as a model for what should be and as a source of generalized cultural advancement, while White showed the benefits of agricultural production but shifted to the plight of industrial workers functioning in an urban environment. White conveyed industry's overwhelming power with a scene devoted to an enormous machine with a single worker reaching into its unseen and therefore mysterious recesses. The behemoth was rendered in a strong red that offered a dramatic contrast to the neutral tones of other

Figure 4. Francis Robert White, *Law and Culture*, detail (1936). Tempera on canvas. Linn County Federal Courthouse (now City Hall), Cedar Rapids, Iowa. Photograph courtesy of City of Cedar Rapids.

sections of the mural, a modernist technique used to heighten emotional content also found in the work of Mexican muralists. This section of the mural concludes with a row of nondescript houses—suggesting a company town where the worker could do little to escape the looming machinery where he labored. A similar trope was employed by many artists in the 1930s, especially those like White who were sympathetic to the working man and inclined to a leftist social agenda for their art. Numerous socially critical images cast these laborers as oppressed by the demands of industry and trapped in a daily grind that extended from cradle to grave.

The dystopian effects of this cycle can also be read in Walker Evans's 1935 photograph *Graveyard, Houses and Steel Mill, Bethlehem, Pennsylvania*, which positions the viewer in a poorly maintained graveyard looking across a valley dominated by blast furnaces (Figure 5).[14] Evans's biographer James R. Mellow described the image as operating as though the large granite cross in the foreground "surveys the workers' houses, the steep descent to the mill, and the array of smokestacks barricading the sky."[15] Similar scenes were taken up by printmakers of the 1930s, and although Evans's image was recorded in eastern Pennsylvania, far from the Midwest, its focus on the steel industry as a powerful symbol of workers' struggles came to be as relevant in the center of the country as it was in the Northeast. Two related prints had strong Chicago connections.

Harry Sternberg's lithograph *Steel Town* (1937) (Figure 6) addresses the hopeless life cycle of the steelworker in a composition comprising many elements similar to those found in Evans's photograph: a modest graveyard in the foreground gives way to a row of worn, charmless houses across the road with blast furnaces looming in the near distance.[16] However, Sternberg adds another element to Evans's inventory of things that make up the narrow, miserable life of the invisible inhabitants of this steel town—a Roman Catholic church rising up between the houses and the mill. Although much more substantial than the workers' homes and grandly decorated with a rose window and a monumental sculpture of Christ on the cross, the church is little competition for the massive bulk of the steel yard. And for Sternberg, and others with a leftist viewpoint in this era, the Church—considered to be complicit with the capitalist system that empowered the mill

Figure 5. Walker Evans, *Bethlehem Graveyard and Steel Mill. Pennsylvania* (1935). Film negative. Library of Congress, Prints and Photographs Division, Washington, DC, LC-DIG-ppmsca-36750.

owners—offered no more meaningful alternative to the reality of the workers' lives than did the local bar located in the same row as the mean buildings housing the workers and their families.[17] Sternberg (1904–2001) was raised in New York City where he began his professional career.[18] In 1936, he received a Guggenheim Memorial Fellowship and spent a year visiting coal mines and steel mills and making prints related to the working conditions he found there. For much of 1937, he was in Chicago involved in similar endeavors. There his career and his interests would have overlapped with those of Carl Hoeckner (1883–1972), a long-time Chicagoan.[19]

Like Sternberg and Topchevsky, Hoeckner had an extensive commitment to progressive social stances and addressed them through his art as well as by his participation in professional artist organizations with strong leftist connections, such as the American Artists Congress. By 1937, he, too, was addressing the circumstances of the oppressed workers in the steel industry. Hoeckner's *Steeltown Twilight* (1937)

Figure 6. Harry Sternberg, *Steel Town* (1937). Lithograph. Mary and Leigh Block Museum of Art, Northwestern University.

(Figure 7) produces a message similar to that of Sternberg's print, as it employs comparable elements but expands the allegorical possibilities in an eerie nighttime image of an industrial area. The silhouette of a Catholic church is set against an expansive industrial landscape filled with electrical transmission towers, factories, and chimneys. Clouds blended with smoke obscure many of the scene's details, setting an atmospheric, even mysterious, mood that is heightened by the mass of

Figure 7. Carl Hoeckner, *Steeltown Twilight* (1937). Lithograph. Mary and Leigh Block Museum of Art, Northwestern University.

people emerging out of the gloom in the foreground of the print. To the right, the crowd is drawn to a glowing cross positioned in front of the church, but just to the left of center, uniformed police armed with billy clubs attack the throng. Once again, workers from the steel industry are shown to be at the mercy of powerful institutions that the artist suggests collude with one another.

That both Sternberg's and Hoeckner's prints date to 1937 should not be surprising. That year saw a concerted effort to unionize the steel industry, and social activist artists responded with an increased interest in the plight of the industrial workers with whom they had long sympathized.[20] The steel industry had attracted the attention of socially concerned artists for decades, especially during the Depression when falling demand led mill owners to press for punishing concessions from their workers year after year. Yet, workers fought back through collective action and, after a long period of unsuccessful attempts to unionize, steel workers gained new momentum in the mid-1930s. At that time, the policy of the American Federation of Labor (AFL) to organize workers according to specific skills gave way to the Congress of Industrial Organizations' (CIO) approach of organizing all workers across an industry. By 1936 the CIO had formed the Steel Workers Organizing

Committee (SWOC) with the explicit goal of extending the success the CIO had found with the mining industry. Famously, Big Steel, as the major steel-producing corporations were known, capitulated to union demands relatively quickly—a significant turning point came on March 2, 1937, when the United States Steel Corporation (U.S. Steel) signed a collective bargaining agreement—yet there were holdouts among smaller steel-producing companies.

One reason for the success of the SWOC was its careful strategy to avoid any racial and ethnic conflicts.[21] Reflecting this reality, artists portrayed racially integrated groups of workers at the mills or involved in union activities. Topchevsky's *Strike Against Wage Cuts* (1930s) (Figure 8) reflects and celebrates this approach. Workers are gathered together at a rally and hold signs to reinforce their specific concerns. One sign states that the laborers are on strike because their pay has been reduced, and another urges the workers to maintain a united racial front. The crowd presses in close to a speaker whose potent message is reinforced by his raised fist, a symbol of strength and resistance employed by the labor movement from the days of the Industrial Workers of the World, and the gesture is echoed by others in the crowd.[22] This still-peaceful assembly is framed by uniformed police who intrude in the lower right and at the back of the crowd; they are armed with billy clubs, suggesting the menace to the workers' solidarity that is actively played out in Hoeckner's print.

Despite the SWOC's effective strategies to unite workers behind its causes and its early success with Big Steel, the organization hit a stumbling block as it sought to win representation for the workers in the so-called Little Steel corporations.[23] Regardless of U.S. Steel's capitulations to worker's demands for union representation, the smaller companies chose to stand firm against similar pressure. When negotiations with Little Steel reached a stalemate, the SWOC called a strike for May 26, 1937. A Republic Steel mill in South Chicago became a focus of tensions as the mill continued to operate despite the strike, leading to one of the most infamous confrontations of the era between steel workers and police.[24] On Memorial Day, May 30, 1937, the SWOC held a rally in support of the strikers. Initially, there was a festive mood, as a number of the workers had brought their families and picnicked near the plant. But later, some in the crowd of approximately

Figure 8. Morris Topchevsky, *Strike Against Wage Cuts* (1930s). Watercolor and pencil on paper, 17 x 13 ¼ in. Former collection of Bernard Friedman, present location unknown.

1500 moved across an open field toward the mill, where a line of 250 Chicago policeman confronted them near the plant's gated entrance; the policemen eventually fired on the crowd, leaving ten workers dead and about ninety injured.[25]

The event received wide coverage by news outlets; the reports were powerfully supplemented by photographic images transmitted across the country by the wire services. In the days immediately following the attack, accounts leaned toward justifying police action as indicated by the *Chicago Tribune*'s banner headline: "Riots Blamed on Red Chiefs."[26] However, the confrontation between police and workers aroused sufficient controversy that Senate hearings were held. Led by Robert M. LaFollette, Jr., of Wisconsin, the official inquiry was responsible for transforming press reaction across the nation such that at the end of the hearings even the *Youngstown Vindicator*—a notorious supporter of the steel industry—referred to the "shocking brutality" of Chicago's police in an editorial.[27]

Not surprisingly, artists on the left responded to these events with powerful images sympathizing with the workers—the best known is Philip Evergood's painting *American Tragedy* (1937) (Figure 9). Some years ago, Patricia Hills pointed out that the painting was influenced by news photographs, identifying a clipping in Evergood's papers that, she argued, served as inspiration for the peripheral figures in the painting.[28]

Figure 9. Philip Evergood, *American Tragedy* (1937). Oil on canvas, 29 ½ x 39 ½ in. Courtesy ACA Galleries, New York.

No doubt the artist gleaned other details that informed his image from news reports of the time. For example, the warm day and festive atmosphere made the workers, most in shirtsleeves, easily distinguishable from the uniformed policemen.

Evergood's painting captures the vastness of the field with the mill in the background and the chaos of the violent attack with police fiercely wielding their billy clubs as most strikers attempt to flee. Consistent with events and reflective of SWOC policy, the unionists are presented as racially integrated and ethnically diverse. Pockets of action are distributed throughout the composition, but the most dramatic confrontation appears front and center, as a red-haired male worker in shirtsleeves raises one arm to hold back a policeman who rushes toward him. With the other arm, he shelters a pregnant woman of Hispanic heritage. Despite her petite size, she, too, is—in Hills's words—"boldly determined."[29] She flexes one arm and wields a tree branch with the other. Hills explains that in Evergood's personal lexicon the dead branch was not just a potential weapon, but "the old order that needs to be replaced and thereby signif[ies] the necessity for social change."[30] Evergood's image then addresses the specifics of the day's events but employs allegorical elements to elevate the massacre to the level of a national tragedy.

Although Evergood's painting has become famous, he was by no means the only artist to take up this subject. Francis Robert White also produced a 1937 image inspired by what the left came to call "the Memorial Day Massacre." His *Memorial Day Massacre: Republic Steel Strike, South Chicago* (Figure 10) offers evidence that he, like Evergood, studied news photographs, as it communicates information already established as relevant to the events of that day. For example, the image captures the lighter-colored clothing of the union supporters and the much darker uniforms of the police—a contrast that only emphasizes the latter's menace. Yet, his tones are muted and do not bring energy to the work as do the clear hues of Evergood's painting. Instead, White relies on a centralized melee of distorted forms with flailing limbs to convey the intensity of the conflict. His expressive, figurative style is in keeping with many of his fellow social realists' approach to modernism filtered through the work of the Mexican muralists. The painting's focus is not on a hero but a martyr—a single figure of a male worker whose

Figure 10. Francis Robert White, *Memorial Day Massacre: Republic Steel Strike, South Chicago* (1937). Present location unknown.

body is torqued in agony as he collapses backward. Presumably he is one of the union supporters shot by police. As he falls, he clings to a large American flag similar to those held by demonstrators at the rally that day and recorded in photo documentation of the event.[31] White's image suggests that the flag is a surrogate for a country that should support the worker but is unable, or perhaps even unwilling, to fulfill the task.

As both martyrs and heroes, for White and Evergood, the unionists were those in the right, those who upheld the values of the country and were true Americans. These artists of urban-oriented social realism presented demonstrators who were not themselves in revolt, but who were victims of police run amok. The laborers were not reliant on the past but were thrust into new situations that necessitated change. Although the workers were from varying backgrounds and diverse ethnicities, both artists and union organizers agreed that rugged individualism would not save them; only collective action could meaningfully transform their situation.

In these ways, then, social realism reinforced a definition of labor and laborers that rendered all but irrelevant the regionalist illusion of peaceful continuity in the countryside. Rural America was not a meaningful alternative nor was it a source of successful solutions to the industrial worker's problems. Their reality was the city, and there was no reason to pretend it could be left behind. If both groups of artists relied on elements of a modernist visual language to communicate their messages—creating a type of abstraction with flattened forms and repeated patterns as a way to organize space and form and similarly eschewed radical abstraction—there were still notable stylistic differences. The regionalists were much more reliant on traditional realism, where the social realists borrowed from modernism characteristics to heighten the emotional power of their images. In spite of these differences in style, it was subject matter that prevailed in distinguishing social realism and regionalism, and it was urban subject matter that conveyed a truly modern spirit in the Midwest.

Acknowledgement

I wish to express my gratitude to Helen Langa, whose insightful comments on a draft of this manuscript helped to clarify my ideas.

Notes

1. The contrasting styles of the social realists and the regionalists are discussed somewhat differently, but most usefully, in Susan S. Weininger, "Completing the Soul of Chicago: From Urban Realism to Social Concern, 1915–1945," in *Chicago Modern, 1893–1945: Pursuit of the New*, ed. Elizabeth Kennedy (Chicago: Terra Museum of American Art, 2004), 53–65.
2. James M. Dennis, *Grant Wood: A Study in American Art and Culture* (Columbia, MO: University of Missouri Press, 1986), 159, 227.
3. The timeless yet modern qualities of Wood's plowing scenes have been thoroughly reviewed by Judith Barter, "Prairie Pastoral," in *America After the Fall: Painting of the 1930s*, ed. Judith Barter (Chicago: Art Institute of Chicago, 2016), 30–56.
4. Grant Wood, *Revolt Against the City* (Iowa City, IA: Clio Press, 1935), 16. The essay is now understood to have been ghostwritten by Wood's University of Iowa colleague Frank Luther Mott but remains an important statement of regionalist attitudes toward the city.
5. Ibid., 18, 31, 32.
6. Ibid., 44.
7. For detailed biographical information on Wood, see R. Tripp Evans, *Grant Wood: A Life* (New York: Alfred A. Knopf, 2010).

8. A thorough discussion of the Fair and its architecture is provided by Lisa D. Schrenk, *Building a Century of Progress: The Architecture of Chicago's 1933–34 World's Fair* (Minneapolis: University of Minnesota Press, 2007).
9. Sarah Kelly Oehler, *They Seek a City: Chicago and the Art of Migration, 1910–1950* (Chicago: Art Institute of Chicago, 2013), 20.
10. Donna S. Korey and Amy Galpin, "Morris Topchevsky: Eyewitness," in *Eyewitness: Works by Morris Topchevsky* (Des Plaines, IL: Koehnline Museum of Art at Oakton Community College, 2012), 4–9. The authoritative study of 1930s American artists and the political left is Andrew Hemingway, *Artists on the Left: American Artists and the Communist Movement, 1926–1956* (New Haven: Yale University Press, 2002).
11. Despite the extensive bibliography on the topic, *Art for the Millions: Essays from the 1930s by Artists and Administrators of the WPA Federal Art Project*, ed. Francis V. O'Connor (Greenwich, CT: New York Graphic Society, 1973) remains a most useful source on the subject of government support of artists during the Great Depression.
12. Information about the University of Iowa murals is taken from *When Tillage Begins, Other Arts Follow: Grant Wood and Christian Petersen Murals* (Ames, IA: Brunnier Art Museum at Iowa State University, 2006).
13. There is little conventional scholarship yet published on White. The best available information about the project is from local reporting by the Cedar Rapids *Gazette* on efforts to restore the murals. The original project was funded by the Treasury Relief Art Project or TRAP. Strictly speaking, TRAP was not a part of the WPA, but a similar source of federal patronage for public art in government buildings.
14. At the time he took this photograph, Evans was working under the auspices of the Farm Security Administration as part of another federally sponsored art project. He was initially assigned to document rural poverty, but he later broadened his subject matter to include impoverished industrial regions of the United States. See Stuart Cohen, *The Likes of Us: America in the Eyes of the Farm Security Administration* (Boston: David R. Godine, 2009).
15. James R. Mellow, *Walker Evans* (New York: Basic Books, 1999), 276.
16. This work has been discussed by Helen Langa in *Radical Art: Printmaking and the Left in 1930s New York* (Berkeley: University of California Press, 2004), 117.
17. On the role of the Catholic Church in 1930s see Michael Denning, *The Cultural Front: The Laboring of American Culture in the Twentieth-Century* (New York: Verso, 1996).
18. James C. Moore, *Harry Sternberg: A Catalog Raisonné of his Graphic Work with Annotations by Harry Sternberg* (Wichita, KS: Edwin A Ulrich Museum of Art at Wichita State University, 1976).
19. Hoeckner has yet to find a scholarly champion, but a fine biographical sketch is provided by Patricia Smith Scanlon, "Carl Hoeckner," *Modernism*

in the New City: Chicago Artists, 1920–1950, http://www.chicagomodern.org/artists/carl_hoeckner/.
20. For important context on labor organizing and the 1930s, see Irving Bernstein, *The Turbulent Years: A History of the American Worker, 1933–1941* (reissued, Haymarket Books, 2010).
21. See Bruce Nelson, *Divided We Stand: American Workers and the Struggle for Black Equality* (Princeton, NJ: Princeton University Press, 2001).
22. *Rebel Voices: An IWW Anthology*, ed. Joyce L. Kornbluh, New and Expanded Edition (Chicago: Charles H. Kerr Publishing, 1988), 25.
23. Little Steel comprised approximately thirty different mills owned by firms including Bethlehem Steel, Youngtown Sheet and Tube, and Republic Steel, and located in towns from the inland valleys of the East to the Great Lakes region of the Midwest. For an authoritative source on this episode in labor history of the U.S.A., see Ahmed White, *The Last Great Strike: Little Steel, the CIO, and the Struggle for Labor Rights in New Deal America* (Berkeley: University of California Press, 2016).
24. A useful perspective on the events surrounding the strike is found in Michael Dennis, "Chicago and the Little Steel Strike," *Labor History* 53 (Spring 2012): 167–204.
25. The numbers are White, *The Last Great Strike*, 1, 2, 136.
26. "Riots Blamed on Red Chiefs," *Chicago Daily Tribune*, June 1, 1937: 1.
27. Carol Quirke, "Reframing Chicago's Memorial Day Massacre," *American Quarterly* 60, no. 1 (March 2008): 150.
28. Patricia Hills, "Philip Evergood's 'American Tragedy': The Poetics of Ugliness, the Politics of Anger," *Arts Magazine* 54 (February 1980): 138–42. The paintings is also analyzed by Kendall Taylor, *Philip Evergood: Never Separate from the Heart* (London: Associated University Presses, 1987), 172.
29. Hills, "Philip Evergood's 'American Tragedy,'" 140.
30. Ibid.
31. News photographs of the marchers show at least two carrying American flags. The flags are referenced by Quirke, "Reframing Chicago's Memorial Day Massacre," 132, 145, 146 and Michael Dennis, "Chicago and the Little Steel Strike," 178, 180.

Gregory Gilbert

Federal Art in the Midwest in the 1930s and the Meeting of Rural and Urban Cultures

A Challenge to Grant Wood's "Revolt Against the City"

In his 1935 essay "Revolt Against the City," Grant Wood articulated a prideful separatist ideology associated with the midwestern regionalist movement, promoting the distinctive social and cultural values of rural American life as worthy of artistic exploration.[1] Citing the isolationist policies of the United States in the 1920s and 1930s, Wood called for the nation's regional centers, in particular the Midwest, to renounce reliance on urban, eastern culture and establish their independent social and artistic character. The federal Public Works of Art Project (PWAP) had been established in 1934 to provide work relief to artists and other creative individuals enduring the economic hardship of the Depression. In his essay, Wood pointed to the PWAP as a regionalist ally, holding the promise for creating regional artistic centers that would encourage the localized art production he envisioned for a flourishing regionalist art movement.

Despite the PWAP's and the later WPA Federal Art Project's endorsement of the American Scene, with its emphasis on distinctive regional locality, the New Deal government of the 1930s developed economic policies and artistic programs that actually ran counter to the autonomous regionalism of Wood's revolt. Interrelated themes of farming and urbanized industry in federal art served the centrist ideological motives of the New Deal to encourage a sense of nationalistic unity through a joining of urban and rural cultures, stressing the interdependence of differing regional economies as crucial to national progress during the Depression. Indeed, many of the New Deal's agricultural and relief programs resulted in the increased dominance of the homogenizing economic and cultural forces the regionalists had hoped to hinder with their vision of geographic pluralism and indigenous folkways.

Owing to the populist mission of the federal art programs in the 1930s, New Deal art aimed to be accessible to a mass public by emphasizing quotidian localized subjects associated with the trend of the American Scene. As a result, art historical studies tend to align the thematic and ideological strains of federal art of the 1930s with the regionalist ethos. Moreover, in charting the development of modern art in the United States from the 1930s through the 1940s, art historians often focus on a developmental paradigm in which the cultural insularity of regionalist art is supplanted by the cosmopolitan internationalism of abstract expressionism. However, these art historical views tend to overlook the role of the New Deal in redefining the nationalistic and modernist character of American art away from particular regionalist values, most importantly the regionalist movement's resistance to forms of political and cultural hegemony and economic centralization, which became associated with many of the reformist policies of the New Deal.

Because Wood's regionalist manifesto "Revolt Against the City" was most likely written with the regionalist advocate Frank Luther Mott, scholars such as Tripp Evans have argued the essay bears little relation to Wood's own regionalist sentiments, which were less polemical and separatist.[2] However, as Wanda Corn and James Dennis have pointed out, the essay's call for liberating regional provinces from the controlling elitist influence of eastern, urban culture does reflect committed regionalist beliefs Wood voiced in interviews and lectures beginning in the early 1930s.[3] Examples of Wood's own art also serve as visual testimony to particular regionalist ideologies voiced in the written polemics of the essay. Moreover, Wood's emphasis on the PWAP as potentially serving to promote regionalist cultural values and aesthetics may have been encouraged by his close association with Edward Rowan. In 1928, Rowan founded the Little Gallery in Cedar Rapids, Iowa, to exhibit and support the work of aspiring local artists. In the summer of 1932 and 1933, Rowan, Wood, and Adrian Dornbush (an art teacher at the Little Gallery) established and operated the Stone City Art Colony in rural eastern Iowa. The colony was envisioned as a communal residency for artists devoted to studying midwestern subjects and locales and served to solidify Wood's commitment to a burgeoning regionalist art movement. In 1934, Rowan was hired to do administrative work for the PWAP in Washington, D.C., and afterward helped to run the Treasury Section of Fine Arts until its dissolution in 1943. From his earliest affiliation with New Deal art programs, Rowan called upon artists to extol the virtues of the American Scene and used his position to foster greater advocacy of regional expression in public art.[4]

Wood's essay seizes on the terms of provincialism and decolonization in describing a midwestern revolt, which links his rhetoric to a longstanding history of confrontation between the region and the East. In the late eighteenth century, the Midwest began as the Old Northwest region, the first territorial colony in North America, whose development was part of a process of national expansion administered by governmental and economic powers in the East. As early as 1828 and continuing through the Populist Revolt of the 1890s, Old Northwesterners began to resist what they saw as the colonizing assimilation and marginalizing of their region by a metropolitan and industrial, eastern culture.[5] Despite its historical roots, Wood's call for a regionalist revolt of the provinces was more closely allied with the "New Regionalist" literary and academic movement of the 1920s and the 1930s, which encompassed the writings of the Southern Agrarians, but geographically closer to Wood were midwestern authors like E.W. Howe, Hamlin Garland, and the folklorist B.A. Botkin. Wood's essay echoes sentiments by prominent agrarian theorists like Ralph Borsodi, whose 1933 book *Flight from the City* touted elemental rural life as an antidote to industrial modernity and urban culture.[6] Wood had also been surrounded by writers on the local Iowa scene, like Herbert Quick and Ruth Suckow, who lamented the passage of pioneer culture in their works, most notably in Quick's *One Man's Life* (1925) and Suckow's *The Folks* (1934). This midwestern literary trend constituted a regional renaissance devoted to maintaining localized difference against the cultural and socio-economic standardization associated with modernization in the industrialized East.[7] Although writers like Garland, Quick, and Suckow critically examined the changing realities of post-frontier life in the Midwest and the region's ambivalence towards modernity, they rejected the satirical and somewhat scornful tone of an earlier generation of expatriate midwestern authors like Sherwood Anderson and Sinclair Lewis. In keeping with the regionalist writers of the thirties, Wood sought to develop a more affirmative, prideful image of the Midwest that challenged the elitist judgements of eastern critics like H.L. Mencken, who deemed the Midwest as overly provincial and lacking a worthy regional culture.

Due to the PWAP's endorsement of the American Scene, Wood viewed federal art programs as aligned with regionalist agendas to promote the distinctive cultural values and folk traditions of localized communities. For Wood, this was perceived as a regionalist current within the New Deal to support a cultural and artistic vision of rural autonomy and sectionalism. However, numerous examples of federal art in the Midwest were later created depicting the interconnection of urban industrial and rural economies. In contrast to Wood's idealized conception of early federal art as devoted to geographic and cultural pluralism, this thematic tendency reflected the reality of New Deal ideologies based on policies of political consensus and socio-economic centralization.

With the economic hardship of the Depression, the inauguration of the New Deal in 1933 not only led to the establishing of federal work relief programs like the Civil Works Administration and the later Works Progress Administration, but also a concerted attack on the problems of rural America. The New Deal government established a host of programs in the 1930s aimed at alleviating farm poverty, modernizing farming regions, and restoring the viability of rural living. Many New Deal policy-makers believed farmers' low rural living standards helped trigger the financial crisis of the Depression and aimed for national economic recovery by restoring farmers' purchasing power to maintain employment for urban industrial workers. Initial efforts to bolster farm commodity prices and income came through the Agricultural Adjustment Act and the expansion of government credit programs. The USDA provided drought relief and subsidized farm exports. The Resettlement Administration (RA) and its successors, like the Farm Security Administration, engaged in large-scale rural development based on Roosevelt's belief in merging agriculture and industry to form what he called "rural industrial groups."[8] The Resettlement Administration was created in 1935 by the agricultural economist Rexford Tugwell, who was a member of a group of Columbia University academics in New York City that served as part of Roosevelt's "Brain Trust" during the New Deal era. Tugwell, who served as Undersecretary of the United States Department of Agriculture, was an outspoken critic of the agrarian "myth" of the virtuous small family farm and promoted a modern restructuring of agricultural production based on technocratic principles of rationalized scientific management and industrial liberalism.[9] Through the RA, destitute farming families were relocated from submarginal lands to subsistence homesteads in planned communities where income from farming was supplemented by industrial employment in rural factories.

During the 1930s, other New Deal programs also led to an increased merging of rural and urban cultures. The Civilian Works Administration funded numerous projects to not only build and repair roads in rural sectors, but also to improve the transportation infrastructure of rural regions that facilitated the shipping of produce from farms to urban commercial centers. It also allowed for the dispersal of industrial goods manufactured in new rural factories and expanded connections between rural and metropolitan economies, creating a regional fluidity that collapsed the kind of country-city binaries championed by Wood.[10] In conjunction with modern roadways, the automobile in the country not only provided freedom of movement but also became an emblem of geographic mobility and transformative social change for both individuals and regions. Established in 1935, the Rural Electrification Administration organized local electric cooperatives to expand electrical service to farming regions, which provided cheap power for farming operations and industrial customers in the country. In addition, it created opportunities for increased industrial production and factory jobs, spurring consumption of consumer goods. Electrification also allowed for the dissemination of modern urbanized mass media in rural areas, in particular radio broadcasts like Roosevelt's "fireside chats" and state-sponsored films. The New Deal government increasingly used such media as a tool for nation building, promoting unifying and centrist political ideals.[11] As John Gould Fletcher, an Imagist poet and a radical member of the Southern Agrarians, noted, "Modern inventions … do not exist separately from the metropolitan ideas which they bring with them … usually … utterly unregional … The moment a region swallows them, it becomes metropolitan in its mind."[12]

The modernizing and hegemonic urbanizing effects of industrial expansion on the rural Midwest represented a reversal of the aims of Wood's regionalist manifesto. In "Revolt Against the City," Wood invoked Frederick Jackson Turner's famous frontier thesis, asserting that the economic instability of the Depression stimulated a movement away from a dependence on what he called the "false prosperity" of urban capitalist centers towards the "old frontier virtues" of self-reliance in the form of traditional rural values, in particular self-supporting agricultural labor.[13] Turner's historical theories on the American frontier argued a form of democratic exceptionalism through pioneering settlement, in which individual initiative and expansionist growth was a revitalizing force liberating the United States from reliance on Europeanized eastern culture. It is important to note Wood's invocation of the frontier ethos coincided with debates in the 1930s on the closing of the American frontier, an anti-Turnerian idea that was featured prominently in the political discourse of the New Deal. Writing during the Depression, the historian Charles Beard argued in his 1931 article "The Myth of Rugged Individualism" that the philosophy of capitalist individualism needed to be modified in an age of economic crisis requiring a cooperative ethos.[14] Henry Steele Commager sounded a similar belief in an essay from 1933 titled "Farewell to Laissez-Faire," in which he observed that the old pioneers of the frontier were the natural ancestors of the businessmen of the post-frontier age.[15] However, in his endorsement of the early phase of the New Deal government, Commager argued the financial failures of laissez-faire capitalism made clear the need to support the economic reforms of Roosevelt's administration. The closed-frontier argument was even highlighted in the speeches and writings of Roosevelt and members of his New Deal administration, such as Tugwell in the Resettlement Administration, the agency responsible for planning rural industrial programs. In an article in 1936 for the *New York Times* Sunday magazine, Tugwell defended what he termed the political and economic experiments of the New Deal by proclaiming that an age of reckless individualistic expansion, which had created an unstable economic structure, had come crashing down and was now closed.[16] In the absence of economic opportunity provided by the open land of the frontier, the government would have to provide a new safety valve in times of economic distress through financial planning and regulation.

Administrators like Tugwell actually began to promote the New Deal programs as a "New Frontier" in which individual success could still be achieved, but within a community framework based on national federally regulated programs and the support of corporate capital.

Just two years after Wood's manifesto renouncing eastern industrial culture, *Life* magazine ran a pictorial titled "The Iowa Farm: A Corn and Hog Business Run by Machinery."[17] *Life*'s editors in the 1930s made a concerted effort to compose a new image of midwestern agriculture and its transformation into a modern business enterprise. As a result, the magazine helped to promote and popularize many of the goals of New Deal farm programs.[18] The 1937 pictorial featured an Iowa farmer named Charles Dewey Woodruff, who did not own the land he farmed but instead worked it under contract with a corporate land company. The magazine promoted the view of the farmer not as a traditional emblem of American economic and social independence, but as a skilled worker or manager beholden to a system of capitalist industrial production. The following year *Life* published an article on the government's Agricultural Adjustment Administration allotment policy. It championed the program's "modern remaking of rural identity" and stated "that by unifying the region's agricultural production into a single program of bureaucratic control, the administration had 'destroyed for good the outworn myth of the American farmer's sturdy independence.'"[19]

American Scene regionalism was endorsed by the federal art projects to visually promote the ideology of the "New Deal Frontier." The interrelated themes of prosperous farming life and industrial production served an edifying, inspirational function for Americans suffering the hardship of the Depression. While these images extolled dedicated collective forms of labor as essential to the nation's economic recovery, they were also intended to promote the liberality and unifying aims of New Deal policies, in particular Roosevelt's rural industrial programs. In their scholarship on New Deal art, Marlene Park and Gerald Markowitz have studied the thematic merging of farming and industry, which represented the experimental goals of the Resettlement Administration to rehabilitate and economically fortify rural regions by introducing industrialization and modernization in farming communities.[20] Federal artists themselves became indoctrinated to New Deal policies on the interdependence of rural and urban economies, as in 1939 when David B. Cheskin wrote to the Section of Fine Arts administrator Edward Rowan that "Today the farmer is not an isolated individualist. Modern transportation has drawn him close to the city ... Without the farmer (and) the modern means of transportation, the city could not exist. Without the manufactures of the city the modern farmer could not exist."[21]

Prominent examples of this theme are found in such WPA and Treasury Section murals as Paul Meltsner's *Ohio* (1937, Figure 1) and Mitchell Siporin's *The Fusion of Agriculture and Industry in Illinois* (1938). In Meltsner's mural, which hangs in the post office in Bellevue, Ohio, the cooperative labor and economic tie between farming and urban industry is signified through the pictorial melding of rural landscape and industrial architecture, as well as the rhythmic, diagonal linkage of field hands with factory workers. Siporin's murals were executed for the post office in Decatur, Illinois, and contain three separate narrative panels. Beginning with *Pioneer Family*, the artist intended his murals to depict the fortitude of the midwestern character and the virtuous history of frontier labor and expansion that culminated in the union of agricultural and industrial power in modern Illinois. In *Workers of Today* (Figure 2) figures ranging from a farming couple with a cornblower to industrious miners stand as laboring comrades, exchanging respectful glances in a productive communal landscape. In the panel *The Exchange of the Products of Agriculture for the Products of Industry* (Figure 3), farmers and factory workers trade goods in a show of social and economic solidarity. As Andrew Hemingway has explained, given Siporin's ties with the social

Figure 1. Paul Meltsner, *Ohio* (1937). U.S. Post Office, Bellevue, Ohio.

Figure 2. Mitchell Siporin, *Workers of Today*, from *The Fusion of Agriculture and Industry in Illinois* (1938). Fresco, 7 ft x 7 ft 6 in. U.S. Post Office, Decatur, Illinois.

Figure 3. Mitchell Siporin, *The Exchange of the Products of Agriculture for the Products of Industry*, from *The Fusion of Agriculture and Industry in Illinois* (1938). Fresco, 7 ft x 7 ft 6 in. U.S. Post Office, Decatur, Illinois.

realist movement and his alignment with left-wing politics, the farming and industrial figures exchange products in an ideal and mutualist relationship, free from an intermediary capitalist market.[22] In his 1936 essay "Mural Art and the Midwest," Siporin distanced his liberal brand of localized art from the regionalism of figures like Thomas Hart Benton, rejecting what he regarded as a "synthetic regionalist vernacular filled with jingoistic nationalism."[23] At the time of Siporin's murals, Decatur was a small industrial city in an agricultural region of the state with thriving manufacturing and coal-mining enterprises. However, during the Depression, there was extensive labor unrest and intra-class violence in Decatur with a series of militant strikes and protests by garment and mining workers against local industries that were opposed to industrial unionism. Siporin's mural clearly references the working-class concerns of the region with its images of the potentially progressive power of unified labor. While the federal art programs discouraged overt reference to labor unrest as well as artists' affiliation with left-wing political causes and radical labor organizations, Siporin's murals followed New Deal political and socio-economic agendas to encourage the mutual gains of agricultural and industrial unification and cooperative systems of labor.

Similar examples of federal murals that thematically aligned factory and farm are Jean Swiggett's 1940 *Local Industry* (Figure 4), done for the post office in Franklin, Indiana, and Herschel Levit's *Farm and Mill* (Figure 5), which dates from 1941 and was commissioned for the Louisville, Ohio, post office. On either side of Swiggett's mural stand illuminated iconic figures of a farmer and factory laborer, who lead a brethren of fellow workers. The equal representations symbolize the necessity of a balanced economy for future national stability, an idea that is further referenced in the background through an integrated layering of agricultural and industrial buildings rendered with a uniform precisionist clarity. In Levit's mural, jovial workmen and farmers seem to form a blissful laboring community, whose joint enterprise is suggested through the interchangeable form of their figures and the virile fusion of curving bodily elements within the scene.

As Park and Markowitz have observed, the idealized cooperative theme of the farm and factory in federal public art served the persuasive strategies of the New Deal to incorporate what would have been perceived as an intrusive and urbanized industrial modernization into rural regions.[24] In these works, government-sponsored forms of industrial labor and production coexist with American Scene portrayals of rural farming, catering to the regionalist ethos to honor the social values, traditions and occupational practices of the local community. This theme was a government formulation that served the ideological motive of rendering New Deal technocracy in the country (and by

Figure 4. Jean Swiggett, *Local Industry* (1940). U.S. Post Office, Franklin, Indiana.

Figure 5. Herschel Levit, *Farm and Mill* (1941). U.S. Post Office, Louisville, Ohio.

extension, its artistic philanthropy) as a congenial new neighbor. In their writings on New Deal art, Jared A. Fogel and Robert L. Stevens have labeled this thematic current "American Idealism," which they not only identify with the federal impulse to merge the rural and industrial, but also a conciliatory effort on the part of the art projects to build a creative coalition between the opposing factions of regionalists and social realists.[25] This reflects the larger ideological imperative of the New Deal to encourage political consensus among differing political, social and ethnic divisions within the United States. Federal programs aimed at constructing broad forms of national citizenship in which Americans were encouraged to view microcommunities of small towns as united with metropolitan urban sectors through shared socioeconomic needs.

Federal art functioned as a hegemonic discourse, promoting a democratic vision of shared concerns and cooperative citizenship as a means to rebuild the nation's resources through collective effort. This New Deal ideology of a nationalized unified identity is not only apparent in the theme of a rural and industrial brotherhood, but also more tacitly viewed in the iconography of the supportive family group included in the murals by Siporin and Swiggett. This archetype of the union of female and male also evokes the gender and cultural dialectic between nature and culture, which further naturalizes and promotes the New Deal's persuasive discourse on the crucial symbiotic relationship between the rural and industrial, the frontier and civilization. As with any ideological construct, the dilemma of the New Deal to endorse a nationalizing program of industrial modernization in the country involved contradictions it sought to resolve through an appeal to regionalist locality and its myths. Karal Ann Marling has commented more broadly on the contradictory aims of New Deal art, stating it "found itself in the anomalous position of directing a homogenizing, national Renaissance in an era of ardent (Regionalist) belief in sectional distinction that were both cultivated and challenged by New Deal programs."[26]

In addition to federal art, photography also played a crucial role within the visual culture of the New Deal to promote governmental policies of bringing modernizing industrial systems into rural regions. In his study of the impact of aerial vision on perceptions of the midwestern landscape, Jason Weems has argued that the defining purpose of the Farm Security Administration was to convince rural Americans of the agricultural benefits of modernization and industrialization.[27] This mission was supported through the persuasive visual rhetoric of documentary photographs by Roy Stryker and Arthur Rothstein, as well as the scopic technologies of aerial surveys conducted by the government. Rothstein's dynamic photographs of Iowa farmers harvesting corn in 1939 with powerful mechanized pickers and shelling equipment was a far cry from Wood's nostalgic regionalist images of traditional hand labor on the farm. These FSA photos focus on mechanized production as an efficient system that transforms crops into commodities dissociated from particular agricultural regions and local farming conditions.[28]

The aerial photographic data gained by the Department of Agriculture and Farm Service Agency in the 1930s was used to evaluate and improve farming practices, providing information on agricultural resources involving land management, crop determination, and soil conservation. These photographs present the rural midwestern landscape as a patterned grid of individual farmsteads, partly signifying the Jeffersonian ethos of independent small landowners. Yet, more importantly, the government's panoptic perspective imposed an abstracted, uniform view on the midwestern countryside, eradicating any sense of regional distinctions. As Weems observed,

> Bolstered by the sense of control and containment offered by aerial photographs, agricultural agents grew increasingly confident they could order the landscape through these images.… In proposing the landscape as a single unified *image*, the government claimed the power to extend regularized agricultural and cultural practices across the prairies.… replacing localized knowledge with a more centralized and technocratic vision of modern life.[29]

This photographic technology influenced New Deal policy-makers to envision the Midwest as operating under an integrated system of agricultural controls and open to the hegemonic expansion of modern commercial industry, roadways, and electric power.

Despite the intentions or the rhetoric of the New Deal towards rural rehabilitation and the preservation of regional farming life, federal agriculture programs largely contributed to what has been called a modern American "enclosure movement," which led to the disappearance of the traditional small farm.[30] While the Rural Electrification Administration enhanced living conditions in rural farming sectors, electric power ultimately improved the prospects for farming enterprises that operated efficiently on a large scale. Agricultural policy-makers realized that small, low-income farmers could not readily adapt to the industrialized and capitalistic methods of production favored by the New Deal and the increasing emphasis on large farm interests. Within rural regions, government relief agencies began to more actively promote policies of out-migration, industrialization, and urbanization, subsidizing the growth of rural industry but also relocating poor rural populations to urban centers, which provided opportunities for industrial employment. The progressive southern sociologist Howard Odum voiced the disappointment of many regionalist supporters on the social and economic outcome of the New Deal's rural industrial policies. Even by the mid-1930s Odum had observed that these federal programs had "resulted in a new and increased dominance of corporate business and centralized power over society, making a new era of concentration, bigness, monopoly, commercialized agriculture and large scale industry."[31]

In taking a broader view of federal art in the 1930s and its relation to the agricultural policies of the New Deal, it is important to return to Wood's essay and consider how his rhetorical revolt against the city was manifested in his own regionalist works. Wood's reference to the regionalist basis of New Deal art programs was influenced by his own appointment in 1934 as director of the Public Works of Art Project in Iowa. This led to the University of Iowa hiring Wood to use his position to organize public mural projects on campus, which were to be executed with the assistance of art students who received federal relief. When the PWAP ended in June of 1934, Wood was appointed for a three-year term as associate professor in the art department to continue with his plans for regionalist murals at the university. According to Corn, Wood envisioned the University of Iowa art department as becoming a model for regionalist art programs.[32] This goal was supported by a flowering of a regional arts movement at the university, particularly in the English department, which had a strong regionalist bent in the 1920s and 1930s.[33] During these years, the Iowa Writers Workshop was established and the regionalist little magazine the *Midland* was based at the university. Despite his initial support of early federal art programs to encourage distinctive regionalist cultural and artistic expression, it is possible to detect in Wood's own art a prescient critical response to the social effects of the New Deal on the rural provinces of the Midwest. Wood scholars, such as Corn and Dennis, have argued that Wood never overtly critiqued modern urban culture and industrial technology in his regionalist narratives. Rather, these forces were either censored completely in favor of pastoral visions of pre-industrial farming scenes or were dealt with in more humorous or oblique forms of disavowal.[34]

As early as 1931 in his painting *Appraisal* (Figure 6), Wood appears to critique the intrusion of the city into rural Iowa through the encounter of a farm woman with a city-dweller who has come to buy a fresh fowl. The painting functions as an anecdotal allegory of the challenge of modernity to rural life through a series of unfavorable contrasts, which includes the disparity between the country woman's humble dress and agrarian offering and the city woman's pampered fashionable appearance and air of privileged consumption.[35] *Dinner for Threshers* from 1934 (Figure 7), one of Wood's major regionalist works, has also been cited as reflecting his critical views of industrial modernization and its association with midwestern farming. Travis Nygard, in his study on agribusiness and its relation to Wood's art, has noted that large-scale

Figure 6. Grant Wood, *Appraisal* (1931). Oil on composition board, 29 ½ x 35 ¼ in. Dubuque Museum of Art, on long-term loan from the Carnegie-Stout Public Library.

Figure 7. Grant Wood, *Dinner for Threshers* (1934). Oil on hardboard, 20 × 81 1/16 in. Fine Arts Museums of San Francisco.

farming in the United States had its beginnings in the late nineteenth century but was greatly expanded by New Deal agricultural programs in the 1930s and the increasing alignment with corporate enterprises and industrial systems of production and distribution.[36] Nygard has argued that while scholars have traditionally viewed Wood's regionalist images as idealized nostalgic renditions of midwestern farming life, they actually represent the artist's strong critical response to the socio-economic realities of agribusiness and their effect on agricultural practices and rural communities.[37] These modern changes were particularly apparent in their impact on the mode of threshing. Traditionally, threshing was a form of cooperative labor in rural sectors, where neighboring farmers would support each other through communal harvests. With the rise of large-scale commercial farming in the early twentieth century, threshing was increasingly being carried out by hired migrant workers. With its depiction of a close-knit rural community of dining laborers, Wood's painting can be seen as a rejection of this modernizing trend, which threatened the traditional regional lifestyle of independent farmers in the Midwest.

While Wood resisted the influx of industrial farming in the Midwest, it is possible to discern subtle traces of modern technological forces in his idealized landscapes. A prime example is *Spring Turning* of 1936 (Figure 8), a panoramic agrarian landscape filled with undulating fertile hills. The scene suggests the kind of large-scale agriculture

Figure 8. Grant Wood, *Spring Turning* (1936). Oil on masonite panel, 24 ⅜ x 46 ¼ in. Reynolda House Museum of American Art.

supported by New Deal agencies in the 1930s and contains massive cultivated fields that would have been farmed with modern mechanized equipment. Yet, Wood only depicts tiny figures laboring with horse-drawn plows. The dramatic elevated perspective of *Spring Turning* and the precise geometry of its fields and roadways also indicate Wood's awareness of the government's use of aerial photography to regulate and restructure farming regions in the Midwest.[38] The artist, however, employed these signs of mechanized modernity to enhance his idyllic vision of human control over nature through traditional, pre-industrial farming practices. This approach follows Leo Marx's concept of "counterforce" in his ideological analysis of American landscape imagery in the nineteenth and early twentieth centuries, in which artists modified and partly disavowed the intrusion of industry into nature, resulting in a modernized pastoralism that served to perpetuate national myths of agrarian purity and the yeoman farmer.[39]

Appearing the same year as "Revolt Against the City," the most pointed example of the rural/urban dichotomy in Wood's oeuvre is *Death on the Ridge Road* (Figure 9) from 1935. In this work, Wood depicts in an almost cinematic fashion the tragic outcome of three vehicles on a narrow winding country road. A modern luxury limousine has sped past a rural Ford and is heading on a collision course with a red commercial truck heading towards it around a cresting turn. A further portent of the impending tragedy of the crash is a brewing storm in the distance and modern telephone poles forming funeral crosses that loom over the countryside. The rectilinear telephone poles clash with the soft organic forms of the rural landscape, which further symbolizes the destructive opposition of cultures. In keeping with his psycho-biographical analysis of Wood, Tripp Evans has interpreted the tragic theme and the cruciform telephone poles as reflecting Wood's own earlier traumas and anxieties of the period: the sudden death of his father and his feelings of being enlisted as an unwilling martyr to the regionalist cause.[40] However, in her social analysis of the work, Corn has more directly addressed the theme of conflict between country and city, as the commercial truck, limousine, and utility lines all signify the threatening intrusion of modernity and its impact on midwestern rural life.[41] However, these same points need to be addressed with another level of historical specificity, namely that the paved country road and telephone poles are all conspicuous signs of the

Figure 9. Grant Wood, *Death on the Ridge Road* (1935). Oil on masonite panel, 32 x 39 in. Williams College Museum of Art.

modernizing effects of the New Deal rural industrial programs. These programs brought the flow of commerce between country and city, the incorporation of electrified technologies, and the burgeoning rural industries that ultimately threatened the localized purity and isolationist sanctity of Wood's regional Midwest.

In one of Wood's major final works, *Spring in Town* (1941, Figure 10), he depicts an idyllic tranquil scene of a man spading the soil of a backyard garden plot by hand. Even as the regionalist movement began to wane, the artist's aversion to modern progress and change in the country is still present, as the smokestacks of a factory have been rendered in the far distance, a troubling, persistent reminder of the steady encroachment of industry and urban culture. Wood's scene of the pristine rural town garden is evocative of his nostalgic regionalist paintings of perfectly tilled farming fields, but it also reflects the increased merging of town and country resulting from the modernizing effects of New Deal programs. Despite Wood's initial faith in the early federal art programs to support the rural ethos of regionalism, the imagery of *Spring in Town* may have

Figure 10. Grant Wood, *Spring in Town* (1941). Oil on masonite panel, 26 x 24 ½ in. The Sheldon Swope Art Gallery.

reflected his awareness that many WPA murals actually promoted the unification of traditional midwestern farming life with modern industry. This painting is perhaps a final resigned statement of his revolt against the city, as the factory is merely a tiny, faint image that is barely discernible on the far edge of the prairie.

Acknowledgment
An earlier version of this essay was presented at the 2014 Grant Wood Symposium "Revolt Against the City: Midwestern Culture in Hard Times" at the University of Iowa.

Notes

1. Grant Wood, "Revolt Against the City," reprinted in *Grant Wood: A Study in American Art and Culture*, James M. Dennis (New York: The Viking Press, 1975). Wood's essay was independently published by Frank Luther Mott in 1935 in Iowa City, Iowa. It was the first of three works by regionalist writers as part of the "Whirling World Series" of the Clio Press.
2. R. Tripp Evans, *Grant Wood: A Life* (New York: Alfred A. Knopf, 2010), 232.
3. Wanda M. Corn, *Grant Wood: The Regionalist Vision* (New Haven: Yale University Press, 1983), 46; Dennis, *Grant Wood: A Study*, 105. Based on information provided by Nan Wood, the artist's sister, and Park Rinard, Wood's secretary-assistant, both Corn and Dennis have stated their views that "Revolt Against the City" was largely composed by Frank Luther Mott using statements taken from Wood's writings and lectures. See Corn, 153n85 and James M. Dennis, *Renegade Regionalists: The Modern Independence of Grant Wood, Thomas Hart Benton, and John Steuart Curry* (Madison: The University of Wisconsin Press, 1998), 255n13.
4. Sharon Ann Musher, *Democratic Art: The New Deal's Influence on American Culture* (Chicago: The University of Chicago Press, 2015), 80.
5. Edward Watts, *An American Colony: Regionalism and the Roots of Midwestern Culture* (Athens, Ohio: Ohio University Press, 2002), xvi.
6. Ralph Borsodi, *Flight from the City* (New York: Harper and Brothers, 1933).
7. For discussions of Wood's embrace of midwestern subject matter and the influence of regionalist writers, see Dennis, *Grant Wood: A Study*, 150–51; Corn, *Grant Wood: Regionalist Vision*, 26; Jason Weems, *Barnstorming the Prairies: How Aerial Vision Shaped the Midwest* (Minneapolis: University of Minnesota Press, 2015), 151.
8. For important studies discussing New Deal Agricultural programs, see Theodore Saloutos, *The American Farmer and the New Deal* (Ames: The Iowa State University Press, 1982); Jane Adams, ed., *Fighting for the Farm: Rural America Transformed* (Philadelphia: University of Pennsylvania Press, 2003), 129–59; Sarah T. Phillips, *This Land, This Nation: Conservation, Rural America, and the New Deal* (Cambridge, England: Cambridge University Press, 2007), 75–196.
9. Dennis Roth, Anne B.W. Effland, and Douglas E. Bowers, *Federal Rural Development Policy in the Twentieth Century* (Beltsville, Maryland: USDA, National Agricultural Library, Rural Information Center, 2002), 20.
10. For an interesting analysis of the merging of rural and urban regions in the United States during the early twentieth century, see Mark A. Robinson, "Transcending the Urban-Rural Divide: *Willa Cather's Thea Kronborg Goes to Chicago*," in *Regionalism and the Humanities*, ed. Timothy R. Mahoney and Wendy J. Katz (Lincoln: University of Nebraska Press, 2008), 190–210.
11. William Uricchio and Marja Roholl, "From New Deal Propaganda to National Vernacular: Pare Lorentz and the Construction of an American

Public Culture," in *Triumph der Bilder: Kultur- und Dokumentarfilme vor 1945 im internationalen Vergleich*, ed. Peter Zimmermann and Kay Hoffmann (Konstanz: UVK Verlagsges., 2003), 8.
12. Robert L. Dorman, *Revolt of the Provinces: The Regionalist Movement in America, 1920–1945* (Chapel Hill: The University of North Carolina Press, 1993), 287–88.
13. Wood, "Revolt Against the City," 231.
14. Charles A. Beard, "The Myth of the Rugged American Individual," *Harper's Magazine* (December 1931): 13–22.
15. Henry Steele Commager, "Farwell to Laissez-Faire," *Current History* 38 (August 1933): 513–20.
16. Rexford G. Tugwell, "No More Frontier," *Today* (22 June 1936): 3–4, 21. For historical and socio-cultural discussion of the "New Deal frontier," see David M. Wrobel, *The End of American Exceptionalism: Frontier Anxiety from the Old West to the New Deal* (Lawrence, Kansas: University Press of Kansas, 1993), 122–42.
17. "The Iowa Farm: A Corn and Hog Business Run by Machinery," *Life Magazine* (20 September 1937): 36–43.
18. Weems, *Barnstorming the Prairies*, 115.
19. "Life on the American Newsfront: Mr. Roosevelt's Farm Bill and Mr. Remsberg's Farm," *Life Magazine* (28 February, 1938): 15; Weems, *Barnstorming the Prairies*, 116.
20. Marlene Park and Gerald E. Markowitz, *Democratic Vistas: Post Offices and Public Art in the New Deal* (Philadelphia: Temple University Press, 1984), 54.
21. Qtd. in Barbara Melosh, *Engendering Culture: Manhood and Womanhood in New Deal Public Art and Theater* (Washington, D.C.: Smithsonian Institution Press, 1991), 64.
22. Andrew Hemingway, *Artists on the Left: American Artists and the Communist Movement 1926–1956* (New Haven: Yale University Press, 2002), 164.
23. Mitchell Siporin, "Mural Art and the Midwestern Myth," in *Art for the Millions*, ed. Francis V. O'Connor (Greenwich, Connecticut: New York Graphic Society, 1973), 64–67.
24. Park and Markowitz, *Democratic Vistas*, 55.
25. Jared A. Fogel and Robert L. Stevens, "The Canvas Mirror: Painting as Politics in the New Deal," *OAH Magazine of History* (Fall 2001): 22–24; "Conflict and Consensus: New Deal Mural Post Office Art," *The National Social Science Journal* 33, no. 2 (2010): 163.
26. Karal Ann Marling, *Wall-to-Wall America: A Cultural History of Post-Office Murals in the Great Depression* (Minneapolis: University of Minnesota Press, 1982), 68.
27. Weems, *Barnstorming the Prairies*, 100.
28. Ibid., 101.
29. Ibid., 84.

30. Roth, *Federal Rural Development Policy*, 12.
31. Howard Odum, "The Case for Regional-National Social Planning," *Social Forces* 13 (October 1934): 8.
32. Corn, *Grant Wood: Regionalist Vision*, 43.
33. Ibid., 44.
34. Ibid., 80; Dennis, *Grant Wood: A Study*, 216
35. Corn, *Grant Wood: Regionalist Vision*, 80.
36. Travis E. Nygard, "Grant Wood and the Visual Culture of Agribusiness," *Athanor* 27 (2009): 79.
37. Ibid.
38. Weems, *Barnstorming the Prairies*, 127.
39. Leo Marx, *The Machine in the Garden: Technology and the Pastoral Ideal in America* (Oxford, England: Oxford University Press, 1964), 25.
40. Evans, *Grant Wood: A Life*, 196
41. Corn, *Grant Wood: Regionalist Vision*, 82.

Dimitrios Latsis | MoMA's Wood

Regionalism and the
Midwest at the Heart of
the Modernist "Beast"

Margaret Scolari Barr (MB): The exhibition was opened by the President of the [French] Republic, I think, and various people. Then Mr. Goodyear had to give an official dinner, which he did—a luncheon in the Salon des Aigles of the Trianon for the same people.... And what did the French like? They liked, above all, the naive pictures and they liked that picture called American Gothic—help me—who is it by?
Paul Cummings (PC): Grant Wood.
MB: By Grant Wood, yes. That's what they liked.
PC: Really?
NB: Yes.
PC: That's fascinating.[1]

Margaret Scolari Barr, the wife of Museum of Modern Art (MoMA) director Alfred Barr, Jr., was still befuddled by the taste of the French when she gave this oral history interview to the Archives of American Art in 1974—thirty-six years after the exhibition of American art that MoMA had organized in Paris.[2] And with good reason: After all, MoMA was supposed to be the arbiter of American modernism, the institution that would bring American art into its own, and in whose circles regionalism (and to an extent the entire so-called "American Scene") were dismissed as "caricatures" or "nationalisms that involved violent propaganda against modern foreign art."[3] Barr's surprise (or feigned surprise) at Grant Wood's popularity in Europe, and her pretense at not knowing who painted one of the most famous American paintings are surely testament to the broader disconnect that scholars like Wanda

Corn and Erika Doss have diagnosed between the representational art of a national character that proliferated during the New Deal and the onset of modern abstraction after World War II. For it was the latter—as promoted by MoMA, the Guggenheim and other institutions and collectors—that became the "license" for New York to "steal the idea of modern art" from Paris.[4]

The clear-cut distinction between pre-war and post-war American art that has tended to anoint abstraction as the real representative of modernism on American soil has been repeatedly challenged by scholars who have recovered an earlier avant-garde during the interwar period and have further connected Pollock and his confrères to earlier stylistic movements like regionalism. What is still far from complete, however, is a revisionist assessment of modernism during the 1920s and 1930s that would uncover how close regionalist sensibilities were perceived to be at the time to notions of "modern art," and how museums and galleries that supposedly denounced anything that reeked of provincialism in American art actually came to champion the chief representatives of regionalist art, especially during the years of the New Deal. Looking for "MoMA's Wood" can help us reevaluate not just the museum's institutional history and that of the American Scene as a movement; it can also inform our conception of what a critical and interdisciplinary regionalism can and should be today. It will lastly go a long way toward mending the major intra-disciplinary cleavage in American art history between so-called Americanists (by whom regionalism has traditionally been studied) and modernists.[5]

The Museum and the State: Regionalism as a State Aesthetic

During the 1930s, the Museum of Modern Art acquired, loaned, and exhibited a variety of works produced under the auspices of government art programs like the Federal Art Program (FAP) and the Section of Painting and Sculpture of the Department of the Treasury. Indeed, its policy regarding American art encouraged acquisition of works by "younger and less known men, from all over the country rather than from New York and works that *seem American* rather than that which shows obvious European influence."[6] In 1936 it staged *New Horizons in American Art*, a major exhibition of work by artists in the Works Progress

Administration programs, many of them from the Midwest. All the while, it pioneered the display of folk arts and crafts with funding and encouragement from the Rockefeller family.

It should be noted that Holger Cahill, MoMA's director from 1932 to 1933, would later become the federal government's "art czar" within the WPA, while his wife, Dorothy Miller, was one of the first curators hired at MoMA. There is thus a complex web of intertwined curatorial and political decisions that demonstrate the government's involvement in crafting an officially sanctioned national aesthetic in art that even private institutions came to embrace—especially when it came to the promotion of American art overseas. Such was the case in the 1938 exhibition in Paris, *Three Centuries of American Art,* organized by MoMA with the collaboration of the federal government (Figure 1). This "official aesthetic" favored works of a resolutely representational style that would be straightforwardly understandable to citizens and allies and that aligned itself with New Deal social politics. MoMA and

Figure 1. Advertisement for *Three Centuries of American Art*, 1938 exhibition in Paris.

other cultural institutions of national prominence inevitably had to toe this line. This is borne out by the fact that the museum felt compelled to defend itself against accusations that "[it] was concerning itself overmuch with the art of foreigners." In 1940, for instance, it published a retrospective consideration and overview of its contributions toward greater visibility for American artists during the past decade in an article entitled "American Art and the Museum."[7]

Within this context, regionalism had a prominent position as a representative of "what is most American about American art." Grant Wood, Thomas Hart Benton, and John Steuart Curry (Figure 2), along with many other artists representing the "heartland," were featured in no less than seven of the museum's exhibitions during the 1930s. Benton's and Wood's works were even highlighted in the show that opened MoMA's new building in 1939, under the banner of *Art in Our Time*. Individual paintings and drawings of theirs were further selected for shows that dealt with modern art more broadly. Thus, for example, Benton's *Homestead* (1934) and Wood's *Daughters of the Revolution* (1932) were hung close to works by Picasso, Cézanne, and De Chirico for *Modern Works of Art* (organized in 1935) and their prints next to those of Toulouse-Lautrec and Matisse for *Modern Painters and Sculptors as Illustrators* (1938).[8]

Figure 2. Grant Wood and Thomas Hart Benton. *The Des Moines Register* (January 20, 1935).

(De-)Centralization:
Geographic Representation in 1930s Exhibitions

There is an irony, to be sure, in the pride of place accorded to regionalism in the heart of the "beast" of modernism in the nation's artistic capital. In his manifesto *Revolt Against the City,* originally published in 1935, Grant Wood had argued for "a widely diffused art among our whole people, ... a growth of non-urban and regional activity in the arts and letters," of "a varied, rich land, abounding in painting material."[9] At the same time, however, his paintings were feted in New York and Paris and his *American Gothic* (1930) had already been snapped up by the Art Institute of Chicago. One can only imagine how Wood would have felt when, for the show *Painting and Sculpture from 16 American Cities* (1933), his work was lumped in under the section dedicated to artists from Chicago instead of the more accurate geographic label of Iowa.

Nevertheless, the very fact that entire exhibitions were designed with geographic representation in mind testifies to how powerful the geographical impulse was as an organizing category in art at this time. In the press materials and exhibition catalogs of the time, the names of the regionalists (and of other American painters not directly allied with the movement) would often appear next to their native places. So, for the 1937 preparatory exhibition of "living artists" invited to submit work for the Paris exhibit of the following year, beside the profusion of names under New York City, one also finds entries for Iowa City, Kansas City, and Madison. The curators stressed that it was their goal to represent "all parts of the United States," as opposed to the East Coast–concentrated modernist schools.[10] In Paris, too, the regionalist trio's work was presented as the culmination of a progression of American art that stretched from the Hudson River School's landscapes to Depression-era representations of the American land and people. Almost all the four regionalists' works chosen were landscapes, including Wood's *Study for Dinner for Threshers* (1934). These were supplemented by works like Charles Sheeler's *American Landscape* (1930), William Groper's *Dustland* (1937), and Edward Hopper's *East Wind over Weehawken* (1934). Among the very few contemporary paintings the French actually chose to acquire for the Musée de Luxembourg after the exhibition was Alexander Hogue's *Drought Survivors* (1936), which depicted the ravages of the Dust Bowl on the land in a decidedly regionalist style.

The discourse accompanying regionalism was not always celebratory. On the one hand, Holger Cahill, who coedited MoMA's survey *Art in America* with Alfred Barr, noted with enthusiasm "the growth of regional art groups devoted to exploring various local aspects of their land," and proceeded to list a long catalog of artists' names arranged by place—a veritable decentralized, rhizomatic atlas of contemporary art in America. (Wood is placed in Cedar Rapids as the "recorder of the scene of the Middle-West, the rolling hills, the farms, the toil-hardened people.")[11] On the other hand, MoMA's senior curator of painting and principal instigator of the 1938 Paris show, A. Conger Goodyear, would not shy away from delivering backhanded compliments: "Since 1930 there has been a swelling of a self-conscious but vigorous nationalistic feeling that has made painting of the American scene abundant to the point of excess.... [T]hanks to obvious sentiment, familiar subject matter and intensive (though mostly unsolicited) publicity the painters of the American Scene have achieved an extraordinary popularity."[12]

It is, of course, true that the regionalists did not shy away from preemptively crafting their own image as overall-sporting country bumpkins (much like Paul Cézanne before them), with their finger on the pulse of middle America.[13] Nor were they naïve to the fact that their art mainly catered to an upper-class, mostly urbane, East Coast audience. The truth, as we now know, is that all three of them were highly educated, having trained in Europe and gone through a considerable evolution in their styles, before becoming practitioners of what they presented as a "democratic art" that common people can embrace and understand. In spite of that, their ubiquity in the New York centers of modernism during the 1930s remains an under-acknowledged aspect of their careers.

In addition to temporary exhibitions, Benton, Wood, and Curry were all represented in the founding collection of the Whitney Museum of American Art, and Benton delivered one of MoMA's inaugural lectures, entitled "Art and the Common Man," in 1932. He was also featured in the museum's first exhibit, *American Painting and Sculpture: 1862–1932*, the second-best attended exhibition of MoMA's first decade, drawing over 100,000 visitors.[14] Moreover, the regionalists were present at every biennial and exhibition that the Whitney organized in the 1930s and

1940s, and their paintings, watercolors, and drawings were acquired for the museum's permanent collection, where most of them remain to the present day.

The extent of this visibility and even celebration of regionalist work as "American modernism" becomes evident if one considers the wider image of regionalism in the press, in popular culture, and in other media, like film. In particular, two documentaries made in the early 1940s and 1950s give a sense of the primacy given to artists like Benton and Wood as representatives of a "national school" in art.

American Art and Cinema: On-screen Representations of Regionalism

Meant as a piece of propaganda to be screened primarily for foreign audiences, the government-produced *Art Discovers America* (1943) was part of a series that "portrayed the artistic, musical and literary background of the United States, the talents of its people, further counteracting Axis propagandists who characterize us as a nation of businessmen and industrialists."[15] Emerging from the Great Depression, re-energized by the ascendant nationalist spirit of the (pre-)war years and purged of a suspect "internationalism," American art was ready to conquer the world on its own terms. The second documentary, the omnibus film *Pictura: An Adventure in Art* (1951), adopted a comparative structure that implicitly argued for the international stature of American art, with its predominant style being the representational work of regionalist artists. Grant Wood was here given a place next to Leonardo Da Vinci and Paul Gauguin.[16]

The American-ness of native-born art is traced in the first film's references to the improved social status of artists (their works no longer sold "for a few dollars, another meager meal" as the evocative voiceover puts it) and the shift away from "alien modernisms" ("no longer dreaming wistfully of Paris and the Left Bank") toward "subjects which Americans understood in life." As a suitable spokesperson of this latter tendency, *Art Discovers America* presents the dean of the American Scene movement, Thomas Hart Benton (Figure 3). He is shown on one of his walks in search of subject matter outdoors, painting *en plein air* or modeling his scenes in plaster before "transferring" them to a two-dimensional canvas,

Figure 3. Thomas Hart Benton. *Art Discovers America* (1943).

a technique that the narrator praises for its fidelity to rural life: "typically Benton and unmistakably American."

Other artists represented as "quintessentially" American range from Joan Sloan (as a representative of "The Eight") to Reginald Marsh, to American modernists like Abraham Walkowitz, Charles Burchfield, Eugene Speicher, Max Weber, and Alexander Brook, and finally to Grant Wood. The narrator finds a way to rhetorically redeem the "native modernists" as distinct from European models ("they are painting New York cityscapes," or portraits of "typical American figures like a farmer's wife"), but there is no mistaking where his preferences lie; when *American Gothic* (1930) comes on screen, he heralds Wood as "among America's best." The artists of the time, the voiceover continues, have "an enthusiasm for everyday American life," which he proclaims to be "the subject matter of a *true* national art."[17]

Moreover, as *Art Discovers America* repeatedly emphasizes, American art had become big business: "it can be sold, it *is* sold." The film thus directly links the narrator's assertion about "a *true* national art" with what sells and what the public is interested in—the press and museum exhibitions (Figure 4) are singled out as popularizing agents alongside cinema. It was this kind of national artistic production, in the final analysis, that would realize "American's destiny in this war-torn world: to assume cultural and spiritual leadership to the end that the pursuit of beauty shall not die." This Lincolnesque adage is spoken over a sunset that elegiacally brings the film to a close.

On the other hand, *Pictura: An Adventure in Art* represented a new concept in documentary feature films, consisting of six episodes based on the lives and works of Hieronymus Bosch, Vittore Carpaccio, Paul Gauguin, Francisco Goya, Henri de Toulouse-Lautrec, and Grant Wood, with well-known actors like Vincent Price, Gregory Peck, Henry Fonda (who narrated the segment on Grant Wood), and Lilli Palmer providing narration.[18] The film attempted to contextualize these individual segments within the larger narrative of the "story of art" and the place of American art (especially midwestern regionalism as represented by Grant Wood) within it. This was symptomatic of the boosterish rhetoric of the New Deal whose influence was still actively felt in the public discourse of the 1950s—especially concerning cultural

Figure 4. Museum exhibition. *Art Discovers America* (1943).

matters. As historians of American art have demonstrated, during the first few decades of the twentieth century, American art and culture went through an intensive period of self-questioning in search of "the Great American thing"—a native-grown version of modernism that would be free of European influence and represent the social and historical makeup of American society.

To achieve this goal, representational art dealing with national or historical themes and landscapes was particularly encouraged by the government's Federal Art Project, and regionalist artists like Benton and Wood became very prominent in this effort during the 1930s and 1940s. From Bosch to Van Gogh to Gauguin, and finally to Grant Wood, the documentary implies that the U.S. had come into its own in the cultural arena, its painters forming a legitimate link in a long cultural chain. Instead of dwelling on the formal or technical characteristics of the paintings, the film emphasizes their narrative and historical aspects, and thus it is only natural that the familiar midwestern scenery and genre paintings of American "types" and folklore as depicted by Grant Wood are placed at the conclusion of this trajectory (Figure 5).

This last segment was the only one produced especially for *Pictura*, in addition to being one of the earliest "monographic" films dedicated to the work of an American artist.[19] It presents a multi-strand story involving Wood's own life as well as the stories behind several of Wood's most famous paintings, including *John B. Turner, Pioneer* (1929), a portrait of a midwestern undertaker; *Woman with Plants* (1929), a study of his mother; and the famous *American Gothic*, in which his sister and his dentist were the models for corn farmers. Using an Aaron Copland–inflected score and with Henry Fonda's stentorian voiceover repeatedly referring to Wood as a "quintessentially American artist," the film features a multitude of symbols and imagery connected to the idea of the region and the nation: maps depicting the "Middle-West" (Figure 6), the rolling hills of Iowa in Wood's paintings, his humorous portrait of the cherry tree episode from George Washington's life, and his other "masterpieces of Americana." Wood finally comes across as a gentle, self-taught "man of the people."[20] He is quoted at the conclusion, which also serves as the end of *Pictura*, in a remark that summarizes the overall film's intentions and place in history: "I had in mind something which I hope to convey to a fairly wide audience in America—the picture of a

Figure 5. Still from *Pictura: An Adventure in Art* (1951), featuring the work of Grant Wood.

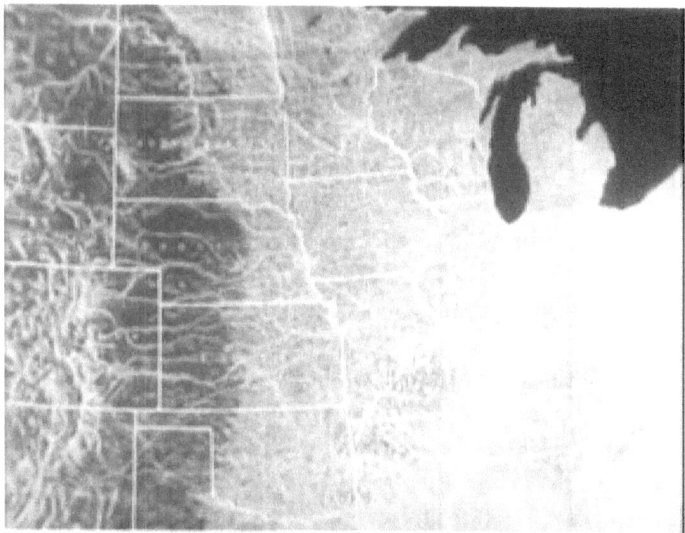

Figure 6. Map depicting the "Middle-West." *Pictura: An Adventure in Art* (1951).

country rich in the arts of peace, homely, lovable, and infinitely worth any sacrifice."[21] This implies that the place of American modernism at the outset of the Cold War would be as the guardian of Western values and as a democratic (and even populist) counterbalance to European modernist propaganda.

Afterlives and Legacy

The regionalists retained a presence in modern art in the immediate aftermath of World War II (and Wood's and Curry's deaths), disproving the myth of their complete disappearance from museums' radars from 1945 until the 1980s.[22] *American Gothic,* the picture by Grant Wood, whose name Margaret Barr could not recall, was exhibited at MoMA for the first and only time in the *Twentieth Century Portraits* exhibition, just months after his death in 1942. In 1953, *Daughters of the Revolution* by the "late American painter Grant Wood" was included among paintings by French masters in the show of the Edward G. Robinson collection.[23] The American Scene had a showing in 1961 with *America Seen: Between the Wars* where "the bumptious regionalism of Benton" was front and center, while Wood's and Benton's prints were regularly included in other shows throughout the 1940s, 1950s, 1970s, and 1990s.[24] They were last seen at the Whitney in exhibitions in 2011 (*Breaking Ground: The Whitney's Founding Collection*) and 2012 (*American Legends: From Calder to O'Keeffe*), and they were included in MoMA's 2013 show *American Modern: Hopper to O'Keeffe.*[25]

It is true that 1938 marked a certain terminus for the place of "land" and "region" as central concerns of representational American art, as well as for regionalism as a prominent stylistic tendency. The Paris exhibition was the first and for a long time would remain the last opportunity to "promote the terms of an artistic Americanism" in an international forum.[26] It also marked the last gasp of the New Deal art programs that were run into the ground by congress shortly thereafter, with the FAP being progressively defunded in 1941. The American Scene movement for a national art "with roots sinking deeper and deeper, day by day, into the soil" had "declined" irrevocably as E.A. Jewell noted in 1939, with the somewhat reductive realization that "just painting farmyard silos or urban skyscrapers or native 'types' will not suffice to bring an artist into his patrimony."[27] Benton later remembered that "as soon as World War II began, substituting in the public mind a world concern for the specifically American concerns which had prevailed during our rise, Wood, Curry and I found the bottom knocked out from under us."[28] From that point forward, artistic representations of the nation would be largely understood as government propaganda of a highly codified and controlled variety. Private initiative, on the other hand, flourished, and MoMA inaugurated its new building in 1939 and contributed considerably to the fine arts section of the World's Fair hosted by New York that year. Grant Wood and Thomas Hart Benton gradually gave way to Norman Rockwell, and soon to Jackson Pollock, both in public consciousness and in curatorial priorities.

Nevertheless, the regionalists never ceased to cause controversy at MoMA—an institution that seemed accepting of their paintings if not their ideology. In 1946, the tides at the museum had already turned, and the show *Fourteen Americans* had not a single figure in common with its 1937 predecessor *Forty Leading American Artists*. The 1946 catalog pointedly remarked that

> [for the fourteen artists selected] the idiom is American but there is no hint of regionalism or chauvinistic tendency. On the contrary, there is a profound consciousness that the world of art is one world and that it contains the Orient no less than Europe and the Americas.[29]

One could well ask if the "local" had been substituted by the "continental" or the "global" in modern art's definition of region and scale.[30]

Seven years later, in 1953, the museum felt compelled to reply to an editorial by forty-four artists in the inaugural issue of *Reality* magazine that denounced "the fast spreading doctrine of non-objectivism."[31] While the museum admitted that in the previous summer's *Fifteen Americans*, there had been "more abstract painters than realists or expressionists," it provided the following rationale:

> In previous decades [the museum] paid heed to the various realistic and romantic tendencies which throve in that period under the names of "regionalism," "social consciousness,"

"neo-romanticism," "surrealism," "American Scene," etcetera. Time moves on and art changes but neither then nor now, as a matter of policy, has the Museum tried to guide or influence artists or favor one direction more than another.[32]

The institution that prided itself on its cardinal role in shaping modern art in America now presented itself as a mere "mirror," while seemingly abrogating its former championing of representational art as if it was now a taint on its reputation. Was regionalism destined to become the butt of a perpetual art historical joke? Had modern art simply outgrown this primitive "representationalism"?

Art and Nation: The Midwest as "Cradle" of Americanism

That the United States expounded its regionalist ideals in the 1938 exhibition in Paris or that MoMA participated in this celebration of Middle America for a brief but important phase of its early history implies a specific definition of the "nation" and its place in art that cannot be divorced from political and ideological considerations, nor from its cognate scales: the regional/local and the global/international. "If America is to become a homogenous cultural unit," noted a progress report of the Federal Art Project in 1938,

> an equal distribution of cultural advantage must be made possible. Not the large metropolitan centers but the underprivileged small towns and cities throughout America must be given the opportunity to share and participate in a well-rounded program: to learn what elements of their own culture are worth preserving and how they can best be replenished and extended.... A firm foundation is being laid for future generations of Americans who will no longer look upon art as something remote from their daily lives but an essential element of survival.[33]

The question, of course, is who would get to define those elements worth preserving as part of the national character. A crucial factor in the establishment of artistic norms and styles is surely public reception, thus retroactively confirming Alfred Barr's estimations that, the New York connoisseurs' tastes notwithstanding, it was after all the "American public" and its enthusiasm for the portrayals of its land that would have the final say as to what counts as "idiosyncratically" American.[34]

In our own day, when the contestation over land, the environment, and their representation is as apt a summary of the state of our polity as any, the link between geography and the politics of representation is more relevant than ever. Artists and scholars, including the contributors to this volume and the series of books to which it belongs, are increasingly taking part in a powerful revival of regionalism and regional studies.[35] Although they cannot be called radical in their politics, the regionalist artists of the interwar years in America were, nonetheless, radical in their ideological reassessment of the role of region in art. They participated in a crucial reckoning with the aesthetics and politics of region, and the Midwest was often at the epicenter of these debates. While their work has too often been dismissed as quaint tokens of Americana or nostalgic portrayals of a land ethos that was rapidly disappearing, they provided implicit critiques of received notions of regionalism-qua-conservatism. These words from Grant Wood's *Revolt Against the City*, written as many years after the economic collapse of 1929 as we are today after the financial crisis of 2008, perfectly echo this spirit:

> Your true regionalist is not a mere eulogist: he may even be a severe critic. I believe in the regional movement in Arts and Letters ... but I wish to place no narrow interpretation on such regionalism. There is, or at least there need be, no geography of the art mind or of artistic talent or appreciation. But for the arts, not until the break-up caused by the Great Depression has there really been an opportunity to demonstrate the artistic potentialities of what some of our Eastern city friends call "the provinces."[36]

Notes

1. Margaret Scolari Barr, oral history interview with Paul Cummings concerning Alfred H. Barr, 1974 Feb. 22–May 13, Archives of American Art, Smithsonian Institution..
2. For the catalogue see Musée du Jeu de Paume, *Trois siècles d'art aux États-Unis; exposition organisée en collaboration avec le Museum of Modern Art,*

New-York. Musée du jeu de paume. Paris, mai-juillet, 1938 (Paris: Éditions des musées nationaux, 1938).
3. Alfred Barr, Jr., "Painting and Sculpture in the United States," in Musée du Jeu de Paume, *Trois siècles d'art aux États-Unis*, 30.
4. Wanda Corn, *The Great American Thing, Modern Art and National Identity, 1915–1935* (Berkeley: University of California Press, 2000); Erika Doss, *Benton, Pollock, and the Politics of Modernism: From Regionalism to Abstract Expressionism* (Chicago: University of Chicago Press, 1995); Serge Guilbaut, *How New York Stole the Idea of Modern Art: Abstract Expressionism, Freedom and the Cold War* (Chicago, University of Chicago Press, 1985).
5. For more on this cleavage see Jason Weems and Joshua Shannon, "A Conversation Missed: Towards an Historical Understanding of the Americanist Modernist Divide," in *A Companion to American Art*, ed. John Davis, Jennifer Greenhill, and Jason Lafountain (New York: Blackwell Press, 2015), 17–33. For a recent attempt to reconsider this divide see the exhibition catalogue *New Forms: The Avant-Garde Meets the American Scene, 1934–1949*, ed. Kathleen A. Edwards (Iowa City, Iowa: University of Iowa Museum of Art, 2013), especially the contribution by Erika Doss. Regarding the current debate on "anti-modernism," alternative modernism(s) and early-twentieth-century American art, see also Pierre Sérié, "New York troisième Rome: pourquoi l'Amérique résista si longtemps à l'idée d'art modern," *Revue de l'Art*, No. 191/2016-1 (2016): 71–80; James M. Dennis has discussed the regionalists' place within American modernism in *Renegade Regionalists: The Modern Independence of Grant Wood, Thomas Hart Benton, and John Steuart Curry* (Madison: The University of Wisconsin Press, 1998).
6. A. Conger Goodyear, *The Museum of Modern Art: The First Ten Years* (New York: Private Publication, 1943), 86 (emphasis added).
7. "American Art and the Museum," *The Bulletin of the Museum of Modern Art* 8, no. 1 (Nov., 1940): 3–26. The author was nonetheless quick to note that MoMA's pro-American art efforts were "in diametric opposition to the hysterically intolerant nationalism which has swept over half of Europe destroying the freedom of art along with the freedom of speech and religion."
8. Although not used pejoratively in this case, the work of the regionalists was often (and still is) characterized as mere "illustrations" by modernist critics. Emphasizing its popular themes and representational character distinguishes it, somewhat unfavorably, from the work of other modernists. For instance, see Robert Storr, *Modern Art Despite Modernism* (New York: The Museum of Modern Art, 2002), 72: "Like Benton—or, for that matter, Rivera—[John Steuart Curry] was more of an illustrator than anything else." This bias against the "illustrative" or intensely realistic style of the regionalists persisted at MoMA; a press release for the 1975 exhibition *American Prints: 1913–1963* recalls that "in the 1930s the abstractions of

Stuart Davis contrasted with the Social Realism of Grant Wood, Reginald Marsh and Thomas Hart Benton and his student Jackson Pollock." MoMA press release no. 118, December 5, 1974.
9. Grant Wood, *Revolt Against the City* (Iowa City, IA: Clio Press, 1935) (originally published as a pamphlet).
10. MoMA press release no. 38418-17, April 20, 1938. Benton's *Romance* (1934), Curry's *The Gospel Train* (1924), and Wood's *Study for "Dinner for Threshers"* (1934) were included in that preparatory exhibition. In the final show in Paris, Benton was represented by two paintings, *Homestead* (1934) and *Going Home* (1934), along with Curry's *The Stallion* (1937) and Wood's *Daughters of the Revolution* (1932).
11. Holger Cahill and Alfred H. Barr, Jr., *Art In America: A Complete Survey* (New York: Reynal and Hitchcock, 1935), 106–07.
12. Musée du Jeu de Paume, *Trois siècles d'art aux États-Unis*, 34, 36. This observation was originally made by Goodyear in *Modern Works of Art: 5th Anniversary Exhibition* (New York: The Museum of Modern Art, 1934), 16. He also adds (somewhat disparagingly) that "the central figure of the movement, Thomas Benton, combines vivid journalistic observation with mannered drawing and dynamic composition."
13. See Henry Adams, *Tom and Jack: The Intertwined Lives of Thomas Hart Benton and Jackson Pollock* (New York: Bloomsbury, 2009), 195.
14. Benton's early work *Agression* (1920), one of five panels illustrating American history, was particularly praised in the catalogue by Holger Cahill for representing a "characteristically American style in mural painting in which [Benton] shows a healthy absorption in contemporary subject matter." Holger Cahill, *American Painting and Sculpture, 1862–1932* (New York: W.W. Norton & Company, 1932), 18–19.
15. Jean A. Miller and Chauncey O. Rowe, "Films Reinforce Hemispheric Ties," *Foreign Commerce Weekly: Journal of International Economy* (June 2, 1945): 9. I would like to thank the staff at the Archives of American Art for providing access to this film. It should be noted that the film was found among the papers of art collector, dealer, and cultural administrator Alfredo Valente; this indicates the lengths to which the federal government went to forge a "unified national aesthetic front" to present to the world, one that involved artists, producers, studios, diplomats, and the military.
16. *Art Discovers America* (MGM, 1943); *Pictura: An Adventure in Art* (The Pictura Company, 1951). Scenes from *Art Discovers America*, a short film co-directed by Alfredo Valente and Hal Frater, were incorporated into the MGM Passing Parade short subject *Grandpa Called It Art*, released in 1944.
17. Several of the paintings shown in the film, such as those by Marsh, Walkowitz, and Burchfield, in addition to Benton's, are landscapes. Even the cover of the book prominently displayed in a bookstore (Peyton Boswell's *Modern American Painting*, first issued in 1939) features a landscape painting on its cover, Benton's *Tornado Over Kansas* (1929). That painting

must have looked particularly evocative to audiences in 1939, the year *The Wizard of Oz* was released in theaters.

18. Wood's and Benton's work was collected by another Hollywood star of the time, Edward G. Robinson. Erika Doss, *Regionalists in Hollywood: Painting, Film, and Patronage, 1925–1945* (PhD diss., University of Minnesota, 1983). Benton's work was featured in two additional documentaries of the period, *Grandpa Called It Art* (1944) and *The Making of a Mural* (1947). These and other films featuring American artists would have been regularly screened in museum auditoria during this period, including at the Museum of Modern Art.

19. The segments on Bosch, Carpaccio, and Goya had been produced (and released) in Italy in 1942, 1948, and 1951, respectively; the portions on Gauguin and Toulouse-Lautrec were made in France in 1950. All segments received new English language voiceovers for their inclusion in *Pictura*.

20. Implicit comparisons with acknowledged artists like Van Gogh (the subject of one of the previous episodes in the film) are also made in the film, as when a pair of shoes, painted by a young Wood, pans across the screen.

21. These words were printed on the cover of the *Saturday Evening Post* of April 18, 1942, and were accompanied by a reproduction of his painting *Spring in Town* (1941).

22. Postwar exhibitions at MoMA that included Benton's and Wood's work (particularly their prints) include *Master Prints from the Museum Collection* (1949), *American Prints of the 20th Century* (1954), *XXVth Anniversary Exhibition: Paintings from the Museum Collection* (1954), *The Artist as His Subject* (1967), *The Artist as Adversary* (1971), *American Prints from the International Program* (1971), *American Prints: 1913–1963* (1974), *Points of View* (1975), *Views Over America* (1979), *American Prints: 1900–1960* (1985), *Recent Acquisitions: Illustrated Books* (1985), *Recent Acquisitions: Contemporary Prints* (1986), *Recent Acquisitions* (1991), *Pastimes in Prints* (1993), *Adding It Up: Print Acquisitions 1970–1995* (1995), *From Henry Toulouse-Lautrec to Andy Warhol: Exploring Techniques* (1997), *Making Choices* (2000), and *Painting and Sculpture Changes* (2007 and 2011).

23. MoMA press release no. 530115-04, n.d. [1953].

24. MoMA press release no. 41, April 25, 1961.

25. As of this writing MoMA's permanent collection includes the following works by the three core regionalists: Benton's *Mine Strike from the American Scene no. 2* (1936), *In the Ozarks* (1938), *Frisky Day* (1939), *Spring Tryout* (1943), *Loading Corn* (1945), and *Island Hay* (1945); Curry's *John Brown* (1939, published 1940); Wood's *Shriner's Quartet* (1933) and *In the Spring* (1939) (all lithographs); Benton's *Homestead* (tempera and oil on composition board, 1934) and *Study for Homestead* (watercolor, pencil, and ink on paper, 1928–1930).

26. Jocelyne Rotily, "Politique des Musées du Luxembourg et du Jeu de Paume face a l'art américaine: histoire de deux grandes expositions dans le Paris

de l'entre-deux-guerres," *Gazette des beaux-Arts* (November, 1997): 188 (my translation). I have explored the context of this exhibition more fully in Dimitrios Latsis, "À la Recherche de Yankee Art: Landscape and Franco-American Exhibition Diplomacy between the Wars," *Transatlantica: Revue d'études américaines*, no. 2 (2014).
27. Edward Alden Jewell, *Have We an American Art?* (New York: Longmans, Green & Co, 1939), 202–03.
28. Thomas Hart Benton, "What's Holding Back American Art?" *Saturday Review of Literature* (December 15, 1951): 10. While that statement rings true, it should be said that the regionalists were represented in multiple exhibitions during the war, both at MoMA—*Painting and Sculpture from the Museum Collection* (1940), *American Watercolors; Lettering and Arrangements in Poster Design* (1941), *How Modern Artists Paint People* (1942), *Twentieth Century Portraits* (1942) (where *American Gothic* was one of the highlights), *Romantic Painting in America* (1943), *What Is Modern Painting* (1945), and *The Museum Collection of Painting and Sculpture* (1945)—and elsewhere.
29. Dorothy Canning Miller, *Fourteen Americans* (New York: Museum of Modern Art, 1946), 8.
30. In his catalogue essay for the exhibition *Romantic Painting in America* (1943), James Thrall Soby placed the regionalists under the banner of American romanticism in art and stressed their "intense localism." He elaborated that "while claiming to free American art from European domination, [their work] often merely changed the source of this influence from the French 19th and 20th centuries to the Flemish 15th century (Grant Wood) or to the Mannerist-Baroque period in Italy (Benton)." James Thrall Soby, *Romantic Painting in America* (New York: The Museum of Modern Art, 1943), 45–46.
31. "Letter to Museum of Modern Art," *Reality* (Spring, 1953): 2.
32. "An Open Letter to 'Reality' Magazine," MoMA press release no. 530424-39, April 24, 1953. The release was signed by Barr, the then-director Rene D'Harnoncourt, and director of painting and sculpture Andrew C. Ritchie.
33. "Progress Report—Federal Art Project: November 1937–April 1, 1938," Federal Art Project General Project File, ca. 1936–ca. 1940, Box 4: Correspondence and Memoranda, Record Group, 69, National Archives and Records Administration (College Park, MD).
34. Barr, "Painting and Sculpture in the United States."
35. See, among others, Tom Lutz, *Cosmopolitan Vistas: The Local, the Global, and American Literary Value* (Ithaca: Cornell University Press, 2004), 151. Lutz's work as well as that of Douglas Reichert Powell, *Critical Regionalism: Connecting Politics and Culture in the American Landscape* (Chapel Hill: University of North Carolina University Press, 2007), have marked a resurgence of theory around the regional and the national in an American context. Arguably at the starting point of this trend is Cheryl Herr's

innovative notion of "twinning" that can be deployed to negotiate the national and international dimensions of "the region" (in her case Ireland and Iowa). Cheryl Herr, *Critical Regional and Cultural Studies: From Ireland to the American Midwest* (Gainesville: University Press of Florida, 1996).
36. Grant Wood, *Revolt Against the City*.

Lara Kuykendall | John Steuart Curry
Regionalism at War

In art the term "regionalism" readily conjures images like John Steuart Curry's *Kansas Cornfield* (1933), Grant Wood's *Fall Plowing* (1931), and Thomas Hart Benton's *Cradling Wheat* (1938), all exaggerated, if not wholly fictitious, visualizations of midwestern fecundity during the Great Depression and Dust Bowl era. These painters were relatively unhindered by the gritty realities that documentary photographers like Dorothea Lange, Arthur Rothstein, and Walker Evans found in the drought-stricken American landscape. Instead, during those years of economic hardship and environmental catastrophe, Curry's, Wood's, and Benton's paintings functioned as evidence of the "usable past" that so preoccupied artists, poets, novelists, and historians in the interwar period and fostered optimism and hope for a restorative future.[1] Consequently, as Elizabeth Broun observed, these regionalists' works have been "considered escapist and nostalgic—a backwards look at an idealized agrarian past full of sentiment or a shield raised against harsh realities."[2]

That assessment is not the harshest criticism that the regionalists faced. Whereas the popularity of nostalgic American imagery and the accessibility of regionalists' realism benefited their careers during the early 1930s, as evinced by the first-ever appearance of a living artist (Benton) on the cover of *Time* magazine in 1934 and Curry's feature in the first issue of *Life* magazine in 1936, as early as 1935 and increasingly in subsequent years, regionalists faced criticism of their work as xenophobic, jingoistic, and even fascist.[3] Detractors complained that these artists' attitudes toward American identity were not sufficiently sophisticated and belied an insidious element in America's patriotic culture. The regionalists' advocacy for a uniquely American art was met with intense skepticism as it became clear that nationalism was breeding dictatorships and war abroad. Artist Stuart Davis denounced the "Fascist tendencies of the American Scene school of Benton, etc." and chided Curry for "willfully or through ignorance" eschewing modernist trends in painting like those of "Monet, Seurat, Cézanne, and Picasso."[4] Writing about cultural regionalism broadly, Lewis Mumford found regionalists' predilection for prosaic subject matter and nostalgic storytelling dangerously regressive and "sentimental," calling it an "attempt to find refuge within an old shell against the turbulent invasions of the outside world."[5] Even after the war, art historian H.W. Janson famously asserted, "almost every one of the ideas constituting the regionalist credo could be matched more or less verbatim from the writings of Nazi experts on art."[6] Scholars like Cécile Whiting, James Dennis, and Erika Doss have done much to complicate and disprove such problematic allegations.[7] But as recently as 2003, historian Bram Djikstra referred to Curry's *Bathers* (1928) as a "manifestation of 'Nordic' superiority" and suspiciously celebratory of the physical ideals lauded in Nazi art.[8] The perception, however misguided, that the regionalists were on the wrong side of art and history in the 1930s and 1940s still has some proponents.

Historian Michael C. Steiner acknowledged "some truth to [the] conclusion," that casts "1930s regionalists as cranky reactionaries building foolish barriers against the acids of modernity and tides of pluralism and progress."[9] However, the notion that Curry, Benton, and Wood were somehow sympathetic to fascism or worked in a mode that resembled Nazi art is incorrect and unconstructive. Despite their commitment to political and military isolationism during the 1930s and early 1940s, after the Japanese attack on Pearl Harbor on December 7, 1941, and the United States' entry into World War II the following day, each artist found a way to make his work relevant to the changing political, military, and cultural situation. Curry's ideological change after Pearl Harbor did not come easily, nor was it a radical about-face. But he did develop a regionalist reaction to the war that was antifascist in subtle and complicated ways, and his work as an artist during World War II both reflected and appealed to the unique concerns of his midwestern audience.

The Roots of Curry's Pacifism

Curry's antipathy toward war began in the 1910s and percolated through 1941. Letters to his parents in 1917 (while he was a student at the Art Institute of Chicago) show that Curry was plagued with indecision about whether to join the Army during World War I. He considered enlisting in an artillery unit, then the camouflage unit, and even mentioned aviation (which he had dismissed earlier as the most dangerous assignment), and watched the news carefully to see whether he might be drafted. His letters reflect a deep ambivalence about the war; his reluctance to give up his artistic studies was in conflict with his youthful sense of patriotic duty.[10] He might also have been struggling with his father's disapproval of his chosen career path; Smith Curry thought being an artist was unmanly, but presumably serving as a soldier would have made Curry's father proud.[11] In 1918, while a student at Geneva College in Pennsylvania, Curry joined the Student Army Training Corps, but he began his preparation too late in the war and never deployed abroad. Still, Curry's limited experience in uniform was unpleasant. He wrote to his parents in December, 1918, "No one can keep his self respect and make the army a life's profession. We had a rotten dose in ways here."[12]

The pictorial statements about war that Curry made prior to 1942 established his early fixation on the tragic consequences of military engagement and his opposition to the nation's entrance into World War II. The first antiwar painting that Curry completed, *Parade to War, Allegory* (1938, Figure 1), is particularly emphatic in this

Figure 1. John Steuart Curry, *Parade to War, Allegory* (1938). Oil on canvas, 47 ¹³⁄₁₆ x 63 ¹³⁄₁₆ in. The Cummer Museum of Art and Gardens, Gift of Barnett Banks, Inc., AG.1991.4.1. John Steuart Curry Estate, Kiechel Fine Art, Lincoln, Nebraska.

regard as the marching soldiers have skulls for faces and are evidently predestined to perish. Curry's daughter, Ellen, remembers that her father was "frightened by what he saw in Germany in 1938" and that listening to the radio broadcasts about the war made him "very edgy."[13] Curry's biographer, Laurence Schmeckebier, attributed the moroseness of this painting and Curry's attitude toward combat to the "surge of popular disillusionment and anti-war spirit of the period" generally and specifically to the haunting language of Alfred Noyes's 1920 poem "The Victory Ball," which describes a celebration of a war's end.[14] "The cymbals crash, and the dancers walk," Noyes wrote, as "shadows of dead men stand by the wall." The poem toggles between the merry revelry of the "Victory Ball" and the laments of young men who are sickened by the jubilance and resigned to their deaths. The regular, yet abrupt rhythm of Noyes's poem—each line is only four to six beats—contributes to its mundane sadness. Likewise, in Curry's painting, the repetition of the men's bodies and their guns and bayonets establishes a menacing, dirge-like pace within the composition that can, in turn, cause anxiety and fear in the viewer.

Curry's *The Return of Private Davis from the Argonne* (Figure 2) was a delayed response to the funeral of a boyhood friend, William Davis, whom Curry knew in high school and who was one of the first Kansans to die in World War I. Davis's stateside burial took place in 1921, three years after he perished in the trenches of France. Curry began this work in 1928, after he visited American war cemeteries in France in 1926, and completed it in 1940.[15] As much as *The Return of Private Davis from the Argonne* honors Davis's and other soldiers' sacrifices and alludes to the triumph over death for someone who has a Christian burial, so does it remind viewers of the costs of a young man's death for his family and farm. The mourning in the foreground is immediate and sincere, but it is also located only in the present pictorial moment. The broad horizontal expanse of farmland in the background bears down on the funeral and represents both the mourners' past and future responsibilities. As demonstrated by the partially plowed field on the left, the farm work has paused only briefly, and the flags that obstruct that view of agricultural productivity are but temporary visual and symbolic distractions. Soon the honor guard will leave, the mourners will pile back into their waiting cars, and life will return to normal. For Curry, the war cut short the life of

Figure 2. John Steuart Curry, *The Return of Private Davis from the Argonne* (1928–1940). Oil on canvas, 38 ¼ x 52 ¼ in. The Museum of Fine Arts, Houston. Museum purchase funded by the Caroline Wiess Law Accessions Endowment Fund, 2011.763. John Steuart Curry Estate, Kiechel Fine Art, Lincoln, Nebraska.

a good and devout farm boy unnecessarily, and, tragically, Private Davis cannot participate in the future of his farm and his family. The curious line-up of clouds on the horizon reads like a parade of soldiers' ghosts who march on infinitely, and Private Davis is but one member in that haunting brigade. The fact that Curry continued to work on this painting until 1940 indicates that the prospect of military intervention in World War II reminded him of the futility of death and the costs of World War I for the agrarian Midwest.

Another pre–World War II painting, *Leaving the Farm for Army Training Camp* (1941), reads like a prequel to *The Return of Private Davis*. In this work Curry portrayed a young farmer surveying his land as he departs to join the military. No one sees him off, and the painting does not suggest any future glories on the battlefield. All Curry offers is a vision of the man's past and a parcel of land to which he may never return. The sun shines on the farm in the background, but the man prepares to stride off-canvas into a dark and stormy future. As he painted such works, Curry worried that another massive war would disrupt the midwestern way of life and the development of American art, effectively halting the progress that had been made since the Great Depression.[16] As Curry explained, "Give us ten years, and if we can escape the paralyzing hand of war we will accomplish something."[17]

Curry held his antiwar and isolationist perspective in common with a majority of people in the Midwest in the 1930s. In large part, this isolationism was a function of the persistent economic hardships with which the region had been grappling since the end of World War I when postwar demobilization resulted in a rapid and severe devaluation of farmland, equipment, and crops.[18] The environmental catastrophe of the Dust Bowl and the devastating economic effects of the 1929 stock market crash only exacerbated the problems that farmers had been fighting since 1920. A March 1941 report on the impact of war on American farms by economist John D. Black warned that the price of and demand for wheat, corn, and other products would fall during the war, and that farmers would have to undergo the "difficult and costly" measure of redirecting their efforts toward more profitable beef, dairy, and poultry to offset such a decline.[19] The prospect of diverting the nation's resources away from domestic economic recovery and toward a surge in military preparedness and reimagining the structure of American agriculture elicited great trepidation in Curry and his fellow Midwesterners, especially as they feared another postwar weakening of the agricultural market. As economist Walter W. Wilcox explained, "[A]griculture did not plan for war."[20] Thus, even after Hitler's Germany invaded Austria, people of the Midwest overwhelmingly agreed that neutrality was the proper response. Not until December 7, 1941, when the United States came under attack at Pearl Harbor, did the conservative, isolationist tide change.[21]

As late as the fall of 1941, Curry expressed his sense of dread in *The Light of the World*, a work that does not inspire action, defense, and readiness on America's part, but depicts a group of curious onlookers standing paralyzed at the edge of a city as a violent storm brews over the nearby ocean. Curry called this image *America Facing the Storm* and, coincidentally, this image appeared in the December 1941 issue of *Esquire* magazine. It is marked by fear and disbelief about the advent of another disruptive military conflict, but it is also the last antiwar image Curry ever made.

Cultivating Heroism in a "War Picture"

Pearl Harbor was a watershed moment for Curry and many other Americans who held fast to their resistance to war throughout the 1930s. While Curry opposed military intervention in works made prior to December 1941, by the spring of 1942, he was making his first foray into government-sponsored war propaganda with the painting and war bonds poster *Our Good Earth* (Figure 3). In the literature this painting has often been dated erroneously 1940–1941, a date that has obscured the fact that Curry designed this painting expressly as a "war picture."[22] At first glance, this painting's fertile farm landscape represents a midwestern family's triumph over the hardships of the Dust Bowl and the Great Depression. The wheat grows tall and golden, and the house, windmill, and barn in the background are intact. Although the farm family in *Our Good Earth* is experiencing a level of prosperity that had only recently become possible again, the landscape is not entirely tranquil. As in *The Light of the World*, a meteorological menace enters as a gusty wind rips through the scene and threatens to blow the children down. The farmer's face registers his concern; he worries that the storm of World War II that brews afar will affect his family and his farm.

Curry's decision to set the farmer and his children in a wheat field in *Our Good Earth* relates to the poster's intended audience of midwestern farmers, to his own experiences growing up on a Kansas farm and living in the Midwest as an adult, and to the significance of wheat as a synecdoche for both the Midwest and the United States. Curry's home state of Kansas was a leading producer of wheat and experimental fields of wheat were readily available to him at the University of Wisconsin, where he had served as artist-in-residence in the Department of Agriculture since 1936. *Our Good Earth*'s working title was *Long May It Wave*, a phrase from the second stanza of Francis Scott Key's "The Star Spangled Banner." The phrase links Curry's wheat field with the American flag, a very regionalist response to his dealer Reeves Lewenthal's request that Curry create a "standard bearer" for the war.[23] In the painting and the first version of the *Our Good Earth* lithograph (a unique impression owned by the Figge Art Museum) the emphatic horizontality and solidity of the clouds make them look like the stripes on an American flag, as well.

Robert Gambone argued that the wheat farmer in *Our Good Earth* represents "fallen humanity, raising this crop to feed GIs who

Figure 3. John Steuart Curry, *Our Good Earth* (1942). Oil on hardboard, 60 ⅛ × 48 ⅛ in. Chazen Museum of Art, University of Wisconsin-Madison, on loan from the College of Agricultural and Life Sciences, University of Wisconsin-Madison (Gift of the U.S. Treasury Department to the College of Agriculture), 3.1999.1. John Steuart Curry Estate, Kiechel Fine Art, Lincoln, Nebraska.

will, after all, fight and kill in the war."[24] On the contrary, the wheat signifies an America worth defending and is key to this farmer's wartime heroism. As the war surged and European farms became theaters of war, provisions had to be imported. After Pearl Harbor, the U.S. government began purchasing its own reserves of food. The 1941 Lend-Lease Act facilitated the exportation of U.S. foodstuffs to Allied forces abroad, and Congress passed legislation in May 1941 that led to a 50% rise in the production of wheat and caused prices to soar proportionately.[25] All of these developments kept demand and prices for wheat high and stable. Wheat was especially significant to the war as it was one crop that Hitler's Germany desperately lacked. A report in *Life* magazine on the vulnerability of Romania to a Nazi invasion explained that Romania's wheat harvest was "its gold" and its expansive fields were "irresistible bait to Nazi Germany."[26] Thus, growing wheat during World War II, as *Our Good Earth*'s farmer is doing, was both a patriotic and a profitable pursuit.

In Curry's *Our Good Earth*, the farmer is intent on harvesting his crop, and there is no indication that he would leave his family and his farm to do battle in Europe or on any other field of war. Unlike Cincinnatus, the Roman statesman who temporarily left his farm to lead the Republic during a crisis and who served as a model for American revolutionaries like George Washington who returned to their plows and fields after serving their country, Curry's farmer is not rushing off to don a uniform and take up arms. The farm in *Our Good Earth* is a family farm and the father is essential to it. His children are too young to be autonomous, and their unseen mother is presumably fulfilling her domestic duties in the house and barn, too busy to join them on their scouting mission or to do her husband's work should he join the military. Instead of leaving his land and family, the farmer in *Our Good Earth* holds fast to his wheat and his children and remains rooted at home.

In this way, despite the "Nordic" or "Aryan" appearance of this family that has compelled some viewers to look askance at Curry's work, Curry cultivated a new type of American war hero that also diverged from the celebrated icons of Nazi art. The quintessential Nazi hero was not the farmer, but the soldier. Third Reich Minister of Propaganda Joseph Goebbels announced, "[T]he most noble consecration and the ultimate glorification [of Nazi ideals is] through the fighting, dying, and victory of the German soldier."[27] When the farmer was heroized in Nazi art he was a peasant, a quaint ancestor of a more modern and triumphant German people.[28] As James Dennis explained, in such works as Oskar Martin-Amorbach's *The Sower* (1937) and *Out to Harvest* (1938), farmers were romanticized and antiquated heroes of the past, not modern heroes of the present.[29] For Nazis of the 1940s, the hero who commanded the most attention was undoubtedly the warrior who sacrificed himself for the good of the nation and the race. As Jonathan Petropoulos argued, in such sculptures as *Comradeship, Warrior's Departure,* and *Sacrifice,* favored Nazi artist Arno Breker "exalted warfare ... as noble and heroic," often to the point of death.[30] As Curry's contemporary farmer appears unwilling to go to war and demonstrates his patriotism on his own terms as a producer of crops on the home front, he would be seen in the context of Nazi propaganda as selfish and disloyal. Rather than creating a blind follower of hawkish nationalism, Curry's war hero is independent and not distracted by the potential glories of combat. His patriotism is nuanced and complicated, something that Nazi propaganda, with its emphasis on "loyalty, honor, unconditional obedience, and readiness for self-sacrifice" would never allow.[31]

In Defense of the Farm

As Curry began his next project for the Office of War Information, Lewenthal told him, "The whole idea to be conveyed in this picture is briefly this—that the farmers of the Nation will be enslaved if we are defeated and come under the Nazi yoke."[32] Curry was indignant as he defended the service of farmers during wartime, reminding Lewenthal, "Farmers are exerting all-out effort and working 70 and 80 hours a week. There is no problem as we see it out here in getting farmers to work as hard as they can, for they are now doing exactly this."[33] Curry did not want to paint a bloody battle, caricature the evils of defeat, or intimidate his viewers in order to promote wartime patriotism. He was leery of sensationalizing the dangers of the war and preferred to praise the efforts of midwestern farmers rather than goad or scare them into advancing the war effort.

In his propaganda pictures of the 1940s, Curry remained closer to the pastoral patterns of his entire oeuvre. As he planned his second war bonds poster design, Curry explained to Lewenthal,

> with patriotic and courageous Americans it seems very doubtful whether it is strategic or desirable to use fear as the motive in picturing to them the needs of the war program. Our people are patriotic. Thousands of our young men are volunteering before they are drafted. Bond sales are

at a high level. Our people expect to win the war and are prepared to pay any price that may be necessary. They do not need to be threatened by some fear complex in order to do their best. They are responding to incentives that are on a much higher plane and more effective than fear. Can't your Writers' War Board develop a theme more positive?[34]

Curry's "more positive" pictorial statement, *The Farm Is a Battleground, Too!* (1943), acknowledges and commends farmers for their continuing efforts and analogizes their labor to the activities of soldiers abroad.

The painting and poster, *The Farm Is a Battleground, Too!*, recall a mural (now lost) titled *Wisconsin Agriculture Leads to Victory* (Figure 4) that he had exhibited at the 1942 Wisconsin State Fair.[35] Featuring a gigantic pitchfork-holding farmer who resembles the man in *Our Good Earth*, this composition visually connects his activities with the infantry on the front lines of World War II. Tractors and tanks roll through the landscape in the background on their respective missions, both

Figure 4. John Steuart Curry with his mural *Wisconsin Agriculture Leads to Victory*, unknown photographer. John Steuart Curry and Curry family papers, 1848–1999. Archives of American Art, Smithsonian Institution. John Steuart Curry Estate, Kiechel Fine Art, Lincoln, Nebraska.

mobilized on behalf of the war effort. Whether viewers stood in front of Curry's gargantuan mural or the more modestly sized painting or poster, they were engulfed in the agricultural landscape and encouraged to be proud of the Midwest's contributions to wartime mobilization.

In his war bonds poster designs, Curry sought to emphasize the urgent need for farmers on the home front. By 1942, the allure of high-paying war industry jobs, military volunteerism, and the compulsory draft had greatly reduced the number of young men working on American farms, and the shortage of labor made fulfilling the demand for wheat and other crops very difficult.[36] As Curry planned his third war bonds commission, *Plant the Seeds of Victory* (1943), he considered painting "a big empty space without a farmer in it." As he saw it, "The main thing on everybody's mind around the cow college is to keep one or two farmers on the ground and out of the Army and Navy."[37] Agricultural deferments became available in November of 1942 to those "essential to the war effort," but they were difficult to secure as individual farmers had to prove that they were the "'key man' on the farm" and that their productivity contributed significantly more resources to the marketplace than their family consumed. Such challenges were compounded by the negative stigma of abstaining from military service; farmers who received deferments were often accused of "shirking" their patriotic duties or called "slackers." Some in the agricultural areas even argued for the implementation of a farm labor draft or a "great land army" featuring farmers in military uniforms to ensure that the work that needed to be done in the fields, in support of the war, was accomplished and recognized as critical.[38]

Curry's images engage these issues and establish the farmer as a leader of the military charge, not a fearful coward or an ancillary contributor. To this end, Curry made a subtle change when he executed the final lithograph of *Our Good Earth*, which transformed the scared little boy to the right of the iconic farmer into a more confident character. In most incarnations of that image—a watercolor, full size drawing, painting, and first stone lithograph—the boy holds his hand up somewhat passively and defensively. In the official lithograph, released by Curry's gallery Associated American Artists in an edition of 250, the boy's hand has become a fist and, like his father, is prepared for a more aggressive protection of his farm. James Dennis argued that even as he made war bonds posters "Curry seemed to remain reluctant to go to war,"[39] which is true, but that stance was justified by the necessity and valor of farmers' service at home. Farmers were fighting, but their weapons were pitchforks, tractors, and crops, and they did not have to go anywhere new or serve in battle to make their contributions.

In *Our Good Earth, Wisconsin Agriculture Leads to Victory,* and *The Farm Is a Battleground, Too!*, Curry maintained his commitment to the authenticity of midwestern agricultural life; he resisted any suggestion to treat farmers as pawns who could be manipulated for propagandistic purposes without regard for the realities of their work. When Lewenthal suggested that Curry turn the pitchfork in *The Farm Is a Battleground, Too!* so that it would align visually with the guns the soldiers carry, Curry consulted colleagues at the University of Wisconsin's College of Agriculture.[40] They agreed that marching with a stabbing pitchfork would be absurd, and Curry explained, "Farming is a skilled trade, or profession, and if you were to show a mechanic swinging his tools around in a wild manner ... it would detract."[41] The resulting message is that the farmer could be a soldier for the Allied cause without leaving his fields or changing his lifestyle. His patriotic duty was not newly mobilized. His task was to maintain the home front, to feed the troops, and to sustain the virtuous agrarian way of life so essential to the definition of America, as he had always done. By extension, as Curry cultivated a new kind of wartime, home front heroism that connected with his prewar advocacy for American farm culture, he, too, was able to perform his patriotic duty as a regionalist artist and make it relevant for this new era.

Curry Goes to Army Camp

The final phase of Curry's career as a war artist began in March 1944, when he participated in an initiative sponsored by the pharmaceutical company Abbott Laboratories, and coordinated by Lewenthal and Associated American Artists, to hire artists to chronicle the training and service of medical personnel during World War II.[42] Curry spent nearly two weeks at the Army Medical Training facility at Camp Barkeley, near Abilene, Texas, observing mock combat scenarios, battlefield rescues, and tent surgeries.[43] The trip yielded multiple paintings of operations and maneuvers, portraits of officers, and up to one hundred additional sketches.⁴⁴ *Medical Training in Texas* (c. 1944–1945, Figure 5) shows how realistic the medical training maneuvers were and features

> a stretcher squad and battalion aid man picking up a patient who has a severe head wound. The peculiar yellow tone of the wounded man's head is because of the malage [sic] which the medical corps sometimes use in their training procedure. These simulate the various wounds which the medical corpsmen will encounter in actual combat.... The setting is in the streets of the mock village.⁴⁵

The explosions, the dirt and dust, and the men rushing diagonally through the composition communicate the seriousness and urgency of these wartime preparations.

Curry dove headlong into his assignment at Camp Barkeley, as he dressed in fatigues and "ate chow with the soldiers." The *Kansas City Star* praised Curry for becoming "one of the men," and he was proud to feel some sense of what it was like to serve in World War II.⁴⁶ Yet, Curry's Army Medical images are not a wholesale repudiation of his earlier

Figure 5. John Steuart Curry, *Medical Training in Texas* (1944). Oil on canvas over hardboard, 31 x 50 in. Kansas State University, Marianna Kistler Beach Museum of Art, bequest of Kathleen G. Curry, 2002.1530. John Steuart Curry Estate, Kiechel Fine Art, Lincoln, Nebraska.

antipathy toward war. In fact, they are best seen as a continuation of his gradual evolution after Pearl Harbor toward making art that could support the war without heroizing combat above all other contributions. As a young man, Curry had missed serving in the military during World War I, and his age and poor health kept him from an overseas assignment as a war artist in the 1940s. He certainly empathized with farmers who had their patriotism, courage, and manliness questioned for not enlisting for active duty, and he may have experienced some lingering guilt about his own lack of uniformed service. In the Army medical servicemen, he found additional kindred spirits, as medics were also criticized for the supposedly less dangerous, and therefore less vital and less heroic, nature of their service.[47] When *Battalion Aid Man* (Figure 6) appeared in the April 1945 issue of Abbott Laboratories' magazine, *What's New*, its caption read,

> Pill-roller from Paducah—Before the fighting started, infantrymen and other combat soldiers bestowed such uncomplimentary appellatives upon the Medical Corps enlisted man. But those days are gone forever. A derogatory wise-crack about a corpsman now will get you a punch in the nose from any doughboy who has seen these courageous men dispensing mercy under blistering enemy fire.[48]

Other drawings published in that issue show medical trainees practicing for hand-to-hand combat with armed enemies. Captions emphasize these men were training both to do the valiant work of rescuing wounded and, though they would be unarmed, to ward off enemy attacks. Combined, Curry's images and their captions give us an expanded vision of wartime heroism, one that does not diminish the valiant combat soldiers' service, but one that celebrates the vital efforts of the medical unit soldiers, too.

H.W. Janson wrote in 1946, "[T]he hey-day of regionalism, to be sure, was in the years before Pearl Harbor."[49] However, Curry's work in the 1940s shows that regionalism could adapt and remain relevant. After Pearl Harbor, Curry's attitude toward the war changed, but his admiration for the American agrarian way of life did not. He found subjects that were still rooted in the American landscape, and his work resonated with rural audiences who were also turning away from

Figure 6. John Steuart Curry, *Battalion Aid Man* (1944). Oil on canvas, 66 x 32 ¼ in. Courtesy of the Army Historical Collection, U.S. Army Center of Military History. John Steuart Curry Estate, Kiechel Fine Art, Lincoln, Nebraska.

their commonly held isolationist stance and becoming more willing to intervene in foreign conflicts. Curry's farms became metaphorical battlegrounds in need of defense and theaters for patriotic action. In such works as *Our Good Earth, The Farm Is a Battleground, Too!,* and *Wisconsin Agriculture Leads to Victory,* Curry transformed the wheat fields of his boyhood in Kansas (and of his adulthood in Wisconsin) into spaces of heroic efforts to defeat the Axis powers. Curry paid tribute to farmers' ongoing labor and to the significance of wheat as a wartime commodity. These images demonstrate his belief the laboring farmer could be just as much a war hero as the soldiers fighting in Europe and the Pacific. Using the farm as a backdrop, the farmer as a fighter, and wheat as a weapon, Curry developed a brand of regionalist war propaganda that allowed him to continue to celebrate and advocate for the rural Midwest while also contributing to the American mobilization during World War II. His Army Medical paintings and drawings followed this vein, too, in that they allowed Curry to contribute to the development of war propaganda by chronicling and heroizing the complicated efforts of Army medics, whose service was highly skilled, dangerous, and extraordinarily valuable. Over the course of the early 1940s, Curry transitioned from being an overall-clad regionalist into a fatigue-clad government propagandist. The evolution was gradual, which allowed Curry to mobilize his talents and his ultimately complicated sense of patriotism and antifascism on his own terms.

Notes

1. Alfred Haworth Jones, "The Search for a Usable American Past in the New Deal Era," *American Quarterly* 23, no. 5 (December, 1971): 710–24.
2. Elizabeth Broun, "Thomas Hart Benton: A Politician in Art," *Smithsonian Studies in American Art* 1, no. 1 (Spring 1987): 59.
3. "Thomas Benton's Thomas Benton," *Time* XXIV, no. 26 (December 24, 1934): cover. "Curry of Kansas," *Life* 1 (November 23, 1936): 28–31.
4. Stuart Davis, "A Medium of Two Dimensions," *Art Front* 1, no. 5 (May, 1935): 6. Stuart Davis, "The New York American Scene in Art," *Art Front* 1, no. 3 (February, 1935): 6.
5. Lewis Mumford, *Technics and Civilization* (New York: Harcourt, Brace and Company, 1934), 292.
6. H.W. Janson, "Benton and Wood, Champions of Regionalism," *Magazine of Art* 39, no. 5 (May, 1946): 186.
7. Cécile Whiting, *Antifascism in American Art* (New Haven: Yale University Press, 1989), 98–132. James M. Dennis, *Renegade Regionalists: The Modern*

      Independence of Grant Wood, Thomas Hart Benton, and John Steuart Curry (Madison: University of Wisconsin Press, 1998), 69–89. Erika Doss, *Benton, Pollock, and the Politics of Modernism: From Regionalism to Abstract Expressionism* (Chicago: The University of Chicago Press, 1991), 116–38.

8. Bram Djikstra, *American Expressionism: Art and Social Change, 1920–1950* (New York: Harry N. Abrams, Inc., in association with the Columbus Museum of Art, 2003), 54.
9. Michael C. Steiner, "Introduction: Varieties of Western American Regionalism," in *Regionalists on the Left: Radical Voices from the American West*, ed. Michael Steiner (Norman: University of Oklahoma Press, 2013), 7.
10. See the various correspondence between Curry and his parents from 1917. John Steuart Curry and Curry Family Papers, 1900–1999, Archives of American Art, Smithsonian Institution (hereinafter "Curry Papers, AAA-SI"), Series 2, Box 1, Folders 10 and 11.
11. Bret Waller, "An Interview with Mrs. Daniel Schuster," *Kansas Quarterly* 2, no. 4 (Fall 1970): 15.
12. Curry to his parents, December 22, 1918. Curry Papers, AAA-SI, Series 2, Box 1, Folder 12, Documents 2–3.
13. Waller, "Interview with Mrs. Daniel Schuster," 16.
14. Laurence E. Schmeckebier, *John Steuart Curry's Pageant of America* (New York: American Artists Group, 1943), 254.
15. Ibid.
16. Patricia Junker, "Twilight of Americanism's Golden Age: Curry's Wisconsin Years, 1936–46," in *John Steuart Curry: Inventing the Middle West*, ed. Patricia Junker (New York: Hudson Hills Press, in association with the Elvehjem Museum of Art, 1998), 206.
17. John Steuart Curry, "Address Before the Art Association of Madison," January 19, 1937. Curry Papers, AAA-SI, Series 5, Box 4, Folder 28, Documents 1–10.
18. Willard Wesley Cochrane, *The Development of American Agriculture: A Historical Analysis*, 2nd ed. (Minneapolis: University of Minnesota Press, 1993), 100–01.
19. John D. Black, "The War and American Agriculture," in *The Wartime Outlook for Agriculture* (New York: National Industrial Conference Board, Inc., March 4, 1941), 1.
20. Walter W. Wilcox, *The Farmer in the Second World War* (Ames: The Iowa State College Press, 1947), 35.
21. R. Douglas Hurt, *The Great Plains During World War II* (Lincoln: University of Nebraska Press, 2008), 1–13, 26–28.
22. Curry's correspondence with his dealer Reeves Lewenthal traces the trajectory of this suite, which began with an idea Lewenthal gave Curry in February of 1942. See Curry Papers, AAA-SI, Series 3, Box 1, Folder 39, Document 16; Folder 40, Documents 6, 8, 10, 25 and 27.

23. Lewenthal to Curry, February 6 and 12, 1942. Curry Papers, AAA-SI, Series 3, Box 1, Folder 39, Documents 10 and 13.
24. Robert L. Gambone, "The Use of Religious Motifs in Curry's Art," in *John Steuart Curry: Inventing the Middle West*, 146.
25. John T. Schlebecker, *Whereby We Thrive: A History of American Farming, 1607-1972* (Ames: The Iowa State University Press, 1975), 212-14. David B. Danbom, *Born in the Country: A History of Rural America*, 2nd ed. (Baltimore: Johns Hopkins University Press, 2006), 231.
26. "Rumania: Its People Await Hitler's Drive," *Life* (January 9, 1939): 40-49.
27. Joseph Goebbels, *Das Reich* (June 9, 1940), as quoted in Jay W. Baird, *To Die for Germany: Heroes in the Nazi Pantheon* (Bloomington: Indiana University Press, 1990), 202.
28. Frederic Spotts, *Hitler and the Power of Aesthetics* (Woodstock, NY: The Overlook Press, 2003), 101.
29. Dennis, *Renegade Regionalists*, 78-83.
30. Jonathan Petropoulos, "From Seduction to Denial: Arno Breker's Engagement with National Socialism," in *Art, Culture, and Media under the Third Reich*, ed. Richard A. Etlin (Chicago: The University of Chicago Press, 2002), 211.
31. Baird, *To Die for Germany*, 212.
32. Lewenthal to Curry, October 5, 1942. Curry Papers, AAA-SI, Series 3, Box 1, Folder 41, Document 3.
33. Curry wrote in pencil "no time and a half or double time either" on this letter, as well. Curry to Lewenthal, October 7, 1942. Curry Papers, AAA-SI, Series 3, Box 1, Folder 41, Document 4.
34. Curry to Lewenthal, October 7, 1942. Curry Papers, AAA-SI, Series 3, Box 1, Folder 41, Document 4.
35. John O. Holzhueter, "John Steuart Curry: A Populist Artist from Kansas Embraces Progressivism," *Wisconsin Magazine of History* 84, no. 1 (2000): 15-19.
36. Daniel Nelson, *Farm and Factory: Workers in the Midwest, 1880-1990* (Bloomington: Indiana University Press, 1995), 140-41. Hurt, *Great Plains*, 189-96.
37. Curry to Lewenthal, March 3, 1943. Curry Papers, AAA-SI, Series 3, Box 1, Folder 42, Document 13.
38. Hurt, *Great Plains*, 154, 171, 199-202, 235.
39. Dennis, *Renegade Regionalists*, 85.
40. Lewenthal to Curry, October 17, 1942. Curry Papers, AAA-SI, Series 3, Box 1, Folder 41, Document 10.
41. Curry to Lewenthal, October 19, 1942. Curry Papers, AAA-SI, Series 3, Box 1, Folder 41, Document 11.
42. Curry was one of twelve artists hired for the "Paintings of Army Medicine Project." Elizabeth G. Seaton, Gail Windisch, and Jane Myers, "'Art of Every Possible Service': Associated American Artists and Corporate

Commissions During the War Decade," in *Art for Every Home: Associated American Artists, 1934–2000*, ed. Elizabeth G. Seaton, Jane Myers, and Gail Windisch (Manhattan, KS: Marianna Kistler Beach Museum of Art, 2015), 124, 130.
43. Curry to Estelle Mandel, April 11, 1944. Curry Papers, AAA-SI, Series 3, Box 1, Folder 44, Document 18.
44. Curry to Phyllis Romano, January 15, 1945. Curry Papers, AAA-SI, Series 3, Box 1, Folder 47, Document 7.
45. Curry to Romano, December 27, 1944. Curry Papers, AAA-SI, Series 3, Box 1, Folder 46, Documents 28 and 29.
46. Sgt. H.O. Dendurent, "Camp Barkeley Trainees Are Models for Artist Curry," *Kansas City Star* (May 7, 1944).
47. Gerald F. Linderman, *The World within War: America's Combat Experience in World War II* (New York: The Free Press, 1997), 133.
48. "The Abbott Collection Paintings of Army Medicine III: Training of Enlisted Medical Personnel by John Steuart Curry," *What's New* 91 (April, 1945): 11.
49. Janson, "Champions of Regionalism," 184.

Contributors

Dustin Gann is a native Kansan whose research examines the relationship between national culture and regional identity. He is especially interested in the processes and individuals that have shaped midwestern communities during the early to mid-twentieth century. His recent research appears in *Wide Open Town: Kansas City During the Pendergast Era*, published by the University of Kansas Press, and *Screening Images of Masculinity in the Age of Postfeminism*, published by Lexington Books. Gann earned a PhD in twentieth-century U.S. history from the University of Kansas and currently serves as Assistant Professor of History and Honors Program Coordinator at Midland University in Fremont, Nebraska.

Gregory Gilbert is Professor of Art History and Director of the Art History Program at Knox College in Galesburg, Illinois. He also served as Senior Curator at the Figge Art Museum in Davenport, Iowa, which maintains the Grant Wood Archive. His specialized area of research is the art of Robert Motherwell and the New York School, but he has published and lectured widely on regionalism and WPA art. His publications in the fields of regionalism and New Deal visual culture include *Harry Gottlieb: The Silkscreen and Social Concern in the WPA Era* (The Jane Voorhees Zimmerli Art Museum, Rutgers University, 1983), *George Overbury "Pop" Hart: His Life and Art* (Rutgers University Press, 1986), and *A New Deal for Illinois: The Federal Art Project Collection of Western Illinois University* (University Art Gallery, Western Illinois University, 2013). He was also a featured speaker at the 2014 Grant Wood Symposium "Revolt Against the City: Midwestern Culture in Hard Times," held at the University of Iowa.

Meg Gillette is Associate Professor of English and department chair at Augustana College. Her articles on modern American literature have appeared in *Modern Fiction Studies, Studies in American Fiction,*

Twentieth-Century Literature, and a book collection on teaching Hemingway and modernism.

Harmony Jankowski, PhD, is a Visiting Lecturer at Indiana University–Bloomington. Her academic research draws from the fields of modernist literature and culture, performance studies, and critical theory. Her current research considers how both modern dance and modernist literature, as experimental forms emerging in the early twentieth century, sparked new ways of thinking about the relationship between bodies, movement, and technology.

Sara Kosiba is Associate Professor of English at Troy University. Her research focuses primarily on writers from the American Midwest, including Ernest Hemingway, F. Scott Fitzgerald, Josephine Herbst, Dawn Powell, and John Herrmann. Her work on Herrmann includes an introduction to the first American edition of his first novel, *What Happens* (Hastings College Press, 2015), and she is currently at work on his biography. She is a past president of the Society for the Study of Midwestern Literature (SSML) and serves on the editorial boards of SSML and *Middle West Review*.

Lara Kuykendall is Associate Professor of Art History at Ball State University in Muncie, Indiana. She holds a PhD in American art history from the University of Kansas and was a Georgia O'Keeffe Museum Research Center Scholar in 2010. Kuykendall's research explores issues of national identity in American visual culture and examines ways in which artists have used heroic (and anti-heroic) imagery to understand and critique the changing social and political fabric of the United States. Recent publications include a chapter on African American artist Palmer Hayden's paintings of folk legend John Henry in *Locating American Art: Finding Art's Meaning in Museums* (Ashgate, 2016) and an essay on John Steuart Curry's World War II war bonds posters in the catalogue of the traveling exhibition, *Art for Every Home: Associated American Artists, 1934–2000*.

Dimitrios Latsis is Assistant Professor at the School of Image Arts, Ryerson University, in Toronto, where he teaches in the Film Studies and Film and Photography Preservation and Collection Management programs. He received a PhD in Film Studies from the University of Iowa and completed a postdoctoral fellowship in Visual Data Curation at the Internet Archive, where he served as film archivist. His work on American visual culture, early cinema, and the Digital Humanities has been supported by the Smithsonian Institution, Domitor, and the Mellon and Knight Foundations among others. He has published and lectured widely in the fields of American visual culture, the historiography and theory of cinema, and archival studies. He recently edited a special issue of the journal of the Association of Moving Image Archivists, *The Moving Image*, on Digital Humanities and/in Film Archives. He is currently co-editing an anthology on documentaries about the visual arts in the 1950s and 1960s (for I.B. Tauris), and completing a monograph on the historiography of American cinema during the early and silent years.

Marcia Noe is the author of *Susan Glaspell: Voice from the Heartland* and over twenty other publications on this Pulitzer Prize–winning playwright. She is a senior editor of *The Dictionary of Midwestern Literature*, editor of the journal *MidAmerica*, and chairs the editorial committee of the Society for the Study of Midwestern Literature, which gave her the MidAmerica Award for distinguished contributions to the study of midwestern literature in 2003.

Meghan O'Dea has a master's in English from the University of Tennessee at Chattanooga with a concentration in Creative Writing, specializing in creative nonfiction, place-based personal essay, and city as text. She has also presented at conferences in the United States and abroad on geography in literature.

Gregory Rose, PhD, has been Dean and Director at The Ohio State University at Marion since 2004. He began his teaching career in 1982 as Assistant Professor of Geography at Marion, served as Associate Dean of the Marion campus from 1994 to 2003, and Interim Dean and Director from 2003 to 2004. Dr. Rose earned his master's and doctorate degrees at Michigan State University and his bachelor's degrees in geography and history from Valparaiso University in Indiana. In addition to his administrative duties, Dr. Rose often teaches a university course or a continuing education course in geography. He continues to work on his research projects, most of which focus on the origins of nineteenth-century domestic and foreign immigrant populations in the Old Northwest, utilizing birthplace information from the 1850 census as the starting point, as well as other historical and census records. He has published articles on these topics and presented papers at professional meetings.

Jennifer J. Smith is Assistant Professor of English at Franklin College. Her book, *The American Short Story Cycle*, appeared in 2018 from Edinburgh University Press. Her work has been published in *Pedagogy*, *The Journal of the Short Story in English*, *Short Fiction in Theory and Practice*, and a number of essay collections.

Ross K. Tangedal is Assistant Professor of English at the University of Wisconsin–Stevens Point. He specializes in twentieth-century American print & publishing culture, textual editing, and book history, with emphases on Ernest Hemingway, F. Scott Fitzgerald, and midwestern literature. His articles have appeared (or are forthcoming) in the *Hemingway Review*, *South Atlantic Review*, *F. Scott Fitzgerald Review*, *Authorship*, *MidAmerica*, and *Midwestern Miscellany*. He has also published essays in the *Teaching Hemingway* series (Kent State UP). He is a contributing editor for the *Hemingway Letters Project* (Cambridge University Press) and publisher-in-chief of the Cornerstone Press at UWSP. He serves on the executive advisory board of the Society for the Study of Midwestern Literature and on the Advisory Council of Younger Scholars of the Ernest Hemingway Society.

Paula Wisotzki is Professor of Art History at Loyola University Chicago. She graduated magna cum laude from Lewis and Clark College in her home town of Portland, Oregon. Having earned her PhD at Northwestern University, she taught at the University of Illinois at Chicago before coming to Loyola. At Loyola she is a member of the graduate faculty and is affiliated with the Women's Studies and Gender Studies Program. She is a long-time board member of the Midwest Art History Society and served a term as President of this regional professional organization of academics and museum professionals.

She was an area editor for the *Grove Encyclopedia of American Art* (5 vols. Oxford University Press, 2011) and co-edited with Helen Langa *American Women Artists, 1935–1970: Gender, Culture and Politics* (Ashgate, 2016). She has published several articles exploring David Smith's art through the lens of his political engagement. Her recent research has focused on Dorothy Dehner's early career and her leftist politics, and "Dorothy Dehner and World War II: Not Just 'Life on the Farm'" appeared in the Spring 2016 issue of the *Archives of American Art Journal*. She was named a "Master Teacher" in Loyola's College of Arts and Sciences for 2006–2007.

www.ingramcontent.com/pod-product-compliance
Lightning Source LLC
Chambersburg PA
CBHW020033120526
44588CB00030B/190